CHURCH AGENCIES

CHURCH AGENCIES

Caring for Children and Families in Crisis

Diana S. Richmond Garland

Child Welfare League of America

Child Welfare League of America, Inc.
440 First Street, NW, Suite 310, Washington, DC 20001-2085

Current Printing (last digit)
10 9 8 7 6 5 4 3 2 1

Cover by Jennifer Riggs-Geanakos
Text design by Deborah Finette
Printed in the United States of America

ISBN # 0-87868-532-4

FOR ALAN KEITH-LUCAS

Outstanding
Christian social worker,
educator, and author;
lover of children

Ⓒ ONTENTS

REFACE

⚓HROUGHOUT SOCIAL WORK'S HISTORY, the church has been recognized as a specialized context for ministry. In the 1940s, the Association of Church Social Workers was an active force in developing standards for social work as a profession and in accrediting "church social workers" [Johnson 1941: 406-407]. With the development of the profession in the next half-century, however, the church as a context for social work practice received relatively little attention. Today that picture is changing, with a political climate emphasizing the purchase of services from private agencies, many of them with church sponsorship, and with an increasing emphasis on home- and community-based services, long a focus of churches and their organizations. In 1984, the first graduate social work education program to specifically address church social work was accredited by the Council on Social Work Education.*

Because social work educators have given little focused attention to church social work, the published professional literature that describes the distinctive characteristics of a church context for providing social services to children and their families is limited. Two notable exceptions are Alan Keith-Lucas' book, *The Church Children's Home in a Changing World*, published in 1962, and *Sacred Shelters: Church-Related Children's Homes*, the proceedings of a conference sponsored by the Johnson Foundation and the

---

* The Carver School of Church Social Work, the Southern Baptist Theological Seminary. For a history of this school's development, see Davis 1988.

Lilly Endowment, Inc., edited by Robert Gillogly and published in 1982. In *Group Child Care as a Family Service*, published in 1977, Alan Keith-Lucas and Clifford W. Sanford described church-related agencies as a major sector of group child care services.

Church-related agencies that provide child welfare services have experienced major changes since these volumes appeared. They have been swept along in dramatic social and professional movements that have affected both the field of child welfare and their sponsoring churches and denominations. The Carver School of Church Social Work and the Gheens Center for Christian Family Ministry of the Southern Baptist Theological Seminary, Louisville, Kentucky, together with six other sponsors, hosted a gathering for leaders in church-related child welfare services in April 1991. This conference, entitled "Church-Related Children's Agencies: Present Realities and Future Directions," examined the church as a context for child welfare practice. Twelve presenters led the conference: Charles Baker, Executive Director, Presbyterian Child Welfare Agency, Buckhorn, Kentucky; Kathryn Chapman, Professor of Christian Education, The Southern Baptist Theological Seminary, Louisville, Kentucky; Dan Gilbert, President, Christian Church Homes of Kentucky, Louisville, Kentucky; Bob Gillogly, Pastor, First Federated Church (Presbyterian and Church of Christ), Peoria, Illinois; David Graves, Executive Director, Home of the Innocents, Louisville, Kentucky; Kathy Guy, Religious Affairs Director, Children's Defense Fund, Washington, DC; Alan Keith-Lucas, Alumni Distinguished Professor Emeritus of Social Work, University of North Carolina, Chapel Hill, North Carolina; David Kirk, Executive Director, ChildServ, Park Ridge, Illinois; Judith Lambeth, Executive Director, Maryhurst, Louisville, Kentucky; Heyward Prince, Executive Director, Connie Maxwell Children's Home, Greenwood, South Carolina; Kerry Rice, Director of the Child Advocacy Project, Presbyterian Church USA, Louisville, Kentucky; and Steve Rumford, Executive Director, Methodist Home for Children and Youth, Macon, Georgia.

These colleagues challenged and inspired me. Their presentations at the conference were the foundation on which I began writing *Church Agencies*. I am deeply indebted to them. I have expanded on the content of the conference and, in many instances, I have launched into content not explored there. Subsequently, these colleagues critiqued what I had written, making many helpful suggestions. Those who read the manuscript often did not see my conclusions, however, and although their contribution has been significant, responsibility for the book's premises, conclusions, and limitations rests solely with me.

This book is not simply a presentation of facts, an assessment of what the church has done and is doing for children and their families in crisis, although even such a presentation and assessment would be far from simple. This book has an additional agenda. It advocates a particular value base for the church's ministry with children and their families, and it makes suggestions for programs and services out of that value base. It is my hope that it reflects accurately the roles and purposes of the church in ministry to children and their families; others will have to judge whether I have been faithful to Christian values and beliefs about the role of the church and the focus of the church's calling as a community of faith.

In addition to the support of the conference presenters listed above, I want to express appreciation to the church agencies that provided support for the conference: the Presbyterian Child Welfare Agency in Buckhorn, Kentucky; Christian Church Homes of Kentucky; Home of the Innocents in Louisville; Maryhurst, also in Louisville; Kentucky Baptist Homes for Children; and the Presbyterian Church USA Child Advocacy Project. Both the Carver School of Church Social Work and the Gheens Foundation provided additional financial support. I am grateful to all.

My colleagues in the Carver School at the time—Anne Davis, Donoso Escobar, Jon Rainbow, and Pat Bailey—have provided personal and professional support throughout this project, as they always do. They have cheered me on and carried some of my responsibilities for me so that I might devote myself to this project. The Southern Baptist Theological Seminary granted me a year of sabbatical leave to work on the manuscript. Much of that time was spent in Australia, where work with church agencies in a different cultural context provided me with new perspectives. Morling College, which is the Baptist Theological College of New South Wales in Sydney, Australia, and its president, Dr. Vic Eldridge, warmly welcomed me and helped me find the resources I needed for completing this project.

Carl Schoenberg and Mary Liepold of the Child Welfare League of America, Inc., have provided valuable editorial assistance and encouragement. I am particularly indebted to Marian Wright Edelman, President of the Children's Defense Fund, whose lectures several years ago on our campus and whose book, *Families in Peril*, set my soul on fire. The issues she presented in her speaking and writing were compelling, and the experience of being in the presence of one person who has made such a difference for children and their families was inspiring. Through her, I met Kathy Guy of the Children's Defense Fund, who introduced me to a wonderful ecumenical network of child advocates and who supported me at every step as I have felt my way into a broader understanding of the church's role in child welfare. I am very grateful for the Children's Defense Fund. Countless churches and church agencies are indebted to its careful research and clear messages about children's issues in this nation.

In addition to the agencies and persons already mentioned, many others have shared their work with me, giving me additional insight into the workings of church child welfare agencies. They have freely offered their time and expertise and what they have learned about working with churches, so that others might learn from their experiences and so that children and families might be served more effectively. They also have read the manuscript and given me the benefit of many helpful suggestions. These persons include C. Anne Davis, Professor of Social Work, the Southern Baptist Theological Seminary; Laura Dean Friedrich of ChildServ in Illinois; Myf Bosanquet, Executive Officer of the National Anglican Caring Organisations Network in Australia; the staff of Careforce, an agency of the Anglican Home Mission Society of Australia; and the staff of the Anglican Counselling Centre of New South Wales, Australia. I am most thankful. I owe also a debt of gratitude to my family—David, Sarah, John, and Dorsie. They lived compassionately with me while I wrote. Writing makes me cranky, but they forgave me.

DRG

Part I

Foundations of the Church's Care for Children and Families in Crisis

CHAPTER 1

An Introduction

MOST OF THE EARLIEST INSTITUTIONS that cared for children in the United States were established by churches and religious orders. For example, in 1727, seven Ursuline nuns arrived in New Orleans to operate a school and a hospital, and soon began accepting orphans into their care [Bremner (1) 1970].[1] In 1867, a group of Baptist churchwomen in Louisville, Kentucky, opened a children's home to care for homeless children orphaned during the Civil War [Leonard 1990]. Throughout child welfare history, well before the advent of the social work profession, churches were often the major, and sometimes the only, societal institution to respond to the needs of children in crisis.

This book offers a view of the history, current work, and future of American churches' child welfare agencies, many of which began as children's homes and orphanages. For simplicity's sake, *church agencies* will be used inclusively in these pages to refer to agencies that are related to churches, denominations, ecumenical organizations, or other Christian religious groups and orders to any extent and in any way.

In a survey of child welfare agencies belonging to the National Association of Homes for Children, Barber [1990] found that over two-thirds of the private child welfare agencies had sponsoring organizations, and 91% of these organizations were religious in origin. Even with the advent of government responsibility and funding for social services in our modern era, churches continue to provide a significant percentage of the financial support for these services. Almost two-thirds (65%) of all the agencies in Barber's study, both religiously affiliated and private nonsectarian, received no government funding at all. A national survey of church-sponsored agencies [Garland 1992] found that the agencies drew an average of 28% of their budgets from the contributions of churches and religious organizations. Some of these agencies received an additional 20% of their budget from private donors and 21% from endowment income. Although most of the agencies do not sort out which of their private donors are members of their parent religious organizations, it is probable that these sources of income also represent the support of members of churches and religious groups.

Despite the historical and current importance of the church in the care of children in crisis, little attention has been given to the distinctive characteristics of a church context for child welfare services. If there are such characteristics, how do they affect the services church-sponsored child welfare agencies can provide? Can these church agencies provide services that may be more difficult, for whatever reasons, to offer through public or private nonsectarian auspices? What practical knowledge about this context for child and family services would help these agencies' professional staff members be most effective in imagining, designing, administering, and providing programs and services? And, most important, based on the church's own foundation of values, beliefs, and self-definition, what role should it take in serving children and families in crisis? This book seeks to answer these questions and to lay the groundwork for understanding and working with church agencies that serve children and their families.

Because churches historically have been the major provider of child welfare services in Western society, their work is particularly visible in any historical overview of the field. Churches are not always viewed as sponsors of innovative, creative social services, however. We evaluate the past by our present knowledge and understanding of children and by our current standards for helpful and effective services. Since churches and their programs have been representative of the cultural context in which they were embedded, including the limitations in knowledge current at the time and the personal experiences and motivations of principal actors, some past practices horrify and enrage us now.

Forrest Carter tells the poignant story of a five-year-old Cherokee boy in his book, *The Education of Little Tree*. Although the truth of this "true story" has been questioned recently, the story resonates with the kind of unfortunate "care" church agencies have sometimes visited on children. The story encapsulates our cultural myths about the church's child welfare services throughout history. Little Tree was born to Native American parents married in a tribal ceremony not recognized as legal by the dominant society, orphaned in the 1930s, and taken in by his wise and loving grandparents. Because his grandparents were aging and had "no education," and because his grandfather had a bad reputation as a "moonshiner," Little Tree was removed from their home by the authorities and sent alone on a bus to an orphanage run by the "Reverend" as an outreach of the "Denomination." He is told he is "the only bastard we have ever accepted." Days pass with no contact from the grandparents, who cannot write letters and who have no telephone from which to call him.

Little Tree tells us about one of his experiences in the orphanage school:

> One time [the teacher] held up a picture that showed a deer herd coming out of a spring branch. They was jumping on one another and it looked like they was pushing to get out of the water. She asked if anybody knew what they was doing. One boy said they was running from something, more than likely a hunter. Another boy said they didn't like water and was hurrying to get across. She said this was right. I raised my hand.

I said I seen right off they was mating; for it was buck deer that was jumping the does; also, I could tell by the bushes and trees that it was the time of the year when they done their mating.

She staggered back'ards a step or two before she got aholt of her total senses. Then she run at me. Everybody got quiet. She grabbed me by the neck and commenced to shake me. Her face got red and she commenced to holler, "I should have known— we all should have known—filth...filth...would come out of you...you...little bastard!"

...We went down to the Reverend's office. She made me wait outside and shut the door behind her. ...In a few minutes she come out of the Reverend's office and walked off down the hall without looking at me ...He said, 'You are born of evil, so I know repentance is not in you; but praise God, you are going to be taught not to inflict your evil upon Christians. You can't repent... but you shall cry out!"

He cut loose with the big stick acrost my back. [Carter 1976, 190-191]

It is painful to read about a child being so abused, with no sensitivity to his emotional trauma over senseless separation from a loving family, and with total discounting of his cultural heritage and personal experiences. Perhaps even more painful, we know that this story reflects the experiences of innumerable children in a history of child welfare services provided by churches and individual Christians who intended to express love and care. Not infrequently, however, they have been ineffective or even misguidedly abusive of children and their families.

Lest we be too harsh in judging the church's past response to human needs, however, we must also ask what other alternatives were being offered by society at the time. Cultural values labeled Little Tree's grandparents as unfit to provide his nurture and education. Young children were often placed in such institutions because they were deemed better than the other alternatives. Though we may despise the teacher and the Reverend, they reflect prevalent cultural attitudes and beliefs of the day about Native American culture, the effects of parents' legal marital status on the character of children, the danger of exposing children to sexual knowledge, and the role of physical discipline in controlling and shaping behavior. Too often, stereotypical caricatures of the church-related children's home, molded on the experiences of Oliver Twist or Little Tree, are deemed to reflect on the church rather than on the overall culture of the day and its understanding and treatment of children.

Unfortunately, however, child welfare professionals know that ineffective, even harmful services are still sometimes represented in the array of church-related services to children and their families. Although state regulations and standards protect children from many overtly abusive practices, some church child welfare agencies offer services that have not been updated to represent current professional thought, values, and practice models. Children may be placed in residential or foster care rather than providing family preservation services that might enable them to stay with their families.[2] Child care workers may have little professional preparation for their important roles in the lives of children and may be given minimal in-service training and updating of their skills. The same can be said, of course, for many state and private nonsectarian child and family service agencies. Evidence shows that some church agencies have been guilty of racial bigotry and of judgmental, harsh, and abusive treatment of children and their families, but so have the larger social structures in which those agencies are embedded. While this does not excuse the record of church agencies, one should not dismiss church agencies because they have reflected the societal beliefs and problems of past eras.

Some church agencies, in fact, have been at the forefront of professional thought and practice, piloting new and innovative approaches to services for families and children. "Their contribution has been consistent, significant, and many times prophetic, although seldom acknowledged or appreciated sufficiently even by sponsoring religious organizations" [Gillogly 1982a: 3]. An agency's context as "church-related" can allow it to offer ineffective, outdated programming; this same context, however, can allow the church agency to be a prophet in the field of child welfare, developing innovative projects and services and effectively advocating for children and their families. The characteristics of a church agency that allow its services to range from ineffective and outdated to prophetic and innovative include: (1) flexible funding, (2) a mandate that does not require it to meet the whole range of needs of children and families in society, and (3) greater emphasis on the processes of caring and less emphasis on efficiency and quantitative evaluation of programs than is required of many public agencies.

First, church agencies have flexible funding, not tied directly to reimbursement for specified individual services. Unfortunately for some agencies, this means they can be virtually inattentive to the impact their services actually have on the children and families they serve. On the positive side, however, these agencies can develop innovative services that may not be currently reimbursable by government funds. For example, in one residential program for children with developmental disabilities, social workers spend the great amount of time it takes to develop and maintain informal social support networks for families who are considering placing their developmentally disabled children in residential care. Consequently, with the aid of periodic respite care provided by the residential facility, some children can continue to live with their families. Although continued family care is not the best plan for every child and family, in those instances in which it is, social work services can make it possible. These options exist because the agency has the flexibility to be innovative.

Second, because they are private agencies, church agencies are not mandated by society to meet the whole array of needs that society's children and families experience. Consequently, on the negative side, some agencies may continue to offer services that are only marginally relevant to the most pressing and current needs of children and their families in a given community. On the positive side, however, other agencies use this freedom to be creative in their response to needs, developing a service niche that is uniquely suited to their resources and meets a need that would otherwise be unmet in their community.

Finally, church agencies are not expected to resolve societal problems, as public agencies often are. Thus, unlike public agencies, they do not have to demonstrate the impact of their programs on social indicators for their communities, such as rates of child abuse, teen suicide, homelessness, teen pregnancy and parenting, or criminal activity of children. This means that some church agencies may be offering services for which they cannot demonstrate any effectiveness. Not having to demonstrate effectiveness, however, can be a source of agency innovation rather than stagnation. Church agencies can risk providing services that may not demonstrate immediate outcomes.

Preventive and family support programs, for example, often have difficulty demonstrating effectiveness against social problems. Preventive and support services for youths at risk of pregnancy, school failure, and delinquency often include community sports and activity programs, the effects of which are most often long term and incremental. It may be hard to screen out the many other variables that affect the youths these programs serve and demonstrate short-term quantitative results. Church agencies may have freedom to offer these kinds of services nonetheless.

Changes in Services to Children and Their Families

Child welfare agencies have been changing dramatically in the past two decades—even those that drag their feet when it comes to innovation and program changes! Conversations among child welfare agency administrators will often turn to the dizzying, sometimes frightening changes in the needs of the children today's agency programs serve. Children coming into residential child care are older than in earlier years and often severely damaged by traumatic home and community experiences, by alcohol and drug abuse, or by multiple out-of-home placements. An early recognition of these changes came in 1958. Alan Keith-Lucas described the feelings of those who worked in child welfare—wishing they were back in the "good old days," when:

> running a church institution was a fairly simple job, when most of the children were orphans who came in infancy and stayed until they were grown, when the institution was a little unit of its own apart from the rest of the community, when all that admin-

istrators had to worry about was raising money, food, clothing, buildings, and maintaining Christian training and discipline in their little flocks.

Not that these were easy tasks—they demanded courage and skill and devotion. But in the main they were clear-cut, uncomplicated tasks whose purposes were easy to grasp. Those days are gone forever. The church can dwell in the past only at the cost of living under an illusion, of forfeiting its rightful leadership. [Keith-Lucas 1958]

That was 1958! Since then, the population church agencies serve has not stopped changing; if anything, the rate of change has increased. In part, this change is cause for celebration. Children are no longer growing up in institutions. Some children who formerly would have spent their childhoods in institutional care now are enabled, by support services provided their families, to stay in their own homes, or to experience only short-term placement away from home while their family situations are stabilized. The average length of stay in residential care has dropped markedly. In 1981, 85% of all the group care agencies surveyed reported average stays of less than two years, and half of those reported average stays of less than one year [Young et al. 1988]. Ideally, current child welfare systems reserve residential care for children whose needs cannot currently be met at home or in family foster care. If children cannot return home, plans are made that will help them live in a family, whether with relatives, with an adoptive family, or when these are not possibilities, in a long-term foster home. We are doing some things right.

Nevertheless, today's agencies serve large numbers of children with complex, difficult problems that require highly professional and intensive responses. "The new philosophies and administrative protections, as well as federal emphasis on and financial aid for adoptions if the family cannot be preserved, have left foster home and institutional care with more disturbed and complex populations, certainly reflective of increased pathology in the society at large" [Kamerman and Kahn 1989: 57]. The scale and severity of problems bringing children into the child welfare system have clearly increased. Significant increases in poverty for young families, especially single-mother families, and the growing drug problem have been major contributing factors.

A high proportion of children entering child and family social service agencies come from low-income, single-parent, mother-only families, overwhelmingly from the caseloads of AFDC (Aid to Families with Dependent Children). It is precisely these low-income, mother-headed families that have increased most during the 1980s. The result has been an increase in the economic, social, and psychological pressures on some families with children and without any compensating supports [Kamerman and Kahn 1989: 22]. Although the goal of keeping children in out-of-home care for as short a time as possible has led to timely and effective services for many children and their families, it has also had some unintended negative outcomes. Many children are caught in a system where they experience multiple foster homes and short-term agency placements, unsuccessful returns to their biological families, and even homelessness.

In trying to respond to the rapidly changing needs of children and families and the mushrooming knowledge about families and effective family services, professional programs and services to children and families in crisis have become ever more complex. Old orphanages have been transformed into centers for an array of services—respite care for developmentally disabled persons, often with additional support services for their families; crisis care for children needing immediate placement away from home while permanent plans can be made; apartments for homeless families as they are helped to work through their housing, financial, and personal crises; group homes, transitional living programs, and independent-living apartments for older youths; intermediate care for children to prepare them for foster or adoptive homes; day care for children of working parents; day care and family treatment programs for children who have been abused; residential treatment for children with emotional problems and/or chemical dependency—and the list goes on. At the same time, church agencies are expanding beyond this range of out-of-home services to include a variety of programs to prevent out-of-home placement, including community family services for crisis intervention and counseling, family life education programs in churches and communities, and consultation to church congregations to help them develop family support services sensitive to particular community needs.

Over the past 40 years, the scope of child welfare services has expanded to include services to children and their families. The term *child welfare* is being replaced by agency titles and program names that reflect services to children, youths, and families. One cannot be concerned about a child's welfare without considering that child in the context of the family; therefore, *child welfare services* and *services to children and their families* are used interchangeably. Services for children and their families—child welfare—include the following: family foster care, adoption, child protection (from abuse and neglect), residential treatment, family counseling, family preservation, family support, adolescent pregnancy and parenting services, parent education and parent aide programs, and adolescent and youth programs [Kamerman and Kahn 1989].

Church agencies are likely to gain, not diminish, in importance with the variety of child welfare services available to families in the near future. Recent federal legislation (including Title XX of the Social Security Act and the 1981 Social Services Block Grant) has encouraged the growth of voluntary social service agencies. The Reagan and Bush administrations implicitly defined private agency service delivery as more efficient and of higher quality than public service delivery; they encouraged government agencies to purchase services from private agencies. Private agencies are not always either more efficient or more effective, however, than their public counterparts. Nor are they usually designed to offer comprehensive services to a community. Relying on private agencies for public services may mean that if no private agency currently addresses a particular need, that need will go unmet.

Including the services of church agencies in the overall package of public child and family social services in a community does offer some advantages, however. First, church agencies often can launch new programs more quickly than public agencies can because they are smaller and have more manageable bureaucracies. Second, they can develop service innovations on a small scale that can be evaluated and, if worthy, implemented extensively by a public agency. Third, they may have resources not readily available to a government agency—the professional staff members, the facilities, and the volunteers and community involvement that are essential to some types of programs. Fourth, they have access to certain population groups not easily reached by public agencies. Fifth, they can address religious faith and value concerns more effectively than government-sponsored programs. Finally, the inclusion of church agencies in the array of a community's child welfare services resonates with a culture that values the use of private resources over government intervention whenever possible, even when those private resources are supported by government contracts.

Even in the '90s, public social service funds are increasingly being spent to purchase services from private agencies, including church agencies, rather than to expand public welfare programs; in fact, purchase-of-care arrangements are predicted to increase [Kamerman and Kahn 1989]. Therefore, it will be necessary for church agencies to define their mission, their identity, and thus their role in the larger array of a community's social service programs in order not to lose their direction in the turbulent environment of public and private child welfare services.

Child Welfare and Family Ministry

Churches do much more in ministry with children and their families than provide professional services to families in crisis. Churches have historically been primary sites for community-based family support services. In 1984, 60% of the United States population were members of congregations; 40% of the adults attended church or synagogue during a typical week [Jacquet 1985]. Churches were preventing family crises before prevention received focal attention from child welfare professionals. Church congregations have been the major providers of preschool education and child care in the United States, often with sliding fee scales or other provisions for low-income families [Freeman 1987]. Churches have also sponsored private schools as one of their ministries to children and families, often with the intent to preserve and pass on to children their culture of religious beliefs and practices. Some of these schools were founded as a reaction to court-mandated busing intended to achieve racial integration of the public schools; parents did not want their children sent to schools "across town."

Other founders of church schools had less controversial and more worthy objectives, however. A decade ago, it was estimated that 20% to 25% of American children were educated in private schools, most of them Christian schools [Richards 1983], and their numbers have since increased.

Churches provide care for children on a limited basis (one morning, evening, or full day per week) in Parents Day Out programs, including children who may be at risk for child abuse or who have special needs that put heavy demands on their families. Sunday schools, originally developed to teach reading to poor children who otherwise would have received no formal education, have continued to involve children and adults in educational experiences and to provide a rich environment for the development of informal social supports. For many children living in troubled families, relating to a caring and nurturing volunteer Sunday school teacher in a small group has been a significant interpersonal experience. Churches also offer summer camps, weekly clubs and activity programs, tutoring, and after-school care. The church serves as one of the few anchors of positive peer group activity for children in many communities.

These services to children and their families—day care, schools, tutoring, after-school care, weekly activity programs, and camps—have been the arena of the Christian education professional. Some large churches employ Ministers of Christian Education who have obtained advanced degrees in this field. Churches have also sponsored settlement houses and their offspring, community service agencies, where professional social workers have developed programs for community children who may or may not participate in a church congregation. In general, however, little direct interaction has taken place between a church's Christian education programs and its child welfare ministries.[3]

Recently, and usually apart from these historical and ongoing services to children, churches and denominations have been developing "family ministries," which are often led by those educated to be pastors or pastoral counselors, although social workers and religious educators have also been involved. Some large congregations and denominational groups have created staff positions titled "Director of Family Ministry" or have added this specialty to traditional church leadership roles. The development of a family specialization in professional ministry parallels what has been happening in other helping professions. Physicians have developed a family medicine specialization; fledgling helping professionals are abandoning traditional professional education programs to train as family therapists; and universities are offering degrees in family science in addition to or in place of the traditional social sciences of sociology and psychology.

These professional developments have been fed by rapid social changes that have created widespread alarm concerning the institution of the American family. Those concerned about children have been most attentive to rising rates of divorce and the increase in the number of single-parent families and blended families. Social scientists have argued over whether these changes simply create opportunities for a greater variety of lifestyles or rather indicate the demise of the family and our society. Most recently, a number of respected leaders in the social sciences agreed that as a social institution, the American family is in crisis, increasingly disempowered to carry out its inherent functions, and as a consequence, American children are experiencing a decline in the quality of life [Blankenhorn et al. 1990].

This concern is not new for churches, however. In a 1923 volume, *Jesus Christ and the Social Question*, Francis Greenwood Peabody voiced his worries about the stability of the family:

> The coherence and permanence of family life are, under existing social conditions, seriously threatened. Domestic instability, it is observed, tends in a most startling manner to become an epidemic social disease. The number of divorces annually granted in the U.S. is, it appears, increasing, both at a rate unequaled in any other civilized country, and at a constantly accelerating rate …The increase of population in those 20 years [1867-1886] was 60%; the increase of divorces was 156%. It may even be computed that if the present ratio of increase in population and separation be maintained, the number of separations of marriage by death would be at the end of the twentieth century less than the number of separations by divorce.[3] [Peabody 1923: 129-130]

Peabody's prediction was surprisingly accurate. In response to the continual rise in divorce rates after the 1950s, churches developed marriage education and enrichment programs to strengthen marriages and prevent divorce [Garland 1983]. Marriage enrichment, originally led by volunteer couples, became a primary focus for ministry with families and a central focus for the developing family ministry specialty in professional church leadership. More recently, other educational programs for families have been added to the array of services churches provide under the umbrella of family ministry, including parent education. In addition, family ministry has come to include cross-generational programs, self-help publications for families, family camps and other recreational programs, crisis intervention, family counseling, and advocacy for families within other programs of the church and with other social systems [Garland and Pancoast 1990c; Sell 1981].

For the most part, these services have been offered by or through local congregations. Although state or national church bodies employ directors of family ministry, these persons often serve as consultants to and resources for local congregations rather than developing family ministry agencies or centers at the denominational level or in ecumenical settings. When congregations have not had the resources to offer these services themselves, they have either foregone them or collaborated ecumenically with other congregations to offer them in their communities. In other words, responsibility for these services has remained almost exclusively with local congregations.

Child welfare services, by contrast, have not often belonged to a single congregation, nor have they been directed by a professional currently a member of a congregational staff. More often, churches have viewed these services as missions to be supported by a denominational body, parachurch organization, or religious order. Therefore, churches have supported them but have not been primarily responsible for them, in much the same way that they have supported other mission endeavors in the United States and overseas. Directors of these agencies have often been members of the clergy, and in many cases they have previously served on the professional staff of a congregation.[4] Consequently, child welfare services have had a distinctly different niche in the church's life than family ministries or congregational children's ministries. Their recent history is most akin to that of the church's community ministry agencies or mission organizations.

The lack of connection between family ministries and church-sponsored child welfare services is sometimes startling. For example, the director of one denomination's statewide child and family service agency, which includes residential care, group homes, and family crisis counseling centers, launched a new program of educational and family support services in various congregations throughout the state. The director and his staff, however, had not even met, much less talked with, the denomination's Director of Family Ministry for the state. This Director of Family Ministry offered consultation to churches in providing such ministries as parent education and marriage enrichment in the very congregations where the agency was offering family support services. Although church leaders responsible for family ministry and child welfare services may not have needed to coordinate their work in the past, developments in services to children and their families indicate that these leaders should coordinate their work, or they will be tripping over one another and missing opportunities to join forces in creative service.

A number of changes in child welfare services have led to a confluence between the work of the church's child welfare agencies and the work of congregational and denominational leaders in family ministry. For the past half-century, attention has been shifting away from rescuing children from "unhealthy" family environments and toward family interventions that can change dysfunctional patterns of relating and increase family members' skills in living and working with one another. In other words, education for family living has become a primary part of the intervention package for many of the children and families who receive services from the church's child welfare agencies. Thus, child welfare services are moving away from the children's institutions, built in rural settings perceived to be healthier for children than the cities from which they had been rescued. Instead, staff members are providing services in the community of social networks where the child and family live and can be supported in their efforts to resolve the problems they face. Congregations, embedded as they are in the communities where people live, are ideal settings for these services. Consequently, professional leaders in child welfare services are involved in parent education and other family life education and support programs that parallel, in many respects, the services of congregational family ministry.

Many church child welfare agencies have expanded their services to include prevention and family support programs—camps for inner-city youths, weekday activity programs, teen pregnancy prevention programs, and day care and after-school programs. Thus, although histories, staffing patterns, relationships with congregations and religious groups and, often, target populations may differ somewhat, the church's ministries to children and youth, family ministries, and child welfare ministries currently are providing many similar programs and services.

Some large churches can hire professional staff members to develop and provide ministries to children and families; most churches cannot. They have the community relationships, facilities, and supportive volunteers, but not the professional resources, for community-based ministries for children and their families. Church child welfare agencies are beginning to provide those professional resources through consultation to church groups who want to begin such ministries [Friedrich 1990]. They lend staff members for these programs and sometimes relocate their own programs in congregational sites. They are developing programs and literature that laypeople can use for family life education and family support programs in their own congregations. They see church members not only as potential donors to support the agency, but also as caring individuals who can play key supportive roles in the lives of children and families in crisis—both those served directly by the agency and others in the congregation's own community.

Church child welfare agencies therefore have a new role to consider, that of leadership in congregational and denominational programs of family ministry. This role has significant potential for raising the visibility of the agency's work and strengthening the financial and volunteer support base of the agency. More broadly, it has the potential for creating an array of preventive and supportive services responsive to the needs of families in a particular community.

Such a role requires more than knowledge and skills in services to children and families. It also requires knowledge of the church as a context for these services—its values and beliefs, its organizational patterns and norms, its historical saga and self-identity, its goals and mission. Particular purposes, program goals, funding mechanisms, populations, and values characterize the church as an environment for services to children and their families. These both constrain services and offer the possibility for creative, innovative approaches to the needs of children and their families that can complement those offered by state and other private agencies. Despite changes in the services they offer and the advent of government grants and contracts that partially fund many of these agencies, a survey of church agency administrators indicated recently that they see their relationship with parent church organizations to be significant, stable, and even increasing in importance [Garland 1992]. To understand and to work effectively with and within these agencies, therefore, their context must be understood.

An Overview of This Book

An effective leader of the church's services to children and families must appreciate and respect the church for itself, not just as a potential site for family and children's services. Historically, the church has often tried to provide itself with such leadership by hiring clergy to direct its children's homes and family agencies. These church leaders appreciated and identified with the church's mission and values, but unfortunately, they did not always have the professional knowledge and skills to administer a child welfare and family service agency. Church agencies have received little support from the helping professions in developing the ability to assess, understand, and build on the distinctive characteristics of the church as a context for child welfare practice.

Church Agencies is designed to address the need of professional staff members in church family and children's services to understand the church as a context for their services. It will seek to articulate the characteristics of the church context for child welfare services and to describe effective practice strategies that are sensitive to this context. It will argue that church-related agencies should understand and strengthen reciprocal relationships with their sponsoring religious organizations rather than seeking to duplicate services that are or ought to be provided by government agencies—or by congregations. This book was written primarily for the professional leadership, staff, and board members of agencies affiliated with Christian religious organizations. In addition, pastors and other leaders of Christian social ministries within congregations will find help in developing bridges between their congregations and their denominations' child and family service agencies.

This volume does not try to address all the practice aspects of developing and providing professional services such as family foster care, adoption services, residential treatment services, emergency shelter care, family preservation services, and family counseling. Other resources are available for conceptualizing and guiding direct services to children and their families. Instead, this book considers the church agency as a specific context for the development and provision of these and other child and family services.

Church Agencies will focus on Christian church agencies and organizations as a subgroup of all social service agencies. Obviously, other faith groups also provide child welfare services. Since theology and faith traditions provide the foundation for describing the unique character of this context for child welfare practice, however, it seems appropriate to focus broadly on the theology and traditions of the Christian church rather than trying to deal with all religious contexts of care for children and families in crisis. Specifically, I will describe the role of Christian scripture and theology as an impetus and a value base for caring for children and families in crisis. In fact, I will argue that to be most effective, church agencies should begin with this value base for the church's ministry with children and their families, not with the needs in the community. Chapter 2, an introduction to the biblical and theological thought that constitutes this base, can assist helping professionals outside this tradition to speak the language and understand the culture of the church as they interact with church leaders and congregations.

Consequently, this book is unapologetically Christian. It seeks to model what it espouses as the approach of church agencies: to embrace and value their foundation in the faith and service of the Christian community, as one would embrace the language and culture of any group in which and through which one serves. It is written from an insider's perspective to others on the inside of the church's agencies and organizations. I hope, though, that those caring for children and families in expression of other faith traditions will be able to generalize the theory and practice principles of this book to their own context.

Chapter 3 reviews the historical role of the church in caring for children and families as it has developed in the United States. Current church-related services to children and their families reflect and are shaped by their own saga and need to be understood in their historic context.

Chapter 4 observes the work of the church child welfare agency today, focusing primarily on agencies that have historically offered residential care. It describes ways in which agency staff members can involve volunteers and community groups in the provision of services to clients and their families, using a social network approach to practice. It examines the particular role of the church agency in the continuum of services to children and their families. It reviews the involvement of congregations in roles such as supportive friends for residents and their families, therapeutic foster care providers, and adoptive parents for children with special needs.

Chapter 5 describes ways in which agency staff members can provide leadership in family ministries offered by congregational and church community agencies. It offers an overview of the knowledge and skills needed for consultation with congregations.

Church congregations and agencies can also be effective advocates for societal programs and policies that support and strengthen families. Chapter 6 describes ways to involve congregations and church agencies in child and family advocacy. Chapter 7 discusses the complex issues of funding, staffing, and governance in church agencies. Chapter 8 concludes the book with a vision for the future of church-based services with children and their families.

Notes

1. Histories of child welfare in the United States have often cited the Ursuline convent as the first American child welfare institution, opened for children left orphaned by the massacre at Natchez in 1729 [e.g., Whittaker 1971]. Bremner [1971 (I): 60-61] has stated that the Sisters were already caring for orphans prior to the Natchez massacre, although they did accept children left orphaned by that event. Alan Keith-Lucas' research has indicated instead that the orphanage was opened for children left homeless by an epidemic [personal correspondence, February 8, 1992]. Keith-Lucas' research also suggests that the Ursuline convent was not the first such institution; it was predated by a short-lived orphanage founded by a sect of German immigrants in Georgia. Bremner notes the founding of an orphanage by German settlers in Georgia in 1738 [Bremner (I): 272]. Whatever the date or the nature of the population served by the Ursuline sisters, this early involvement of religious groups and orders in caring for children exemplifies the historic role of the church in child welfare.

2. For simplicity's sake, this book uses *children* to encompass both children and youths.

3. For example, Lawrence Richards' 1983 book, *A Theology of Children's Ministry*, a significant review of children's ministries, makes no mention of child welfare services and programs.

4. Although no research has been done to determine the extent to which these agencies are directed by clergy, Ellen Netting [1993] collected data on the leaders of church-affiliated retirement communities and found that 28% of them are clergy of the sponsoring religious body, 5% are clergy of other religious groups, and an additional 27% are members, although not clergy, of the sponsoring religious body. A majority of the chief executive officers of these agencies, therefore, are clergy or members of the parent religious group.

CHAPTER 2

A Theological and Biblical Foundation

THE AGENCY PROFESSIONAL has to take into account the cultural context, values, and beliefs that shape the agency and its response to clients. These values and beliefs explicitly and implicitly influence the agency's structures, its mission and goals, and even its methods and processes, and therefore influence the professional's work. The professional in a church agency has to be comfortable with a theological and biblical foundation for the agency's service in the same way that a professional employed by a Latino community service agency founded and sponsored by community groups has to be comfortable speaking Spanish and working in a Latino cultural setting.

At a 1982 conference on church-related children's homes, Martin Marty addressed the topic, "The Difference in Being a Christian and the

Difference It Makes." Concerning what is distinctive about residential child care offered by Christians under the auspices of the church, he asked:

> If there is no difference, and if Christian involvement implies an extra expenditure of energy, why bother? Why call on Christian support in the form of sacrifice and spiritual activity if public or secular residential care is in every respect identical to Christian versions except for the names? What about the morality of asking people to draw upon a specific set of religious emotions to do something that other people are doing as well? Isn't it immoral to exact or extort prayer, voluntary effort, funds, and hours from people if there is no difference? [Marty 1982: 12]

Marty argued that Christian auspices for professional child care services create distinctive characteristics of service but do not indicate uniqueness from the work of other agencies. Some agencies are certainly more distinctive than others. Brendtro [1982][1] has identified five myths about church-related agencies: that they are church-controlled, church-funded, religiously focused, theologically/politically/professionally conservative, and more demanding of those they serve than nonsectarian agencies. In fact, church agencies may be distinguished by all of these characteristics, a mix of these, or none at all.

Some are totally governed by local congregations or their denominational structures; others are totally independent of church control. Some are totally church-funded; others are totally funded by endowments or government grants and fees for services. Some require strict religious adherence of their staff and clients; others are so secularized that one could ferret out little evidence of religious influence in the actual programs and practices of these agencies. Some are extremely conservative; others are extremely progressive or liberal in their professional practice, political leanings, and/or theological foundation. (What's more, an agency may be very conservative theologically and very progressive with regard to politics and professional practice. Other mixes on these dimensions are also possible.) Some expect high levels of client loyalty to the agency, evidence of significant life changes, and commitment to the faith community represented by the agency—they may require children in residential care to attend church or memorize scripture passages; others have expectations that differ little from those of nonsectarian agencies. Most agencies range somewhere within these extremes.

Some agencies do not emphasize their religious connections; the organizational sense of self as a church ministry is peripheral. Such an agency may play down its church ties when it seems necessary to do so for the achievement of its goals and objectives, as in approaching government funding sources that ban discrimination on the basis of religion in the hiring of staff. If its identity as a church agency is central, however, an agency will find it difficult to lower its colors when sailing into areas that do not welcome services clearly influenced by a particular faith or religious group.

An agency that was founded and continues to be supported by a church or group of churches may have little freedom to determine its own identity as a church agency. Even for an agency in which church control is total, however, the agency as a social system interacts with that control and shapes, to some extent, its own identity. It can see itself as a social service agency whose funding happens to be from a private, religious source, a happenstance that has little effect on its methods and practices with clients. At the other extreme, the agency can see itself as an extension of the church into the lives of clients and their families; its staff members may consider themselves church leaders and/or representatives. The varying requirements for religious identification and behavior on the part of staff members employed by these agencies can be viewed as efforts to ensure this fundamental identity with the church.

An agency's self-perception often changes over time. For the most part, it appears that agencies begin as direct extensions of the church community or religious order and its ministry. As agencies grow and come to rely on a professional staff instead of church volunteer workers, however, they tend to become secularized and identify more closely with the human services network of the community than with the church group that founded them.

The force of secularization has been very strong in the Christian churches over time. The arguments for its opposite—defining the agency's role in terms of Christian mission—have often been poorly expressed, have lacked theological rigor, and have alienated many when put into practice. At the heart of the debate, however, is the question of how the Christian community is to share, in its practical works, the Christian hope it is called to live out [Pollard 1991: 8].

This chapter encourages the agency to embrace its identity as a direct extension of and a leader of the church in its service to the community. To the extent that the agency embraces such a role for itself, effective agency leadership begins with an understanding of the church's mission and how the agency can best guide the church in its response to the needs of children and families.

Church agencies that embrace their relationship with the church community and take on a role of leadership within it can exercise that leadership in two ways. Most agencies have seen themselves, primarily, as serving in behalf of the church community. The role of serving in behalf of the church is most like the church leadership role of missionary; the professional serves in a capacity that is closed to the laity because of geographical or social distance, or because of the professional expertise effective service requires. For example, the agricultural missionary in a third world country may serve primarily as an agricultural expert, teaching farming methods, irrigation, and animal husbandry. The missionary is there to live out the biblical mandate to "feed the hungry," using professional expertise in behalf of the church too distant geographically and culturally to be able to serve directly. Although the missionary's practice may differ little from that of any other agricultural professional, the values and meaning that motivate that practice and provide support from the home church group are distinctive. Similarly, the professional programs and methods of the church agency that serves children and their families in crisis do not seem to differ much from those of other professional child and family service agencies. The values and meaning that undergird and thus influence that practice, however, are distinctive.

The second role of the church agency, however, does result in uniqueness in practice. This role is most like the church role of spiritual guide. The spiritual guide is one who leads others through the practice of particular spiritual disciplines (prayer, fasting, worship) in a process of spiritual development and obedience to God. Service to others is a key spiritual discipline in Christian growth. Agency staff members who equip church members to respond to the needs of children and their families are thus guiding those members in their spiritual development; they are "disciplining" Christians (i.e., making disciples). Agencies that accept responsibility for spiritual guidance have two principal concerns. They are concerned with providing needed services to children and their families. Just as important, however, they are concerned with fulfilling the commission from the church to lead its ministry—not to serve in its place, but to lead the church itself in serving. The agency actively seeks ways to link members in the churches it serves with the needs of children and families, so that the needs are met and the members grow through serving and caring for others.

The missionary role for the agency suggests beginning with the needs for ministry, then going to the church for commissioning and support for that ministry. The spiritual guide role begins with a dual focus on the church's need to minister, which is one of its basic purposes for existence, and on the needs of children and their families. Those in this role must recognize that the church can never respond to all the unmet needs of society at any given time.

Instead, they recognize that the call to serve is part of the discipleship of every Christian, and it is the professional church leader's responsibility to find ways Christians can be discipled in response to the needs of the community. Service is "an expression of the search for God and not just of the desire to bring about individual or social change" [Nouwen et al. 1983: 31].

The role of spiritual guide emphasizes the church as the agency's context for practice, even though the agency may offer standard child welfare services such as foster care, residential care, adoption services, and crisis counseling. The mission of public human service agencies springs from the unmet needs of the community to which they are mandated to respond. For example, the rationale for state foster care services begins with the need—a given number of children need temporary placement because of court decisions, and the state carries responsibility for these children. In contrast, the rationale for a denominational agency's foster care services begins with the mission of the church to receive children in the name of Jesus, because to do so is to receive Jesus (Mark 9:37).[2] The church is to lead its people in living the life of service to which it has been called as a living witness to the lordship of Christ. In short, the church concerns itself with needs after recognizing and responding to God's call to service; the needs themselves do not drive the service.

Service, however, may identify needs that lead to a new sense of being called to respond. The relationship between responding to a call and serving needs is thus mutually reciprocal. Each should balance and contribute to the other. An exclusive focus on the church's need to serve with no attention to the needs of the community results in ineffective, self-centered projects that are not truly service at all. An exclusive focus on the community's unmet needs, however, would limit the church to a social service agency without attending to its wider mission and identity. In the words of C. S. Lewis: "Men or nations who think they can revive the Faith in order to make a good society might just as well think they can use the stairs of Heaven as a shortcut to the nearest chemist's shop" [Lewis 1942: 120].

Most church agencies embrace both of these roles to a greater or lesser extent, although the missionary role has predominated historically. Whichever role is dominant, however, agency staff members often find themselves turning to supporting churches and nurturing in them the motivation to care about and respond to the needs of children and their families. In both roles, agency professionals should articulate in presentations to religious groups who support the agency the scriptural and theological basis for caring for children and their families. To be most effective in nurturing an ongoing relationship between church and agency, they should begin with the scripture and theology, not simply provide a "proof text"[3] that rationalizes what the agency is doing or planning to do.

To that end, this chapter explores in a rudimentary way some of the Christian scriptures and theological beliefs that can help church agencies think about and articulate to congregations and other church organizations why they should care for children and their families in crisis. Churches can express caring both by supporting the professional staff members who serve in their name and by involving themselves personally in the crises of children and their families. To begin, we will discuss the need for professional staff members to involve congregations directly in service to children and their families in crisis.

Leading the Church in Ministry to Children and Their Families

When child welfare professionals beckon the church into ministry, much attention goes toward finding the resources to meet the needs of children and their families. In short, the professionals frequently approach churches with the purpose of gaining their financial support for social work. The life of Jesus, however, was spent not only in direct ministry to the poor and oppressed (Matthew 11:5), but just as importantly, in preparing his followers for ministry (Matthew 10:5). Many pages of the Gospels describe him calling his followers, instructing them, and showing them how to minister. His focus seemed to be not just on getting the ministry accomplished, but also on the growth of persons in the process of ministering to others. The calling of Zacchaeus is such a story.

> Jesus entered Jericho and was passing through. A man was there by the name of Zacchaeus; he was a chief tax collector and was wealthy. He wanted to see who Jesus was, but being a short man he could not, because of the crowd. So he ran ahead and climbed a sycamore-fig tree to see him, since Jesus was coming that way.
>
> When Jesus reached the spot, he looked up and said to him, "Zacchaeus, come down immediately. I must stay at your house today." So he came down at once and welcomed him gladly.
>
> All the people saw this and began to mutter, "He has gone to be the guest of a sinner."
>
> But Zacchaeus stood up and said to the Lord, "Look, Lord! Here and now I give half of my possessions to the poor, and if I have cheated anybody out of anything, I will pay back four times the amount."
>
> Jesus said to him, "Today salvation has come to this house, because this man, too, is a son of Abraham. For the Son of Man came to seek and to save what was lost." (Luke 19:1-10, NIV)

Zacchaeus was different from many of the individuals the Gospels record Jesus ministering to; he was not seeking healing for blindness or disease, nor was he a child wanting Jesus' blessing. He was a wealthy oppressor, not one of the oppressed. He was curious about Jesus, watching from a safe distance high in a tree. Zacchaeus was needy in his own way, however; he was wealthy, but he was despised by his own people. They considered him a "sinner" because of his occupation as a tax collector for the oppressive regime, which meant that he became rich at their expense. Because they eschewed any relationship with him, he was most probably a very lonely man.

Some helping professionals of today might have looked at Zacchaeus as an untapped funding source. Jesus did not. He responded to the deepest need in Zacchaeus; by coming to Zacchaeus' home, Jesus reached out to him and broke through his isolation. We do not know what they talked about at Zacchaeus's house, but the results are a social worker's fantasy: Zacchaeus gave half of everything he had to the poor and promised to do all within his power to eliminate social injustice. By attending to Zacchaeus's deepest needs, Jesus empowered him to turn and care for others. Providing leadership in a church community requires caring enough to see the needs and the worth of each of God's children, including the wealthy, above-it-all onlookers, and touching them in ways that nurture their ability to respond with care and with a concern for justice.

Jesus focused on empowering his followers for ministry. Once, when the disciples pointed out the hunger of the crowds who had followed him to an isolated place, Jesus said, "*You* give them something to eat" (Matt. 14:16, emphasis added). When the disciples' resources were not enough, Jesus blessed the five loaves of bread and the two fish they did have and gave them back to the disciples, and the "disciples gave them to the crowds" (Matt. 14:19). Jesus blessed and prepared what they gave—and them as servants—to meet the needs of the crowd. Effective church leaders do not take the church's gifts and serve in their place. Instead, they bless and transform the gifts of the church, turning them back to the members—the disciples—for their ministry to others. They do not professionalize ministry; they empower others to be ministers. They can then share in the joy and amazement at what God is able to do through them.

To be employed in a church agency, therefore, means not only responding to the needs of children and their families, but also responding to the needs of the self-sufficient in supporting congregations. Their needs are to learn to care and to give, to respond to the needs of their "neighbors," the wounded and hurting ones in their community (Luke 10:29-37). First, it is necessary for churches to hear what the scriptures say about children and their families. Second, they have to feel challenged to respond as individuals and as a community to the needs of children and their families in crisis. Third, they must be helped to understand what spiritual development means for children who are in crisis or living in turbulent environments. And finally, they need help in presenting their gifts to God to be blessed and transformed into effective ministry to the needs of children.

Children in Christian Thought

In the Roman world of Jesus' day, children had little worth. If the father did not lift up his new baby when the baby was placed at his feet, the baby was *exposed*—that is, left to die in the garbage dumps of the city. Unwanted children, especially girls, were routinely exposed.

The Jewish world, however, never adopted the Roman practice of exposure. Jews held children, especially boys, in much greater esteem than did the Roman world. Male children were considered full members of the covenant community; all males were commanded to appear before the Lord (Exod. 23:17, Deut. 16:16); and children participated in religious celebrations such as the Passover (Exod. 12:24, Deut. 6:20). Even so, Jesus' teachings about and response to children were no doubt considered radical.

As helpless, nonproductive dependents, children were, at best, second-class citizens in the eyes of both classical Roman gentiles and believing Jews of the first Christian century. One day these children might grow up to be productive and protective of their parents. But until then, they stood far down the social ladder—behind even women, the poor, the sick, and the lame [Willimon 1985: 1109]. The very fact that Jesus took time to be with children can be considered a dramatic statement; for a scholar to spend time with children, outside his formal instruction of them, would have been considered a waste of time. [Weber 1979]

But Jesus did more than simply make time for children; he turned the social order upside down and placed children first.

At that time the disciples came to Jesus and asked, "Who is the greatest in the kingdom of heaven?"

He called a little child and had him stand among them. And he said: "I tell you the truth, unless you change and become like little children, you will never enter the kingdom of heaven. Therefore whoever humbles himself like this child is the greatest in the kingdom of heaven." (Matt. 18:1-4 NIV; see also Mark 9:34-35)

Jesus used his relationship with, and sayings about, children to communicate the very heart of his message. The incidents recorded in Scripture are not of Jesus telling stories to children, but of Jesus using children to communicate radical challenges to adults. Unlike others in his day, Jesus did not see the child as raw material for education and a future support for the family. Instead, he viewed children as the very symbol and model of discipleship. In Jesus' teaching, the child was not the one to receive instruction, but the one whose very presence was the clue to answering the disciples' question, "Who is the greatest in the kingdom of heaven?" [Weber 1979].

Jesus was not idealizing childhood, however; he was transforming social structures, so that the smallest becomes the greatest, the powerless empowered, the valueless of highest value. The new world order belongs to children. In diametric opposition to his contemporaries, his peers, and the spirit of his historical period, Jesus lifted up children and placed them in the center of his teaching about the way God intends us to order our lives with one another. To be a disciple means to become like a child, to recognize one's dependence on God. Jesus told his listeners, "Anyone who will not receive the kingdom of God like a little child will never enter it" (Luke 18:17 NIV); "Whoever humbles himself like this child is the greatest in the kingdom of heaven" (Matt. 18:4 NIV). He used children as examples because they cannot exist without the help of others. Jesus was criticizing the presumed independence and self-sufficiency of adulthood. "Persons can only become human through their neighbors" [Müller-Fahrenholz 1982: 15].

Jesus also taught, however, that children are more than simply models of discipleship; they are to be the focus of our care. Jesus said, "If anyone causes one of these little ones who believe in me to sin, it would be better for him to have a large millstone hung around his neck and to be drowned in the depths of the sea" (Matt. 18:5). Moreover, Jesus taught that at the end of time, God will count our care for the hungry, the thirsty, the stranger, the naked, the sick, and the imprisoned as our care for Christ himself.

> Then the King will say to those on his right, "Come, you who are blessed by my Father; take your inheritance, the kingdom prepared for you since the creation of the world. For I was hungry and you gave me something to drink, I was a stranger and you invited me in, I needed clothes and you clothed me, I was sick and you looked after me, I was in prison and you came to visit me."
>
> Then the righteous will answer him, "Lord, when did we see you hungry and feed you, or thirsty and give you something to drink? When did we see you a stranger and invite you in, or needing clothes and clothe you? When did we see you sick or in prison and go to visit you?"
>
> The King will reply, "I tell you the truth, whatever you did for one of the least of these brothers of mine, you did for me." (Matt. 25:34-40 NIV)

The amazing message of Jesus was that the child is the representative of Jesus and of God in our midst. Caring for children profoundly expresses our love of God.

> He took a little child and had him stand among them. Taking him in his arms, he said to them, "Whoever welcomes one of these little children in my name welcomes me; and whoever welcomes me does not welcome me but the one who sent me." (Mark 9:36-37 NIV)

According to Jewish thinking, the representative of the king is as the king himself [Weber 1979]. The child is not simply a symbol or metaphor for our discipleship. Jesus commended children to our care as the way we can demonstrate our love for him.

Undergirding the specific sayings of Jesus about children, the call of biblical writers in both the Old and New Testaments for justice for the poor and the oppressed provides a powerful foundation for involvement of the church in caring for children and their families in crisis. In our own nation, many of the poor are children. The scriptures clearly point to God's concern and presence with the poor, the oppressed, the orphan. The orphans in our own culture are not only those children who have no biological parents, but also those who have been socially orphaned, those left without an inheritance of hope, resources, and opportunities for the future. Our orphans are today's throwaway children—the homeless, the school dropouts, the chemically dependent, the poor, the abused, the troubled and troubling. God listens to their plight.

> You hear, O Lord, the desire of the afflicted; you encourage them, and you listen to their cry, defending the fatherless and the oppressed, in order that man, who is of the earth, may terrify no more. (Psalm 10:17-18 NIV)

> A father to the fatherless, a defender of widows, is God in his holy dwelling. God sets the lonely in families. (Psalm 68:5-6a NIV)

Repeatedly, the Old Testament prophets called for the people of God to work for justice for the oppressed.

> Do not mistreat an alien or oppress him, for you were aliens in Egypt. Do not take advantage of a widow or an orphan. If you do and they cry out to me, I will certainly hear their cry. (Exodus 22:21-22 NIV)

> Speak up for those who cannot speak for themselves, for the rights of all who are destitute. Speak up and judge fairly; defend the rights of the poor and needy. (Proverbs 31:9)

> Is not this the kind of fasting I have chosen: to loose the chains of

injustice and untie the cords of the yoke, to set the oppressed free and break every yoke? Is it not to share your food with the hungry and to provide the poor wanderer with shelter—when you see the naked, to clothe him, and not to turn away from your own flesh and blood? Then your light will break forth like the dawn, and your healing will quickly appear; then your righteousness will go before you, and the glory of the Lord will be your rear guard. Then you will call, and the Lord will answer; you will cry for help, and he will say: Here am I.

If you do away with the yoke of oppression, with the pointing finger and malicious talk, and if you spend yourselves on behalf of the hungry and satisfy the needs of the oppressed, then your light will rise in the darkness, and your night will become like the noonday. The Lord will guide you always. (Isaiah 58:6-11a NIV)

The biblical foundation of the church's responsibility to care for children is strong, therefore. This tradition needs to be joined with current knowledge that caring for children most often means caring for their families. Church agencies can help churches recognize the significance of families as the context in which children are inextricably embedded, and consequently, the most significant context of care for children.

An example with which many churches are familiar is buying Christmas toys for children of poor families and delivering them on Christmas Eve. The child's delight and appreciation more than reward the givers. But such "caring" is shortsighted and misguided because, in trying to show care for the child, it invades and weakens the child's family. If the benefactors are asked to place themselves in the role of that child's parent observing church folks in such gift-giving, they may well be able to imagine the devastating sense of powerlessness and impoverishment: other adults are giving their children the good gifts that they are unable to provide. Quite unintentionally, the gift-giving lowers parental self-esteem that may already be close to rock bottom.

A ministry that provides the means for parents themselves to give good gifts to their children is ultimately more caring of both children and parents. This may mean providing shopping vouchers, or setting up a church-sponsored toy fair in the weeks before Christmas where donated and purchased new toys are given to low-income parents or sold to them at much reduced prices. This recognizes and respects the role of parents as the experts on what their own children need and want and as the ones who rightfully give gifts to their children. Because it strengthens rather than diminishes the role of parents as caregivers, it is a meaningful and loving way to show care for children—and for the Christ whom they represent.

The Family as the Context for Caring for Children

As the agency serves children, it must take into account that children—even children who have been placed in out-of-home care—are inextricably embedded in their family context. The family is the primary ecology of the child, and it must be addressed as primary if services are to be as effective as possible. In addition, agencies are increasingly involved in the family ministries of congregations. Therefore, church agency staff members need to understand the role and nature of the family in Christian thought.[4]

In understanding Christian thought about family relationships, one must begin with Jesus' teaching that nothing must come between disciples and their God, not even family relationships (Matt. 10:34-39; Luke 12:51-53). Here again, Jesus' teaching turned the culture of his environment on its head. In the ancient Mediterranean world, the family was the cornerstone of life and the center of all one's goods, security, hope, and even religious faith. Flying in the face of this culture, Jesus demanded absolute loyalty from his disciples, forbidding one even to return home to bid farewell to his family (Luke 9:61-62). The New Testament consistently stresses that, as important as family relationships are, the relationship with God is ultimate (Mark 12:25; Rom. 7:2; 1 Cor. 7:31). All else, even those loyalties considered to be of utmost significance, including the family, paled in light of the inbreaking of the kingdom of God.

If Jesus had chosen an institution of lesser importance to make his point, the impact of his message would have been weaker. For example, if he had said, "Leave the rest of the garden club to plant the roses and come follow me," or "Anyone who loves boss or work colleagues more than me is not worthy to be called my disciple," no one would have been surprised.

Instead, Jesus said that "anyone who loves his father or mother more than me is not worthy of me; anyone who loves his son or daughter more than me is not worthy of me" (Matt. 10:37). Jesus claimed that his calling to kingdom service superseded the family precisely because the family was highly valued, not only by his listeners, but by Jesus as well (Garland and Garland 1989).

In addition, Jesus revolutionized the definition of the family. While he was teaching, he was interrupted and told that his mother and brothers were outside wanting to talk with him. He responded, "Who is my mother, and who are my brothers?" (Matt. 12:48; Luke 8:19-21). He answered his own question by pointing to his disciples and saying, "Here are my mother and my brothers. For whoever does the will of my Father in heaven is my brother and sister and mother" (Matt. 12:49-50). Jesus' family had heard the word going around that he had lost his senses, and they had come to end his ministry and take him home (Mark 3:21). Jesus used this moment to make it clear that nothing can interfere with the calling of God, not even one's own family. He transformed the very definition of the family. No longer were family relationships limited to the ties of blood and marriage; for Jesus, family encompassed all those who do the will of God.

This same theme is repeated and brought to fruition in Jesus' words from the cross. He spoke to his mother and to one of the disciples, saying to them "Woman, behold your son," and to the disciple, "Behold, your mother" (John 19:26-27). This passage from the Gospel is full of events noted because they represent the fulfillment of Old Testament prophecy.[5] The Gospel writer inserts in the midst of this passage the words from Jesus to his disciple and mother. The writer thus saw Jesus' death as the fulfillment of God's intentions for the family [Bampfylde 1969; Garland and Garland 1990]. Jesus had said during his ministry that he had come not to abolish the law but to fulfill it (Matt. 5:17). We may also say that Jesus had come not to destroy the family but to fulfill God's original intention for the family. It is to be the source of nurture and the channel of God's love for all of God's children, even those who have been deprived of the traditional family relationships of blood and marriage.

The model of family in Jesus' teaching and example, therefore, was not the biological family but the adoptive family. He claimed those who followed him as his family. He joined the disciple and his mother together in an adoptive family relationship. The possibilities for family care are no longer limited to whatever biological relations one has with others. Adoption, family foster care, and adoptive grandparenting can serve as exemplars of this promise. In the community of faith, all children are *our* children. We have responsibility for all children not just as if they were our own, but because they are our own.

But not only are they our children; their mothers and fathers are also our sisters and brothers. It may be that the most loving, caring response to a child's needs is to reach out to the parents with friendship, with nurture, with challenging programs that raise self-esteem and build competence. Abusive, neglectful parents are often isolated parents, with little or no social support network.[6] To care for them is to care most deeply and meaningfully for their children.

The role of the church as articulated in the message of Jesus is to help children and their families move from being strangers and sojourners to become fellow members of the household of God. Martin Marty has suggested that residential child care is "sacramental," speaking of the "sacrament of residence" as a means by which the church can reflect upon how God's grace is shared with the stranger, with homeless children and their families [Marty 1982: 18]. According to Hebrews 13:2, believers are to provide shelter for strangers, and thereby entertain "angels unawares." Even agency services that do not provide physical shelter provide emotional shelter for children and families, and, to the extent that they help these families develop supportive, family-like relationships with one another and/or with a faith community, they fulfill the mandate for Christians to offer hospitality to one another and to strangers.

Certain questions help church congregations and professional staff members personalize this responsibility for all children as our own.

- If some tragedy occurred and your family needed the services of your agency, if it was necessary for your child to be placed away from you in one of your foster homes or residential facilities (or receive other services offered by the church or agency), how would you feel?

- In what services that are being offered (after-school care, weekday programs, etc.) would you be willing and pleased for your child to participate?

- Would you be satisfied that your child was receiving the very best care possible?

- Would you feel supported and strengthened in your role as your child's parent, or ignored and supplanted?

After all, these are indeed our children.

The Responsibility of Faith Communities— Caring for Children

Charles Baker, the executive director of a church residential treatment facility, described the mission of his agency with the following statements:

The most neglected, most needy children need the people of God; nothing less will do.

We must minister to those who are most in need and those who are most at risk.

We have to be passionate [an allusion to Jesus' passion and our following him in that passion] in our care for children. [Baker 1991]

Baker was describing a mission of the church, a specific calling or vocation of a particular community of faith to care for "the least of these," lived out in the work of his agency. Involving churches in caring for children and their families, particularly children and families in crisis who struggle with multiple problems, requires not just an appreciation for the importance of children and families in Christian teaching, but also a clear, passionate calling and a strong, enduring sense of responsibility to address the needs of a particular group of children and families.

Responding out of Christian Responsibility and Discipline

Generosity and pity are not an appropriate base for the church's ministry;

too easily they become condescension and a means of expiating guilt for undeserved good fortune [Keith-Lucas 1962]. Instead, the base for ministry is Christian responsibility and discipline, that we are called to serve whether or not children and their families are "grateful," even whether or not in the end we can demonstrate effectiveness in achieving the aims of service.

> In other words, Christian care does not begin with an attempt to resolve the need of the other. Serving the world simply because the world has needs can be done on entirely non-Christian assumptions. It is the end point to which the secularization of Christian welfare agencies leads. Not that the existence of, or functioning of, the secularized welfare agency is to be criticized. Its problem is, though, that it lacks the radical depth and breadth of vision of the Christian agency, and potentially (in many cases actually) lacks any real vision at all. [Pollard 1991: 9]

Christian care should begin instead with the Christian's response to God's commandment to love God first and above all, and to love neighbor as self (whether or not the neighbor changes as a result of that love). "Anyone can care for a neighbor, and many non-Christian people do better than most Christian people" [Marty 1982: 14]. Care that begins with the other and the other's need is at risk of the other being deemed unlovable, not worthy of care, because of the other's response. Marty has called this kind of love, which begins as a response to the other's need, "soft" love. "Soft love is not durable in the face of the unlovable—and anyone in child care knows the problem of unlovability face to face" [Marty 1982: 15]. Christians are mandated to care, regardless of the response of the cared-for. "Two similar actions can be grounded in impulses of care, but the Christian version wants to draw on the carefulness of God, who lets no sparrow fall nor hair of the head go uncounted" [Marty 1982: 17].

Christian response to an other does not wait to find qualities in that other worthy of response; it is driven not by the lovableness or acceptability in the other, but by response to God's love given to us "while we were yet sinners," while we were unacceptable, unlovable. The children we care for may seem too damaged by life to have much potential for redemption, but because God is the creator, not even one should be overlooked or allowed to slip through the system unnoticed.

> As long as the help we offer to others is motivated primarily by the changes we may accomplish, our service cannot last long. When results do not appear, when success is absent, when we are no longer liked or praised for what we do, we lose the strength and motivation to continue. When we see nothing but sad, poor, sick, or miserable people, who, even after our many attempts to offer help, remain sad, poor, sick, and miserable, the only reasonable response is to move away in order to prevent ourselves from becoming cynical or depressed. Radical servanthood challenges us, while attempting persistently to overcome poverty, hunger, illness, and any other form of human misery, to reveal the gentle presence of our compassionate God in the midst of our broken world. [Nouwen et al. 1983: 31–32]

In the culture in which the New Testament was written, the relation between a benefactor and a beneficiary consisted of reciprocal obligations. The recipient's gratitude was not only expected but ensured a continuing obligation from the benefactor [Talbert 1982]. The caregiver expected some kind of repayment; the kindness was in fact viewed as a loan. Because of the expectation of tangible gratitude, the choice of someone to help was considered carefully. A benefactor was more likely to help the well-to-do than the poor, because one could expect an appropriate response. Benevolence therefore made little penetration into the lower classes [Mott 1974: 72].

In sharp contrast, Jesus taught that his followers must transcend this principle of reciprocity.

> If you love those who love you, what credit is that to you? Even "sinners" love those who love them. And if you do good to those who are good to you, what credit is that to you? Even "sinners" do that. And if you lend to those from whom you expect repayment, what credit is that to you? Even "sinners" lend to "sinners," expecting to be repaid in full.

But love your enemies, do good to them, and lend to them without expecting to get anything back. Then your reward will be great, and you will be sons of the Most High, because he is kind to the ungrateful and wicked. Be merciful, just as your father is merciful. (Luke 6:32-36)

When you give a dinner or a banquet, do not invite your friends or your brothers or your kinsmen or rich neighbors, lest they also invite you in return, and you be repaid. But when you give a feast, invite the poor, the maimed, the lame, the blind, and you will be blessed, because they cannot repay you. You will be repaid at the resurrection of the just. (Luke 14:12b-14)

The norms in our own culture differ little from the norms in Jesus' day. Caregiving comes with the expectation of response; recipients should use the care they receive (tangible help, counseling, shelter and support, friendship) to resolve their problems and become "functional" citizens and families, as indicated on sundry program evaluation outcomes. At the very least, clients should seem grateful for what they receive. Yet children and their families are often not grateful and often seem unable to rise above the problems that plague them, even with help. We readily identify this attitude, and the quick discouragement that follows, in volunteers, who want to see immediate results in the lives of others because of the care they give. Yet our professional services are by no means beyond the principle of reciprocity. Programs that cannot show demonstrable outcomes—as demonstrated in changed lives—are often cut.

Certainly, we want well-intended efforts to succeed, not to damage others or have no impact on their suffering. We want to help, not just to go through the motions to absolve ourselves of responsibility for the neighbor's pain. Many of the problems confronting the children and families we serve, however, do not lend themselves to quick resolution, to short-term demonstrable change. We do not have strategies for intervention that are effective in all situations, particularly in some of the more complex and long-standing situations of family abuse and disintegration. Support for public services often depends on their ability to demonstrate an impact on highly visible social problems—Head Start programs on school dropout and failure rates, protective services on the numbers of children experiencing repeated physical abuse. The church operates from a different value base, one that calls for care regardless of the response. Christ called his followers to discipline themselves to respond to others in love as a response to His love, without any expectation of reciprocity or even response from the other.

The focus is on the disciple's growth as a Christian and connection to the source of continuing love, which is Christ. The disciple's love of others is the fruit of that love:

> Remain in me, and I will remain in you. No branch can bear fruit by itself; it must remain in the vine. Neither can you bear fruit unless you remain in me. I am the vine; you are the branches. If a man remains in me and I in him, he will bear much fruit; apart from me you can do nothing." (John 15:4-5)

To rely on the response of the one loved is folly. To expect and need a reward from the child and family served as the impetus for continuing service inevitably will lead to disappointment, resentment, and even burnout. Perhaps Jesus was the first to describe burnout, with a somewhat different meaning: "If anyone does not remain in me, he is like a branch that is thrown away and withers; such branches are picked up, thrown into the fire and burned" (John 15:6).

Placing Children and Families First

A second emphasis from Christian thought and scripture concerning care for children and their families includes concern not only for groups categorized by issues and crises—the homeless, the abused, the developmentally disabled, the severely emotionally disturbed—but for individual children and families who may slip through the cracks of society's responses to its problems. Certainly, Christian scriptures and church history clearly demonstrate a mandate to speak out in behalf of the poor and oppressed. This kind of speaking out and caring for poor and oppressed persons is most often in response to a group of persons who have experienced a particular kind of oppression, whether societal (racism, poverty, denial of educational opportunities) or personal (chemical dependency, family violence). No less important, however, is the church's attention to individual children and individual families, especially those who do not fit established categories of service.

In Jesus' culture, "Keep holy the Sabbath" was a most significant law, one of the Decalogue, spoken directly by God to Moses (Exodus 20:1a, 8). When Jesus was accused of breaking the Jewish law, by healing on the Sabbath and by allowing his disciples to pluck grain when they were hungry, Jesus made it clear that the Sabbath was made for people, not people for the Sabbath.[7] Such a reinterpretation of the religious law infuriated the religious authorities; it was at this point that they began to plot to kill Jesus (Matt. 12:14; Mark 3:6).

Some of today's social policies and program stipulations concerning services to children and their families seem almost as sacrosanct as Sabbath observance was in Jesus' world. Professionals in both the public and private sectors of child welfare service inevitably confront brick walls of legalities that prevent some children and their families from receiving needed services. Those legalities usually focus on ensuring the general welfare, being sure that those who need services the most or can most benefit from services receive them. The goal is a system that works most of the time for most children and their families. Unfortunately, this means that some children and families do not meet the criteria for receiving service, or fall outside the capabilities of existing programs, and thus cannot be helped by the established systems. Because of the growing crisis in public child welfare, almost all attention now goes to the most serious problems of child abuse and neglect. Families with chronic or multiple problems that do not include abuse may thus be excluded from receiving services. Out of their national research on public child welfare services, Kamerman and Kahn report the following:

> A repeated theme in interviews around the country is that the social service system has become so constricted that children can gain access to help only if they have been abused or severely neglected, are found delinquent, or run away. Doorways for "less serious" or differently defined problems are closed. Even for

these situations, of course, the help may not be forthcoming, or if it is, may not be adequate. [Kamerman and Kahn 1989: 9]

Church agencies, too, can become narrowly focused on the most serious crises confronting children and their families, particularly when they are providing contract services for state agencies. But the value system of the church and its agencies, and their location in the network of social services, can be the basis for attention to needs that may not be as visible as child abuse and do not fit within any current program or service category.

Jesus' teaching about the Sabbath can be the foundation for our position that no rule, policy, or knot of red tape is more important than a single child. Responding to the needs of persons—loving the neighbor— takes priority over the rest of God's laws. How much more firmly can we say, then, that human rules and program policies must never stand in the way of caring when a child's needs are at stake, even when those needs do not fit our categories of service. Sister Mary Paul, working with seriously troubled families in Brooklyn, has said that only needs—not professional preferences or bureaucratic rules—can be allowed to determine the nature of services to families. She has said that, in her program, "no staff member is ever put in the position of denying help to a family on bureaucratic grounds or of having to justify to a cost accountant the time they take to develop a relationship" [Schorr 1988: 176-177].

Saving Souls

A third emphasis from Christian thought and scripture concerning care for children and their families has been embodied in the evangelistic task of the church, bringing persons outside the community of faith into relationship with God and God's son, Jesus Christ, and into membership in the church community. Coupled with the mandate for Christians to serve neighbors in need, evangelism has provided the motivating force behind the church's historic involvement in child welfare services.

Evangelism has been particularly important in church traditions in which children are not considered "innocent" until an age at which God holds them accountable for their sin. The church has reached out to troubled and troubling children not only to save them from the difficulties in this life, but also to save them from damnation in the next life.[8] Christian traditions that emphasize the ultimate importance of a conscious decision to become a follower of Christ focus their care of children on the children's coming to verbalize such a decision. The "reverent and hopeful agnosticism" [Kingdon 1973: 98] about what happens to children who die before they make such a decision and the worry that children will grow into adults without Christian faith turn to comfort in the joyful accomplishment of the church's mission.

To this end, children in residential care have been required to attend church, chapel services, and religious education programs. Careful attention has been given to overt decisions by clients to become Christians. Helping professionals employed by church agencies have often reacted with frustration and exasperation to pressure from supporting churches, who want to know the status of the souls of the children being served.

Gillogly has argued that we ought to rethink the concept of "saving souls" in our care for children, and to help churches to do so. Gillogly defines the soul as the presence of God within us and among us. The soul is the capacity to care, to love, for "God is love" (1 John 4:16). The soul is "not a thing, not an object, not an entity, not a datum, not something that can be quantified, or measured, or weighed or encapsulated, but a capacity—the God-given capacity to care" [Gillogly 1991: 19]. Child abuse and neglect, whether by persons or insensitive social systems, destroy the capacity to care; they are "soul murder" [Gillogly 1991: 20].

The role of the church, then, is to save souls by restoring the capacity to care. There can be no salvation unless care is experienced and trusted. Children's faith is built on experiences of love, commitment, redemption, and reconciliation they share with significant others in their lives. The potential for faith is destroyed by experiences of love and trust betrayed, promises and commitments broken, forgiveness denied, and relationships severed. The basis of faith is trust in others.

From his study of children's concept of God, David Heller concluded:

> Trust is the process which makes it possible for faith to emerge
> in the child. By laying the groundwork for stable representations,
> trust permits a deity representation to have consistent meaning

in the child's inner world....It is most difficult for a child saddled with overbearing family problems...to confront the question of a God's existence. [Heller 1986: 142-143]

In sum, those who cannot trust cannot have faith. Many of the families in our care cannot trust. The child cannot trust the parent to provide nurture, protection, or even material sustenance. Parents may have learned their untrustworthiness from their own experiences as children and adults with people on whom they relied for nurture, protection, and sustenance. It is a primary task of the church agency, therefore, to provide experiences in which clients' trust is earned and honored. Human beings—whether children or parents—must learn experientially in human relationships what love, trust, reconciliation, and commitment mean before they can experience such a relationship with God. Moreover, Newbigin has posited, there can be no salvation for an individual except by being restored to the wholeness of relationships for which God made us.

If each human being were ultimately understood as an independent spiritual monad, then salvation could only be through an action directed impartially to each and all. But if the truly human is the shared reality of mutual and collective responsibility that the Bible envisages, then salvation must be an action that binds us together and restores for us the true mutual relation to each other. [Newbigin 1978: 78]

The focus of soul-saving in the church's child welfare services, therefore, should not be primarily on inculcating a set of beliefs into individual clients. "A church agency exists as an expression of faith and not to require certain beliefs, and behavior, in the people it serves—we call ourselves Christian or Jewish not because of how we insist that our clients behave, but because of how we behave towards them" [Keith-Lucas 1982: 33]. This behavior toward them, relating to them in ways that are loving, trustworthy, committed, and redemptive, is, in essence, evangelistic.

Church agency professionals deal overtly with questions of faith in their work with children and their families. Children in our care are dealing with life questions that have theological significance: "Who can I trust? Is there anybody I can count on?" Their parents may be wrestling with similar questions, to which their own life experiences have never offered satisfactory response. They may never express interest in the nature of God, and would be surprised, perhaps, if an agency professional drew a connection between their life experiences of being let down, of finding others untrustworthy, and their perceptions of God. Working through hurtful experiences and incorporating them into a functional strategy for living involves not only corrective experiences but also putting words and meaning to those experiences. Children and families try to understand not only what is happening to them, but why, and in doing so, they call upon the religious life they have experienced and the spiritual values they have received.

Robert Coles has studied the spiritual development of children and concluded, concerning children—and adults—who have catastrophic experiences:

> They may not so much become undone as become aroused psychologically—prompted to look with the utmost intensity at their past life, their present condition, and their future prospects, if any. Under such circumstances, psychological themes connect almost imperceptibly, but quite vividly at moments, with a spiritual inwardness. [Coles 1990: 101]

Religion and psychology in a sense merge in a process of "defensive spirituality" [Coles 1990: 107]. At such times, the professional helper cannot avoid dealing with spiritual concerns, cannot refer such matters to the clergy, but must recognize that they are interwoven with the client's interpretations of intrapersonal experiences and interpersonal relationships. Whether the professional caregiver recognizes it or not, to work with clients means to deal with spiritual issues.

Professional caregivers also deal with the spiritual dimension of clients' lives by helping them learn to give. Spiritual growth comes not just from experiencing trust, love, and forgiveness, but also from giving of self to others. There is nothing more impoverishing than to receive without being able to give. To enable persons to give is to empower them. "Adult efforts to restore youth so that they can someday be useful citizens will not be enough. We must strive to involve them in service to their communities so that they can be restored. In helping others the young person creates his own proof of worthiness: being of value to someone" [Brendtro 1982: 48-49].

Youths in residential facilities and treatment centers are being guided in their own spiritual growth when they operate recreation programs for neighborhood children, volunteer at day care centers, conduct Special Olympics events for developmentally disabled persons, visit senior citizens in nursing homes, or restore and revitalize their own communities. Parents are being guided in their spiritual growth when they work toward greater competency and understanding in their relationships with their children. For some, opportunities for spiritual growth come when they offer friendship and support to others who come behind them in the experience of family crisis. This may occur in parent support groups when parents stay on after they have resolved their own family crises to encourage and support others. It occurs when a parent who has experienced the support and friendship of a church volunteer in a "befriending" program volunteers in turn to befriend another parent in crisis.

Staff members in a church agency do not necessarily experience any greater sense of freedom in speaking with clients about spiritual matters than those in state or private nonsectarian agencies. The situation is often just as complex, with subtle but very real expectations about professional conduct. For example, staff members may be keenly aware that their spiritual beliefs, or their understanding of how those beliefs ought to be communicated to others, sharply deviate from those of supporting churches, even though they may be members of those churches. They may have to live with clear mandates about such matters. For example, a Catholic residential treatment facility for adolescent girls may have strict guidelines for discussing birth control and abortion, with which staff members may or may not agree. In other cases, a staff member may have to use considerable discretion and expend enormous energy in communicating to supporting religious groups the agency's interpretation and response to evangelism as an agency goal. "Thus staff in a church-related agency may only be free insofar as they share a defined outlook in the community of believers" [Brendtro 1982: 40]. With considerable work, the professional may be able to shape that "defined outlook."

Professional agency staff members can often help shape an understanding of effective evangelism with children by serving as a resource (leading parent workshops or providing program materials to parents and church leaders) for the spiritual development of the children in their midst. Parents and other caring adults respond with great interest to workshops and materials that deal with such questions as "Will our children have faith?" and "How can we best nurture the spiritual growth of our children?"

In church agencies, confronting the spiritual development of children and families sometimes comes in direct response to the actions of one or more of their clients in the church community. For example, many church agencies strongly encourage or require clients living in a residential facility to participate in the life of a local congregation. A child may quickly learn that the most vulnerable spot for the staff—where the child can create the most pain for others—is in matters of religion and faith. Children may express their pain, their anger at separation from family, by lashing out at the church and by expressing their disdain for religion and spiritual matters. Nothing will quite get the attention of the church community like symbols associated with demonology spray-painted on a church wall by residents of the church agency's residential child care center. The professional skill required for explaining such behavior to concerned supporters is no less than the skill required to help the agency's clients. However difficult, such occasions provide opportunities for the agency staff to educate the church about the nature of spiritual development in children and the meaning of "saving souls."

Seeking Justice Inside and Outside the Church

Churches understand ministries of care to children and families in crisis and are motivated by their evangelistic mission. They find it harder, however, to embrace the biblical mandate to seek justice, to speak out against oppressive social systems. It is easy to love children; it is possible to care about and respond to the needs of rebellious teens; congregations can show compassion for hurting and hurtful parents. It is more difficult, however, to understand and take action in response to the complexity of issues and social policies and institutional practices that insidiously destroy children and their families.

Jesus took children in his arms, but he also attacked the systems in his society that burdened people to the point that they could not care for one another. He spoke out against those who hindered children from knowing God:

> But if anyone causes one of these little ones who believe in me to sin, it would be better for him to have a large millstone hung around his neck and to be drowned in the depths of the sea." (Matt. 18:5-6 NIV)

To sin is to live estranged from God's love. Reducing children's capacity to love and to care, therefore, causes them to sin, to "lose their souls" [Gillogly 1991]. Systems that destroy parents' ability to love and care for their children, therefore, deserve to have millstones tied around them and be thrown into the sea. Some economic systems keep people poor; some educational systems deny children hope; some welfare systems oppress people rather than empowering them to deal with their circumstances. Such systems are the result of social sin, "a hardening of the consequences of personal sin into the structures of institutions" [Lane 1984: 128].

The people of God are called to seek justice and mercy (Micah 6:8). They are to "turn the hearts of the fathers to their children" (Luke 1:17), making ready for their Lord. Jesus' message was a call for observance of Jubilee, for liberation:

> The Spirit of the Lord is upon me, because he has anointed me to preach good news to the poor. He has sent me to proclaim release to the captives and recovering of sight to the blind, to set at liberty those who are oppressed, to proclaim the acceptable year of the Lord." (Luke 4:18-19)

This good news is not something that Christians simply receive passively; it is good news they are called on to live actively.

Christian hope speaks to everyone's sense of powerlessness to change the system. (Subjectively, we are all proletarians.) Faithful hope overcomes the prevailing sense of fate. It gives a vision to people who were nobodies and empowers them to act humanely in the face of oppressive policies and institutionalized violence. [Hessell 1982: 61]

New Testament writers present Jesus and his church as trying together to live out a social ethic. The first responsibility of the church is to be the church, to be a community that demonstrates to the world, through the way its members deal with one another, what social relations directed by God are like. The church is to be a creative minority, a witness to God's mercy [Hauerwas 1974; Nouwen et al. 1983; Talbert 1982]. Any ministry with or advocacy in behalf of children and their families must flow from this communal life.

Family ministry is thus neither a new ministry—an extra for the church that can afford it—nor the last thing to be added when everything else is in place. The apostle Paul saw it as integral to the gospel, central in his ministry with churches. One can even say that Paul was the first family minister. His "family life education" was an integral part of his writings to the churches; his letters to the churches are filled with instructions for living rightly in families and relating to one another in the community of faith as family.[9] Christianity is a faith that deals with the nitty-gritty of life—how to handle anger in family life, how husbands and wives are to relate to one another sexually, how parents are to discipline their children. Out of this life together, then, voices and actions can be raised in response to the structures and the ways of life of the larger society that hurt families and children.

The Relationship between Volunteer Ministry and Professional Services in the Name of the Church

What is the role of the helping professions in the ministries and programs of the church that respond to needs of children and their families? Earlier, I explored the roles of serving on behalf of the church (the missionary role) and of empowering congregation members themselves to respond to the needs of children and families (the role of spiritual guide). Should the church respond with programs of community service based in individual congregations and staffed primarily by the congregation's own volunteers? Or should churches be encouraged to fund services offered by agencies employing a professional staff, agencies at least partly independent from the congregations themselves? Does an examination of biblical texts suggest that one should receive more emphasis than the other?

The main biblical material that can be used in relation to such questions comes from the work of the apostle Paul and his relationship to the churches scattered over the Mediterranean world. Paul carried on his ministry while he supported himself at his trade. He also accepted support from others, like the Phillippian congregation (Phil. 4:10). As many as 40 persons sponsored him and his coworkers in various ways. His letters are filled with thanks for their hospitality and financial support. Paul also had a team of coworkers. Some of them were permanent members of his team; others were deployed temporarily from local churches for particular responsibilities or served in his behalf when he was imprisoned or otherwise constrained.[10] In addition to his sponsors, then, Paul had a temporary and permanent "staff." His work existed alongside, but also somewhat separate from, the churches he had founded. Like the churches, Paul used family terminology extensively when writing about his colleagues, calling them mothers, sisters, brothers, and sons.[11]

Despite the close relationships between Paul's ministry and the church communities, there were also clear differences [Banks 1980]. Paul's mission had a specific and limited purpose different from that of the church. The ministry team was called together not primarily to share in a common life, but rather to work together in a common task. "Paradoxically this may have led to their sharing 'all things in common' more than the communities founded by them" [Banks 1980: 162]. Even so, the work was not focused on the community they shared but was inherent in their tasks and goals—preaching the gospel and establishing and consulting with churches. Despite the cooperative nature of the ministry team, Paul had a position of authority and direction. For example, he was the one who "sent" or "left" his colleagues to engage in various activities.[12] This organizational structure differed from the coming and going of one's own accord to be expected of unpaid workers in a church community. In his analysis of Paul's ministry, Banks concludes:

> Though the churches and the work are integrally related, each has an ongoing life apart from the other. The purpose for which each exists, the skills upon which each depends, and the authority through which each lives are not identical, even though they share a great deal in common. The two groups are interdependent and in a whole variety of ways assist one another in their work. [Banks 1980: 165]

Paul and his colleagues spent considerable energy maintaining the interdependence between their work and the supporting congregations, yet also balancing this with the specialized ministry to which they were called. They set the precedent for churches to sponsor specialized ministries that go beyond the expertise and resources of any one congregation, or even a consortium of congregations.

Church agencies can use this early church experience to inform their work. It provides grounding for specialized ministries beyond the reach of congregations. In Paul's day, that "beyond" was based primarily on geography, but also to some extent on language, culture, and other social characteristics. Today's church agency serves children and their families who are often beyond the reach of congregations, families who need specialized professional services as the language through which they can experience the church's caring.

The challenge for today's specialized ministry team in church agencies is often not in providing the services, but in maintaining an interdependent relationship with the congregations. It is too easy to take the money and run, to treat the church as a source of funding for the agency rather than to take on the task of nurturing congregations toward Christian maturity, a task just as significant to the work of the agency as providing quality professional services to its clients.

The parallel purpose in Paul's ministry was the nurture of the communities he had founded, leading the churches toward Christian maturity. He did so by visiting them, writing letters to help them with problems they faced, sending staff members to them, and praying frequently and consistently for their progress. However, he was also pioneering new areas, reaching out with the Good News. The United Methodist Association of Health and Welfare Ministries has used Jesus' parable about the wounded traveler and the Samaritan to illustrate this partnership in ministry between the congregation and the professional (Luke 10: 29-37). "The Good Samaritan had a partner in his mission of caring love for the man who had been mistreated. That partner was the Innkeeper. The Innkeeper represents the professional who helps us...express our caring love for children, youth and families who are 'beside the road'" [United Methodist Association (undated): 1].

The answer to the question of which is more important, then, is that both the community-based services of congregational members and the specialized services of professional agency staff members are needed in the church's care for children and families in crisis. The greatest challenge to both church and professional is to maintain the integration and involvement of each in the work of the other. The maintenance of this integration and the articulation of the shared task of church and agency requires professional skills in assessing the worldview of the congregation, in communicating sensitively and empathically, in articulating the relationship between the congregation's values and the mission of congregation and agency, in consulting with clergy and congregational members concerning their work with families and children, and in resolving conflicts and maintaining working relationships over time and tasks. These skills are no less demanding than the skills of family intervention, crisis management, and child welfare decision-making necessary for working with children and their families in crisis.

Conclusions

"The church has and seeks no monopoly on social justice, virtue, or care. It has no theology, motivation, or charter—and certainly no credentials— for doing so" [Marty 1982: 21]. Similarly, church agencies are by no means the only repository of Christian care for children and their families. Public and private nonsectarian agencies employ many Christians who give selflessly to children and their families, motivated by their own sense of calling to ministry to "the least of these," these being Jesus in our midst.

Even so, the church makes a distinctive corporate response to children and their families in crisis through its agencies. Its leaders and staff members can recognize this response for what it is, respecting and articulating the values and story of the church as a community of faith living in response to a God of love. Otherwise, Marty's question quoted early in this chapter—What is the difference between church agencies and other child welfare agencies?—could be answered "not much." An agency that allows or encourages the role of the church to become peripheral in its work should include the church group that has sponsored it in planning for this change in the agency's mission. Sometimes this seems to be the best direction. Sometimes churches bring a societal need to the attention of the community through their response and then give away that response system to the public sector and move on to other targets for their service. Professional integrity suggests, however, that the agency be conscientious in including the sponsoring church group in the decision to make this kind of change in agency mission.

Most church agencies will continue to claim their identity with the church, and to strengthen that identity. This means that church agency staff members will need to study the church and its scriptures as they would study any culture in which they practice professionally. They can learn to speak in words and images that carry particular communicative power in that culture. Christian helping professionals who can talk the "language of Zion" have the advantage of being able to become a part of the church as a social system. It is similar to the advantage experienced by the Mexican American, Spanish-speaking professional who practices in a Latino community on the Texas border.

This chapter is only an introduction to the rich biblical and theological foundation for services to children and their families that professional staff members can appreciate and articulate to the church as the basis for ministry. To ignore the connection between the agency and its religious heritage is to attempt to live as a branch apart from the vine, to risk being thrown away from the foundation and source.

In addition to the content of this chapter, the Bible and the history of the church are full of stories that express the nature of Christian faith, and that can connect today's care of children with the experiences of great biblical figures and the stories of God's working throughout the church's history. As a starter, Appendix 1 contains suggestions for using biblical stories in communicating with churches about caring for children and their families.

Notes

1. Brendtro [1982] drew the myths about church-related agencies from an application of Merrimon Cuninggim's 1978 article, "Myths of Church-Relatedness," which addressed church-related educational institutions, not child welfare agencies. Brendtro recognized the similarity that church association confers on organizational cultures, despite the difference between child welfare and educational institutions.

2. Unless otherwise noted, all Scripture refences are to the Revised Standard Version. _NIV_ denotes the New International Version.

3. _Proof texting_ is the process of deciding what one thinks or is going to do, and then searching the scriptures for a passage that backs up that decision. It is more faithful to the intent of scripture to instead begin with a thorough knowledge of biblical themes and the writers' intentions, and to proceed from that knowledge to a consideration of what one ought to do in response.

4. A myriad of books and articles have articulated a theology of family and guided a study of the family in the Bible. See, for example, Anderson and Guernsey 1985; Curran 1980; Garland and Conrad 1990a; Garland 1990a; Guernsey 1982; Kaplan et al. 1984; Olson and Leonard 1990; Sell 1981; and Sheek 1985.

5. John 19:23-25, 28-30, 31-37.

6. See, among others, Cobb 1976; Colletta and Gregg 1981; Garbarino 1979; Gottlieb 1981; Pilisuk 1982; Pilisuk and Parks 1983; and Scheinfeld et al. 1970.

7. For example, see Matt. 12:9-13; Mark 2:23-27, 3:1-5, 7:6-8.

8. Kingdon asserts what many Christians believe: "Unless God saves children by free grace they are and will be eternally lost ...The ground of our hope is

not the supposed innocence of children but in the grace and mercy of the God and Father of our Lord Jesus Christ" [Kingdon 1973: 94].

9. For example, see Eph. 5, 1; Thess. 4:3-8; 1 Tim. 3:5, 5:4-8, 12; Titus 2:4-5; 1 Cor. 13.

10. For coworkers who were permanent members of Paul's team, see Rom. 16:21-22; and Col. 4:10-14. For those who were deployed temporarily from local churches for particular services, see Phil. 4:18; 1 Cor. 1:11; and Phil. 2:25-30. For those who served in Paul's behalf when he was imprisoned or otherwise constrained, see 1 Thess. 3:6; 1 Cor. 4:17, 16:3; 2 Cor. 7:6-15, 8:16-23; Phil. 2:19-23; Col. 4:7-9; and Eph. 6:21-22.

11. Rom. 14:13, 16:1; Phil. 2:22; Philem. 2, 10.

12. 1 Thess. 3:2; 1 Cor. 4:17; 2 Cor. 8:18 ff; Phil. 2:19, 23, 25, 28; Col. 4:8-9; Philem. 12; Eph. 6:22.

CHAPTER 3

The Historical Roots and Development of American Church-Sponsored Child Welfare Services

PROFESSIONAL SOCIAL WORK and child welfare services are only a century old, yet the church has been actively involved in child welfare for its entire 2000-year history. Prior to the conversion of Roman Emperor Constantine in the fourth century, when Christians represented a tiny minority of the population, they astounded others with the ministry they extended to many oppressed groups, including widows and children abandoned on the trash heaps of Roman society. Christians considered it their first concern to care for those who had no one else to care for them. Consequently, the history of the church's involvement in child welfare in the United States began in the Roman world in which Christianity developed. The church spread throughout the Roman Empire and continued to grow in influence and responsibility throughout Europe after the fall of the Roman Empire and beyond, up through the transplantation and development of Christianity in America.

In modern times, the church has played two basic roles in child welfare services. First, it has had a pervasive impact on both sectarian and public child welfare services because of its impact on individual Christians, nurturing in them a valuing of service to the poor and oppressed, the victims of society. Some of these persons have made vocational commitments to caring for children and their families and have become pivotal figures in child welfare services, either by leading the church in response to current needs or by serving through other channels. The ranks of professional child welfare staff members in public and private agencies continue to include Christians who see their professional practice as an expression of their personal faith and Christian calling. Others have served as volunteers in social service programs in response to the claims of Christian faith on their lives.

Second, the church as a community of faith has involved itself directly and corporately in specific ministries with and in behalf of children and their families. Individual congregations, denominations, and ecumenical and parachurch organizations have responded to the needs of children and their families by developing and supporting service programs, agencies, institutions, and coordinated child advocacy campaigns.

Children in Society

In the early centuries of the church, the most critical problem in child welfare was an elementary one—saving the lives of children who had been left without support by the death of parents or who had been abandoned to die. The church's care for infants and children is remarkable because it took place in a society largely unaware of, and apparently unconcerned with, the needs of children, a society that did not recognize any community responsibility for children.

As European society developed during the early centuries of the church, infants were not even counted among the family members. Perhaps this was due in part to high infant mortality rates; families could not expect their children to survive infancy. As late as the mid-eighteenth century, Caulfield [1931] noted that 75% of all infants christened in London were dead before they reached the age of five. Others have said that the infant mortality rate was not typically that high, suggesting that 80% to 85% of babies survived at least the first year or two of life [Pollock 1983]. In times of famine or plague, however, the rates climbed much higher. Parents may well have felt affection and love for their children, even though disease often killed one after the other. It does appear, however, that young infants were not mourned as deeply as older children [Pollock 1983].

If the uncertainty of life discouraged a recognition of childhood as a separate stage of life and encouraged parents to distance themselves emotionally from their offspring, it is somewhat surprising that ideas about childhood began to change to some degree as early as the twelfth century, when infant mortality rates were still quite high. Yet Aries' 1962 study of the development of childhood through art reveals that dead children began to be memorialized in individual paintings in the twelfth century. They also began to be included in family portraits, often holding a cross or a skull to indicate their death. Infants began to count, then, as family members. At the same time, the idea of "necessary wastage," that certain numbers of children would inevitably die and, therefore, a high birth rate was needed, did not finally disappear in all social classes of Europe until the eighteenth century.

Many historians suggest that childhood was "discovered" in the twelfth century [e.g. Caulfield 1931; Aries 1962]. Even so, in those harsh times of subsistence economies and short life spans, there could be no luxury of prolonged childhood. Medieval art pictured children simply as miniature adults. If they survived infancy, children whose parents could not support them became responsible for self-support at approximately age seven. This was true even into the sixteenth century. A statute enacted in England in 1535 declared that poor children over the age of five could be put to work by the city and town governments.

Until modern times, in spite of continuing high infant mortality rates, many parents had more surviving children than they could support. Because children were solely the responsibility of their parents and because infants were not highly valued, infanticide continued to occur even into the eighteenth century, as it had throughout the church's history [Kadushin 1974]. Infanticide often took the form of abandonment. Parents who were unable to care for a child simply left the child to die or to be found and accepted by others. The story of Hansel and Gretel is a story of attempted abandonment; the stepmother and the acceding father "lost" the children in the forest because they did not have enough food for both children and parents. Throughout the centuries, other desperate parents sold their children into slavery or indentured them as servants. These practices often were more a consequence of the hardness of life than of indifference to children. Bossard and Boll note the story of a Greek father who was asked, "Why do you expose your children?" He responded, "Because I love the children I have" [Bossard and Boll 1966: 614]. Abandonment was also practiced in America. As late as 1873, 122 infants were reportedly found dead in the streets and rivers of New York City [Radbill 1968].

The Church's Response

In striking contrast to the culture's blindness to children, Christianity espoused their great value. Children represented the presence of Christ, who said, "Whoever welcomes one of these children in my name welcomes me" (Mark 9:37). From its beginning, the church took on the major task of caring for abandoned and orphaned children. Early Christians took these children into their own homes. As its moral theology developed, the Catholic Church declared infanticide a mortal sin. Consequently, abandonment of children by leaving them surreptitiously at the steps of churches or monasteries increasingly replaced the practice of exposing them to die [Unsworth 1991].

To care for a growing number of children, churches began to establish institutions. As early as 325, the Council of Nicaea prescribed that an institution be established in each Christian village to care for the sick, the poor, and the abandoned children. "At the seventh-century Council of Rouen, the priests of each diocese were instructed to inform their congregations that women might leave at the door of the church any children for whom they could not care" [Kadushin 1974: 41]. A basket to receive abandoned infants was placed in each church. A fourth-century church manual urged childless couples to adopt orphans and instructed bishops to provide full support until the children reached adulthood [Hinson 1988]—the first subsidized adoptions.

Hinson has suggested that it may have been pressure from Christians that led to legislation under Constantine prohibiting removal of abandoned children from the care of those who took them in. Although the church struggled throughout the centuries to respond to the needs of children, their needs were often greater than the resources the church could muster. As an example of the size of the problem, Minuchin and Elizur report [1990: 44] that the order of St. Vincent De Paul in France sheltered 312 children prior to the invention in the eighteenth century of the turret, a turntable on which an infant could be placed and then anonymously passed into the foundling home. After this simple invention was installed, the home received 2,150 children in 1740, 40,000 in 1784, and 131,000 in 1833.

Training and Educating Children and Youths

During the sixteenth and seventeenth centuries, Christian religious orders began to teach children and young people and developed schools. Spanish-Dutch humanist Juan Luis Vives (1492-1540) argued that compulsory education should be provided for poor children. In Ypres, the reorganization of poor relief required children to be apprenticed privately or be sent to school, where, under a strict regime that ordered every aspect of life, they were to be taught trade skills [Michielse and van Krieken 1990]. At the same time, parents were taught that they were responsible before God for the lives of their own children. They could no longer prepare only one child or a few of their children for adult life; by the late seventeenth century, both church and state held them responsible for training all their children, even the girls. "Henceforth it was recognized that the child was not ready for life, and that he had to be subjected to a special treatment, a sort of quarantine, before he [sic] was allowed to join the adults" [Aries 1962: 412]. This concern for children was not entirely selfless. During the Middle Ages, gangs of predatory children roamed Europe. Many of the "knights" of romantic stories were actually young adolescents seeking their fortunes, often at the expense of the citizenry. One of the aims of strengthening the family unit's responsibility for its children and developing schools was to contain, support, and socialize children [Westman 1979].

This emphasis on training and education has continued to be a driving force in the church's response to the needs of children. For example, after the emancipation of slaves in the United States, in the late nineteenth century, African American churches in the South established schools, often staffed and run by African American teachers. This investment in schools resulted in a sharp decrease in the African American illiteracy rate [Billingsley and Giovannoni 1972]. Sunday schools were originally founded by churches for poor working children, who otherwise would not have the opportunity to learn to read. In many African American communities, these first lessons in reading and writing were given to both children and adults [Niebuhr 1932; Lincoln and Mamiya 1991].

Education and training have also been focal points in the church's care for dependent children in the United States. From the nineteenth century and well into the twentieth, providers of child welfare services argued that religious instruction was the key ingredient in their services, and that proper religious training was necessary to prepare children for this world and the life beyond. According to one supporter of church institutions, "all the efficient, lasting work for children today is accomplished under the direction of the various churches. The best results attained in institutions are to be found where religion is the groundwork of the system" [Mulry 1898: 365]. Many church leaders were particularly adamant on the value of a religious education in a church institution for society's waifs and strays.

Dependent Children in Early American History

This concern with giving society's dependent children a religious education in a church institution was not an early response of churches in colonial America, however. Institutional care for children in the United States was relatively slow to develop. During the first century of the colonization of America, English settlers established almost no institutions for dependent children. Most infants and sick children, and sometimes small children of widows, received support in their own homes at the expense of the town or parish; others were boarded out to families willing to take them. Usually, however, children were "bound out" or indentured as early and as cheaply as possible. In public auctions, members of the community were asked to tender a figure for the support of a child for the coming year and the child was given to the lowest bidder [Tiffin 1982]. This approach to caring for dependent children fit a pioneer society where life was hard and labor was scarce; as soon as children could work, they did. This remained the preferred way of caring for dependent children into the late eighteenth and early nineteenth centuries.

By the 1800s, orphanages were still rare and young children were increasingly housed in almshouses, where they lived with older paupers and the mentally and physically ill until they could be indentured. In the 1820s, reformers were recommending that children be placed on "poor farms," where their labor could be overseen by a superintendent, rather than in almshouses. The great age of orphanages began in 1830. In the next 20 years, benevolent individuals and religious groups founded 56 orphanages and other institutions for children. The end of the Civil War brought further impetus to get all dependent children out of almshouses and into situations better suited to their needs, with the orphans of soldiers and sailors a primary target group [Bremner (I) 1970]. African American churches and religious organizations developed institutions for dependent African American children after emancipation [Billingsley and Giovannoni 1972]. Bremner [(I) 1970: 269] estimates that 90% of the children's asylums were established and run by religious denominations or nonsectarian groups, rather than by governments.

Social Action

From the Reformation until the present, the church has confronted many challenges that called for examining the social implications of the Christian faith. Although care for orphans and abandoned children continued, some churches and church members also addressed the social causes of suffering. From its beginnings in seventeenth-century England, the Society of Friends (commonly known as Quakers) actively supported care for the poor and opposition to slavery, including the slavery of children and consequent separation from their families. During the American colonial period, John Woolman traveled throughout the American South convincing Quakers to manumit their slaves. Quakers petitioned state legislatures to enact laws against slavery and boycotted products produced by the labor of slaves [Leonard 1988].

Poverty had become an inescapable reality for many Americans by the early nineteenth century. New immigration and the uncertainties of employment in an infant industrial economy meant that large segments of the population were living in destitution. The lot of children continued to be perilous, dependent almost solely on the provision and protection of their parents. In early nineteenth-century New England, poorhouse children as young as four were working in the textile factories 16 to 18 hours a day.

Church leaders had little to guide them toward an understanding of the forces that were causing poverty. The focus was on personal factors such as "improvidence, intemperance, and discouragement" [Smith 1957: 163]. An understanding of larger societal forces had not emerged; the social sciences had not yet taken shape. Even so, church leaders seemed to be groping for a more satisfactory answer than blaming the poor for their plight. At a revival in Boston in 1842, evangelist Edward Norris Kirk preached: "When men love their neighbors as themselves, the causes of poverty will be sought out, and the remedy applied as far as possible…and that in any case, none had the right to allow children to suffer for their parents' sins" [Smith 1957: 162]. By the time of the Civil War, the conviction had become commonplace that society must be reconstructed through the power of the Christian gospel and the evils of cruelty, slavery, poverty, and greed must be destroyed [Smith 1957].

At the same time, personal benevolence was a constant theme in antebellum treatises and sermons. Great revivalists like Charles Grandison Finney strove to inspire charitable voluntarism on a national scale and at all levels of society by preaching hellfire and damnation and demanding that social action follow conversion. The financially successful were considered obligated to serve the community in which they had prospered. Contemporary authors extolled the virtues of the "Christian Gentleman," pointing to particularly exemplary individuals. Freeman Hunt, a popular author, wrote books about charitable businessmen such as Stephen Girard, who personally cared for the sick during the yellow fever epidemics of 1793 and 1797 and founded a college for poor orphan boys.

George Cadbury exemplified the individual Christian responding to the needs of individuals as well as to the social factors that oppressed many. Cadbury was born in 1839 to a Quaker family in England and became a model philanthropist, making a fortune in the family's chocolate business. He gave away all his money, believing it immoral to harbor wealth. According to Cadbury, wealth was slavery and the lack of it, freedom. He argued that giving away almost everything he earned was a selfish act, because in the process, he gave away his worries. He was an innovator in providing for the needs of his workers and their children in an era when an employer was not considered responsible for the economic and social plight of employees. According to Cadbury, "the mere giving of money is of small value in the sight of God without personal self-denying service as well" [Nightingale 1973: 133]. He established a vacation home for poor children. He would often visit them in the evenings, slipping chocolate bars under their pillows and telling them stories. It is estimated that he entertained 25,000 children each year, over a million in his lifetime [Nightingale 1973: 134].

For many, the dramatic and overwhelming suffering of the American Civil War and the social consequences of rapid industrialization shattered the somewhat simple earlier view of benevolence. The chief distinguishing feature of American religion after 1865 was the rapid growth in attention to the societal causes of poverty and other social problems. The concern had already been present; the development of the social sciences provided the conceptual framework church leaders had been seeking. Seminaries reorganized their programs to stress sociology. Community settlement work became prominent in the cities. Crusades for the rights of oppressed groups absorbed the energies of hundreds of the clergy [Smith 1957].

In 1842, Albert Barnes declared that "sin is never solitary, nor can it be banished piecemeal from society" [Smith 1957: 152]. William Arthur, a Methodist, was another spokesman for the movement. Arthur most clearly expounded the social implications of belief in deliverance from all sin and entire consecration in his book *The Tongue of Fire*, which appeared in a half-dozen editions in England and America after 1854. He warned that the two most dangerous perversions of the gospel were to look upon it as salvation for the soul after it leaves the body, but no salvation from sin in this life, and as a means of forming a holy community in the world to come, but never in this [Smith 1957: 154].

Seeking to diminish human suffering, both evangelical Christians and their more liberal counterparts campaigned to reconstruct social and economic relations on the basis of their understanding of the biblical Kingdom of God. In particular, evangelical religion and revivalism "nourished the impulse to social reform" [White and Hopkins 1976: 5]. Charles Grandison Finney, known as the "father of modern revivalism," urged converts to move from personal conversion to social mission. Voluntary associations, or "societies," developed in which individuals (not churches) joined together in social action to support a common cause. The abolition of slavery and racial caste was one such cause. These societies were the forerunners of organizations that would flourish later under the social gospel, some of which would become child welfare agencies [White and Hopkins 1976].

The industrial era of the late nineteenth and early twentieth centuries, with the growth of slums, labor unrest, urban blight, and unrestrained business practices, had also been accompanied by the growth of pseudo-Darwinian views, perhaps best represented by Andrew Carnegie's "gospel of wealth." In the view of the steel baron Carnegie and others of like mind, God had given certain persons the ability to make money and use it effectively for the benefit of all. With proper stewardship, the material blessings of the rich would trickle down to the impoverished many.

Andrew Carnegie became an archetypal figure. According to Carnegie:

> The first requisite for a really good use of wealth by the millionaire who has accepted the gospel, which proclaims him only a trustee of the surplus that comes to him, is to take care that the purposes for which he spends it shall not have a degrading, pauperizing tendency upon its recipients, but that his trust shall

be so administered as to stimulate the best and most aspiring poor of the community to further efforts for their own improvement...; and the duty of the millionaire is to resolve to cease giving to objects that are not clearly proved to his satisfaction to be deserving. [Carnegie 1962: 31]

Carnegie believed that poor persons could "make it" as he had, if they worked hard enough, and that wealth should be used to encourage them in that work. He believed that the wealthy should invest in universities, libraries, and other public institutions that would encourage and enable individuals to strive harder.

Others sharply disagreed with the supposition that some people had to accumulate wealth to ensure the economic health of the social structure. For example, in a lecture entitled "Christianity and the Social Situation" at Ohio Wesleyan University, George Peck Eckman, Pastor of St. Paul's Methodist Episcopal Church in New York City, said:

Enormous possessions by any man are not required for the advantage of society. A whole people lifted above the level of grinding necessity would accomplish all that civilization requires...Let all the people be exalted in material conditions, and let us all be permeated by the spirit of culture and religion, and the monuments which their generosity and devotion shall rear will reflect far greater glory...than all those separate contributions...to the beauty and order of our times which are made by the gifts of enormously wealthy individuals. [Eckman 1908: 131]

Foremost among those attacking the social problems that created the grinding poverty and suffering of the cities at the turn of the century was Walter Rauschenbusch (1861-1918), a German Baptist who spearheaded the social gospel movement.[1] Serving a congregation on the edge of Hell's Kitchen in New York City, Rauschenbusch despaired of individualized attempts at social service because they perpetuated the corrupt social system. He believed that sin was both individual and corporate. He wrote in *A Theology of the Social Gospel*, "Society is so integral that when one man sins, other men suffer, and when one social class sins, the other classes are involved in the suffering which follows on that sin" [Rauschenbusch 1917: 182]. Rauschenbusch used this example to emphasize the social implications of sin:

> A health officer of Toronto told me a story which illustrates the consciousness of sin created by the old religious teaching.
>
> If milk is found too dirty, the cans are emptied and marked with large red labels. This hits the farmer where he lives. He may not care about the health of Toronto, but he does care for the good opinion of his own neighborhood, and when he drives to the station and finds his friends chuckling over the red labels on his cans, it acts as a moral irritant. One day a Mennonite farmer found his cans labeled and he swore a worldly oath. The Mennonites are a devout people who take the teachings of Christ seriously and refuse to swear, even in law-courts. This man was brought before his church and excluded. But, mark well, not for introducing cow-dung into the intestines of babies, but for expressing his belief in the damnation of the wicked in a non-theological way. When his church will hereafter have fully digested the social gospel, it may treat the case this way: "Our brother was angry and used the name of God profanely in his anger; we urge him to settle this alone with God. But he has also defiled the milk supply by unclean methods. Having the life and health of young children in his keeping, he has failed in his trust. Voted, that he be excluded until he has proved his lasting repentance." The result would be the same, but the sense of sin would do its work more intelligently. [Rauschenbusch 1917: 35-36]

For Rauschenbusch, the Kingdom of God was not only a central theological concept, but also and primarily the historical and current action of God to be joined. "The institutions of the Church, its activities, its worship, and its theology must in the long run be tested by its effectiveness in creating the Kingdom of God" [Rauschenbusch 1917: 143].

He and others led their churches in response to the social gospel, battling child labor and other oppressive forces in the lives of children and families.

Others sought to follow their understanding of the gospel beyond the confines of the institutional church. In the 1890s, Edgar Gardner Murphy, an Episcopalian parish priest, organized the Southern Society for the Promotion of the Study of Race Conditions and Problems. He resigned from the Episcopal ministry, "but his letter to the bishop made it clear that his own sense of ministry would continue now freed from misunderstandings that stemmed from society's ideas about the nature and role of the minister" [White and Hopkins 1976]. Murphy led the Alabama Child Labor Committee, the first such committee in the nation. Although Alabama had enacted a law in 1887 to regulate child labor, the number of children under 16 in the labor force actually increased, until children represented one-fourth of the workers in the rapidly expanding textile industry. Murphy marshaled support for child labor laws in the state legislature and publicly exposed and challenged northern mill owners who were blocking the legislation [White and Hopkins 1976].

The Development of Voluntary Societies

In response to the social concerns and religious awakenings of the last half of the nineteenth and early twentieth centuries, Christians organized voluntary associations to address the problems of slum life and the needs of orphans and poor children. Denominations began to take shape in nineteenth-century America, and with their development came denominational organizations and agencies. Many of these organizations were concerned with the abolition of slavery and with temperance [Leonard 1988]; others confronted the needs of dependent and orphaned children.

Churches were developing child care institutions. Many of these institutions placed children in family homes. Often, in fact, efforts to place children in family homes preceded the building of institutions; institutions were built because the number of children needing care could no longer be absorbed into the foster homes available. For example, the Kentucky Baptist program of child care began in 1866. The Ladies Aid Society of Walnut Street Baptist Church in Louisville had been paying the board of several homeless children who were living in private homes. The

Catholic orphanage in Louisville approached the Baptist pastor requesting funds, however, because many Baptist children were being cared for
at the Catholic orphanage. The women of the church realized that subsidies for placement in homes could no longer meet the needs of a growing
number of needy children; a new Baptist orphans' home was opened in
1869 as a joint effort with other Baptist churches [Turpin 1962].

In Chicago, the cholera epidemic of 1849, which left many children
orphaned, was the impetus for the development of church institutions.
Protestant churches appealed to families to take the children in as appren-
tices. When it became clear that this was not enough, Chicagoans met on
August 3 in the First Baptist Church to consider the fate of the orphans.
They decided to build an asylum, passed the hat and raised $400, ap-
pointed a board of directresses, and admitted three children by September
11 [McCarthy 1982]. Women volunteers controlled and staffed this institution, like similar asylums and institutional homes sponsored by churches
across the country, often in response to the needs of children orphaned by
war and epidemics. As board members, "They made the clothes and
bedding themselves, purchased supplies, investigated and admitted in-
mates, hired and fired the staff, nursed the children, placed them, taught
them, mothered them, and when necessary buried them as well" [McCarthy
1982: 8]. The women worked relentlessly to raise enough money to keep
the asylums open. They often adopted children into their own families,
cooked for the asylum in their own kitchens, and nursed children even
during cholera epidemics that threatened their own health.

Men were drawn into voluntary services and charitable causes by
their hobbies, business considerations, and political interests, as well as
their religious convictions. Businessmen were cautioned to act in their
own best interests, "preserving their character and mercantile integrity by
guarding the public weal. The ultimate issue was one of power...; they
assumed the steward's role as part of their larger economic, political, and
civic duties" [McCarthy 1982: 174].

Women, however, rallied to the cause of children and families almost
solely in response to their faith and their church. Like institutions elsewhere, the Chicago Orphan Asylum drew the majority of its women
volunteers from the city's Protestant congregations. Each church had a

number of places to fill on the various boards. The women were generally the wives of businessmen and professionals, although, because congregations varied in the economic status of their members, there were also wives of blue collar workers. Almost all were married, many with small children of their own [McCarthy 1982]. They were urged on in their volunteer work by clergy who exhorted women to join forces in charitable caregiving. "This holy vocation of charity has been committed to her; it is her task, her lot, her ministry, her special destination; and it constitutes one of her highest claims to our gratitude and admiration," preached Reverend Alexander Young of Boston [McCarthy 1982: 13].

Religious service gave meaning and focus to the lives of women, and enabled them to express themselves and wield some power in a world that otherwise rendered them powerless. Although wives could neither own nor give away money before the passage of the Married Women's Property Act in 1861, their skills in sewing, shopping, and nursing were valued and necessary in the work of the asylums [McCarthy 1982]. Excluded from decision making and influence, through their service they gained the ability to shape the world around them, at least the world of the church's institutions.

Not all child welfare concerns were expressed through the development and support of institutions, however. The seeds of today's community-based services for children and families were being sown as early as the 1830s. Evangelism was often coupled with social reform expressed in local community projects. For example, Phoebe Palmer, a holiness evangelist, conducted revivals and small group meetings in New York in the 1830s. With the support of the Ladies Home Missionary Society and its advisory committee of Methodist men, she founded the Five Points Mission, the first Protestant community-based ministry center in the slums, in New York City in 1850. The Five Points Mission offered day schools for children, free housing for the poor, and other services for children and families [Leonard 1988; Smith 1957]. Others quickly followed; by the close of the Civil War, New York alone had 66 such missions [Smith 1957].

Charles Loring Brace, an 1852 graduate of Union Theological Seminary in New York, worked with the Five Points Mission. Brace became deeply concerned about the hundreds of youngsters drifting on the streets, without apparent supervision or protection. With several of the city's clergymen, he founded the New York Children's Aid Society in 1853. It offered children religious meetings, workshops and industrial schools, lodging, and employment outside New York City. Most significantly, it initiated a program for "placing-out" dependent children in rural homes throughout the nation. Seeing family life as necessary for the reform of vagrant children, Brace sent groups of city children to rural communities all across the country. In the first 20 years of its activities, the New York Children's Aid Society placed over 20 thousand children [Lundberg 1947; Tiffin 1982].

After a preliminary screening process to weed out "the mentally defective, diseased, and incorrigible," the children were washed, clothed, and sent with an agent to communities along the east coast and in western and southern states. According to Brace, the sight of the little company of unfortunate children always touched the hearts of the naturally generous population, and his staff had no problem in disposing of all their charges [Tiffin 1982: 89].

The placing-out program of the Children's Aid Society was the first large-scale attempt to place children in homes since colonial days, when children had been auctioned. Brace's program was an innovation because it focused on the needs of the child. It provided the basis for the development of today's family foster care services. The placing-out program developed major problems around its inferred religious mission, however; although both Catholic and Protestant homes were offered to children, antipathy among Christians reared its ugly head. Many Catholic children were necessarily placed with Protestant families because Catholic homes in rural America were comparatively rare, but some Catholics believed that this was a deliberate attempt to convert children to Protestantism [Tiffin 1982]. The New York Catholic Protectory was founded in 1862 to prevent the exporting of Catholic children to Protestant families in the West. Unlike most other institutions of the day, it harbored large numbers of children—over 2,000 at any one time [Tiffin 1982]. In addition, in 1875, New York Catholics began transporting children by train to Catholic homes in the west [Coleman 1991].

Taking another approach, the Salvation Army and the Volunteers of America, which developed out of a breach in relations among leaders of the Salvation Army, both responded in dramatic ways to the needs of children and their families in the slums. Serving in pairs, "slum sisters" moved into residences in the most depressed neighborhoods. "Here they lived all year round, visiting the sick, looking after the children, showing the women how to keep themselves and their homes decent, often discharging the sick mother's duties themselves," all within the context of evangelism [Magnuson 1977: 34]. The slum workers discovered that mothers often faced the alternatives of leaving infants and children alone all day while they worked or starving because they had no income. As a consequence, nurseries (day care centers) became characteristic features of their ministries before the turn of the century. The Salvation Army and Volunteers of America developed settlement houses as their resources allowed, usually including a large nursery, a laundry room, a sewing room, and a kindergarten. Their work was perhaps the most visible, but by no means the major portion of what many evangelical welfare groups were doing on a relatively unstructured basis for very poor families and children [Magnuson 1977]. The most striking feature of their work was their self-sacrifice, which often meant giving up their own beds and meals in response to the needs of those they served.

Not all clergy greeted these developments with affirmation. Because help was increasingly being based on the developing social sciences, some conservatives feared that it might be too successful and bring an end to the spiritual growth that Christians reaped from being charitable. Canadian editor Jules Tardivel wrote that "a country where there are no beggars is a veritable branch of hell" [Marty 1980: 464]. Other Protestants, such as Dwight L. Moody, the most noted evangelist of his day, considered organized efforts to improve society as futile distractions from the important task of saving souls for life hereafter.

Professionalization of Church Agencies

In the midst of tensions between those who believed the church's focus should be exclusively on the eternal state of souls and those who believed that the gospel called for response to social and physical needs, formalized responses to poverty and the needs of children and their families continued to develop.

Friendly Visiting

"Friendly visiting" developed around the turn of the century in response to the changing ecology of cities. Earlier, rich and poor had lived in the same neighborhoods or within walking distance of one another, so that help was given in natural, informal ways. That situation changed as cities grew; the rich in their neighborhoods were geographically distant and emotionally insulated from the desperate poverty of the slums. Friendly visiting was designed to restore right relations between the classes [McCarthy 1982]. Friendly visitors were volunteers, mostly middle- and upper-class women, who worked conscientiously to develop trust and friendship with a poor family, then used this relationship to bring about positive change. The aid they offered included advice, material resources such as food and coal, medical referrals, and individualized family life education. Ideally, both parties benefited, as the poor received encouragement and aid and the visitor grew more compassionate as a result of her contact with the less fortunate. By restoring "neighborship" between the classes through personal contact, proponents of friendly visiting hoped to bridge the "social gulf," promoting enhanced understanding and circumventing the problems of anonymity, anomie, and unrest [McCarthy 1982: 132].

It was a church visitor in New York City, Etta Angell Wheeler, who discovered the plight of Mary Ellen Wilson, a seven-year-old girl who had been indentured to Mary Connolly and her husband since the age of 18 months. Mary Ellen was severely whipped and left alone for long hours. Her cries carried through the thin partitions of the tenement apartment to the ears of other building occupants. Mrs. Wheeler took it upon herself to rescue the child. When the Department of Charities, which had placed Mary Ellen with the Wilsons, and other agencies expressed no willingness to intervene, Mrs. Wheeler called on the President of the New York Society for the Prevention of Cruelty to Animals, who involved himself as a private but influential citizen. In a case highly publicized by the *New York Times*, the court forcibly removed Mary Ellen from her home. Since no relatives could be found, Mary Ellen was placed in a home for grown children who were being trained for service. Mrs. Wheeler, dissatisfied with this decision, asked the court for custody of Mary Ellen and received it. From the persistence of this church volunteer came not only rescue for Mary Ellen but also the impetus for the child rescue movement and the development of the Society for the Prevention of Cruelty to Children [Costin 1985; Watkins 1990].

The Changing Role of Volunteers

Volunteers, from friendly visitors to the board members of church institutions, were extremely important in the growing array of formal social services. With the growth of institutions and community centers, however, funding became more sure and professional staff members could be hired. States were passing laws allowing women to own and dispose property; they could now pay others to do the less appealing tasks of caregiving. Staffs and facilities grew, and work passed to paid professionals. During the late nineteenth century, the rate of increase for professionals in child welfare was approximately double that of the total labor force [Tiffin 1982].

These professionals worked diligently in the first decades of the twentieth century to narrow the role of the volunteer, unwilling to rely on the volunteers' sometimes sporadic, unskilled, religiously motivated goodwill. Volunteers increasingly found themselves assigned to clerical jobs or to administrative committees rather than to work with poor families. McCarthy describes this process in the children's "asylums": "Rather than drawing directresses into the slums in search of candidates, asylum work now insulated them from the poor. ...Once a week applicants journeyed there to file past the admission committees, telling their tales of deprivation and woe. But employees did the actual work of investigation, sparing the board the unpleasant task of venturing themselves into unsavory neighborhoods" [McCarthy 1982: 29].

Social workers, anxious to guard their claim to professional knowledge and skill, questioned the ability of laypeople to set policies. That required professional expertise. They hoarded information about their work and their clients, excluding board members from meaningful roles in what had been their institutions. As one board president commented with frustration, "I have been told that our staff is so well organized that there is very little for our Board Members to do, but I am sure that there still remains much to be done and the work can be made very interesting" [Chicago Home for the Friendless 1935: 237].

Replacement of volunteers with professionals was taking place in community services as well as in the institutions. Professional homemaker and home health aide services inherited the in-home family caregiving functions of the earlier volunteer friendly visitors. As early as 1892, the Little Sisters of the Poor in New York City and employees of other similar service programs went into homes during the day to clean house and help care for children whose mothers were absent, ill, or perceived as not providing adequate care for their children [Robinson 1985].

Employees of these agencies were first called "visiting housewives." They did housework, shopped, cooked meals, and met the emotional and physical needs of children [Kadushin 1974]. Unlike the volunteers who preceded them, homemakers were often older residents of the same low-income neighborhoods as the families they served who had raised their own children. Their training was their own experience as competent homemakers. These community homemakers helped to educate professional agency staff members about the realities of slum living. Their services have continued and have grown enormously, although virtually all the growth has been in home health care services provided to the elderly, not to families with children. In 1978, a survey of all public social services showed that only 7% of the clients on record received homemaker service [Shyne and Schroeder 1978]. Even so, a review of program evaluations suggests that homemaker and home health aide services have been the most effective component of multiple service interventions with families at high risk of disintegration, enabling children to stay at home rather than be placed in foster or institutional care [Ziefert 1985].

The professionalization of child and family services no doubt provided more effective and efficient services to many clients. While volunteerism was waning, monetary giving was on the rise. Something was lost in the shift, however. The personal relationship between religiously motivated volunteers and recipients of their care was being destroyed, "the act of giving transformed into a bloodless operation requiring neither effort nor commitment" [McCarthy 1982: 178]. Service no longer made neighbors out of strangers. Professional ethics of confidentiality reinforced this process:

> Back in the country...relief was personal, direct, frank, and aboveboard. ...In the cities...the giver never sees the object of his bounty, nor is witness to the act of dispensing what he has provided. ...Whether the recipient is made happy or is embittered by the gift, is unknown to him. Giving is impersonal, indirect, mechanized. ...The process is as cold as the payment of taxes. ...Under modern conditions, particularly in the cities, we must call upon our powers of imagination to help us obtain by proxy, so to speak, the emotional response that our nature requires. [Herrick 1940: 201-2]

Volunteers became primarily donors, not agency decision-makers or friends of the poor.

The role of the volunteer continues to be an issue for church agencies, and deserves attention in any discussion of the future of church-related child welfare services. As the 20th century advanced, volunteers continued to work in a variety of ways directly with children and their families, though their role was constricted, and to serve on the boards of agencies. Today, attention to the importance of informal networks of social support and the indispensable role volunteers can play is bringing volunteer services back to center stage. According to Alec Dickson, who created Great Britain's Voluntary Service Overseas, the criterion for the excellence of social services is the imaginative use of volunteers. As one volunteer commented, "If you have given half a day, it is soul-destroying just to paste labels on envelopes or arrange the flowers; I could pay somebody to do that who needs the job. I wanted to do something to help."

Personal Faith and Religious Calling—Motivation for Professional Service

In recent decades, many church volunteers who wanted to serve the poor and children in crisis and who had sufficient resources went to social work school. As in the decades and centuries before them and into the present, many chose to commit their careers to needy children and their families in direct response to their Christian faith and personal spiritual calling. Hastings Hornell Hart, Homer Folks, and Jane Addams exemplify the personal faith that has motivated many who have led in the development of child and family services. They have served not in abandonment of but rather as a fulfillment of their Christian faith and calling.

Hastings Hornell Hart trained at Andover Theological Seminary and was ordained as a minister of the Congregational Church. Two years later, he left the pastorate for a career in social work. In 1898, he was appointed superintendent of the Illinois Children's Home and Aid Society. He helped transform the society into one of the nation's most advanced children's agencies. He also directed the child-helping department of the Russell Sage Foundation from 1909 to 1924, framed the nation's first juvenile court law, and was among the organizers of the first national gathering on children, the 1909 White House Conference on the Care of Dependent Children [Tiffin 1982].

Homer Folks, a prominent child welfare worker, considered becoming a clergyman. He took undergraduate courses under Francis G. Peabody, a famous theologian, and felt strongly that social problems are essentially questions of ethics, the answers to which are to be found in charity and Christian cooperation. His life was spent in work with the Children's Aid Society of Pennsylvania and the New York State Charities Aid Association. He was a significant supporter of child labor regulation, the juvenile court, and the Children's Bureau [Tiffin 1982].

Similarly, Jane Addams chose professional social work as the channel for her religious faith. For her, Christianity was not "a set of ideas which belong to the religious consciousness, whatever that may be," but a faith that sought expression in the very life of the community [Addams 1910: 122-124; see also Davis 1973]. In 1889 Addams founded Chicago's Hull House in an antebellum mansion in the middle of one of the city's worst slums. She and her colleagues lived at the settlement house, offering a range of services not unlike those of today's family resource programs—children's groups designed to provide opportunities beyond what the schools offered, clean water and milk (critical in fighting high infant mortality), and a public playground, gymnasium, and swimming pool that were probably the first in the nation [Addams 1910; see also Brieland 1990].

Hull House was initially modeled after Toynbee Hall, founded in London in 1884 by clergymen Frederick Denison Maurice and Charles Kingsley. They had as their goals the replacement of competition by cooperation and the establishment of the Kingdom of God on earth [Davis 1967]. Jane Addams developed those ideas in the context of turn-of-the-century Chicago and, more broadly, the United States. She figured prominently in the major social justice campaigns of the era, against child labor and supporting improved race relations, woman suffrage, better wages and working conditions, and public health.

By 1912, Jane Addams had become "the conscience of the nation" [McCarthy 1982: 109]; she served as a role model for others in her day and in generations to come. In describing the foundation of her work, she wrote about what she saw as a renaissance of the early Christian humanitarianism, which was taking place "without leaders who write or philosophize, without much speaking, but with a bent to express in social service and in terms of action the spirit of Christ. Certain it is that spiritual force is found in the Settlement movement, and it is also true that this force must be evoked and must be called into play before the success of any Settlement is assured" [Addams 1910: 124]. For her and many other reformers, Christianity was a religion of social action and a faith that demanded service to the poor.

Caring for Children in the Context of the Family

Later in the twentieth century, the focus on children broadened to include children's families. The social work profession began calling for progress beyond removing children from dangerous influences toward services designed to prevent family disruption. As early as 1901, Mary Richmond, the general secretary of the Philadelphia Society for Organizing Charity, stated that the old cry of "save the children" had to be superseded by a new cry, "save the family." Child-savers turned their attention to preserving and reconstructing the family unit in the hope of reducing the number of dependent and neglected children in institutions and foster homes [Tiffin

1982]. The groundwork was laid, then, for community services aimed toward preventing out-of-home placement and reserving institutional and family foster home care for those in greatest need.

Part of this emphasis on keeping children in their homes derived from growing concern about the future of the family as an institution. Divorce rates were skyrocketing during the early twentieth century; for several decades, the divorce rate had risen five times as fast as the rate of population growth. The number of voluntary separations and desertions was assumed to be even greater, although there was no way of determining these rates [Tiffin 1982]. The institution of the family seemed in danger. Consequently, attention turned to rehabilitating the family in its own environment rather than removing and treating individual members.

Community Work

Many church agencies were far ahead of what was considered a new focus in the fledgling social work profession. Although the emphasis on family support was construed as a challenge to the work of asylums and child-placing agencies, some church-sponsored community work and settlement houses had already been caring for children in the context of their families for 50 years or more. In addition, friendly visiting, visiting nurses, and infant welfare societies were all attempts to shore up the biological family.

One such program, Chicago's Infant Welfare Society (IWS), developed in response to high infant mortality rates. IWS recognized that the infant mortality problem involved more than infant nutrition. The society used a map to chart the location of infant deaths and noted the interrelationship between overcrowding, substandard housing, poverty, and infant deaths. In the neighborhoods where the greatest number of deaths occurred, they located "fresh air stations for sick babies."

Each station was actually a tent, outfitted with beds and hammocks for 10 to 20 infants and staffed by two nurses. The tents were inexpensive and could be easily and quickly assembled in the areas where they were most needed. The neighborhood locations allowed mothers to maintain contact with their infants and the staff, which would not have been possible in a large institutional hospital across town. The openness and accessibility of the stations created trust and a willingness to use available services. (Hospitals, in contrast, were terrifying; it was rumored among immigrant families that they used children for medical experiments.) The staff of each fresh air station provided classes in infant care, sewing, cooking, and health care. The emphasis was on saving a baby by reaching parents with the information, skills, and resources they needed [McCarthy 1982]. Programs such as these are the antecedents of the current family resource programs.

Family Foster Care

The earliest children's institutions developed because there was a shortage of families willing or able to provide homes for orphaned children. By the late nineteenth century, they had become a common placement for dependent children who could not be cared for by their own families. Orphanages used foster care as a supplementary resource. Before the advent of pasteurized milk and infant formula, infants had to be wet-nursed, so orphanages often placed infants in family foster homes until they had been weaned. When children reached adolescence, they were again placed in foster (boarding) homes, this time often working for their keep until they were old enough to live apart from the institution's supervision [Kadushin 1974].

In the early 1900s, professional opinion began to support family foster care over institutional care as the placement of choice for children of all ages who had to be removed from their homes. With vigorous preliminary examination of foster homes, careful matching of children with families, and consistent supervision, family foster care was considered the best out-of-home care available.

In the late nineteenth century, Martin Van Buren Van Arsdale, a Presbyterian minister in Illinois, had established the National Children's Home Society, one of the most influential family foster care programs of the era. While a theological student, he had been concerned with the plight of children in almshouses, who had to remain there until they could be placed out on contract at no expense to the county. Although he apparently had little intimate knowledge of the work of the earlier children's aid societies, he followed his inspiration from scripture, "God sets the lonely in families" (Psalm 68:6). His first solution to the needs of children was to place them in Christian homes through his own personal effort. Finding the work too great for one person, he founded an organization to serve a wide range of dependent and neglected children.

Receiving homes were set up to admit children and prepare them for placement in various localities. Initially, children were voluntarily surrendered by their parents, but after 1899, the newly established juvenile court committed children to the society. Van Arsdale wanted his work to be a national effort, and by 1907, 28 societies were operating in 32 states and territories. The national headquarters in Chicago provided a publication, *The Children's Home Finder*, that published professional articles and information of general interest. When the Child Welfare League of America was established in 1920, most of the members of the National Children's Home Society joined it. The society was finally dissolved in 1939, having served a significant pioneering role in services and professional communication among child welfare workers [Lundberg 1947; Tiffin 1982].

Although Catholic agencies clung longer to their institutions as the care of choice for dependent children, primarily because of the difficulty of finding Catholic family foster homes, changes occurred that eventually made foster care more feasible to the Catholic welfare system. First, massive immigration provided a growing number of potential Catholic foster families. Second, the fear of proselytizing had receded because of insistence by Protestant and nonsectarian children's agencies that, whenever possible, the child's religious beliefs should be respected. Catholic leaders began to recognize the desirability of having organized foster home programs operating conjointly with institutional programs. By 1897, the Catholic Home Bureau had become a clearinghouse for the majority of New York's Catholic institutions. The bureau placed 2,500 children in its first ten years. It also contributed to the formation of similar agencies across the country, until by 1938 there were 72 Catholic child-placing agencies with approximately 15,000 children in family foster care, and 326 institutions for dependent and neglected children with a total population of 39,545 [Keegan 1941; Tiffin 1982].

Other institutions, such as the Boston Church Home Society, also began to place children in family foster care. Founded in 1855 by members of the Episcopal Church of Boston, the society had earlier considered placing out but instead developed a farm school. By 1896 it had returned to the idea, and began to cooperate with the Boston Children's Aid Society in selecting and investigating homes and placing children. The program was so successful that by 1915, the work of the entire agency was devoted to family foster home care. In 1923, according to a census report, there were 339 such placing agencies in the United States [Tiffin 1982], and many of these had church connections. The 1909 White House Conference on the Care of Dependent Children, attended by representatives from all the leading religious bodies, reached a consensus that when children must be cared for outside their own homes, they should be cared for, insofar as possible, in families [Jones 1989].

Despite the favor given to foster care, institutions retained considerable influence. It was more than 35 years after the 1909 White House Conference before the number of children in orphanages began to decline; for the first 25 years after the conference, the number of children in institutional care actually increased [Jones 1989]. According to 1923 census statistics, the first accurate account of child placing, 64.2% of all dependent and neglected children were still in the care of institutions. In comparison, 23.4% were cared for in "free" homes and 10.2% in boarding family homes. After that date, the use of family foster care accelerated, but this did not lessen the number of children in institutions, because the number of children needing out-of-home care continued to increase. In fact, during the 1930s, not only the number of children in care but also their length of stay increased to record highs, due mainly to the Great Depression [Jones 1989].

Nevertheless, by 1962, only 31% of placed children were not in families [Tiffin 1982]. Some church agencies felt threatened by this decrease in the number of children referred for institutional care, seeing it as competition for the "easiest" and most rewarding children to serve, those who could love and be grateful. In addition, church children's homes were facing major financial problems. The passage of the 1935 Social Security Act led many to believe that the care of dependent children would now be the responsibility of public agencies, for which the public was paying taxes, so fundraising became more difficult [Jones 1989]. At the same time, many foster care social workers questioned the value of the institutional children's home, which they considered a damaging setting for children. For a time, the value of the contribution that both institutional care and family foster care can potentially make to meeting the needs of children and their families became lost in the fray, and church institutions suffered declining support and increasing professional ambiguity.

The Federal Government Takes a Role

The passage of the Social Security Act of 1935 marked a major turning point in the church's identity and role in child and family services. From that point on, the church would no longer be the major or only provider of care for children and families in crisis. By 1958, for every child in the care of a church "children's home," there were two in government-sponsored family foster homes and 20 other families receiving public aid so that children could remain at home. No longer were children placed in alternative care solely because of the family's poverty.

Government took the primary role in family support and family foster care, often leaving institutional care of children in the hands of church agencies.[2] Kadushin has noted that most institutions' auspices are private, usually denominational; in 1966, 23 states listed no public institution for dependent or neglected children [Kadushin 1974]. The two services—group care in an institution and family foster care—became inadvertently identified with the current providers of each type of care—the church and the state. Child care professionals began to value or attack one or the other care system "not for its intrinsic merits or demerits, but because they [were] pro- or anti-church" [Keith-Lucas 1962: 7]. Although church agencies also provided family foster care, institutions have continued to serve as the mainstay of the church's child welfare services, particularly in the American South. As late as 1950, one could say of children in the South that if they fell into the hands of the state they found themselves in family foster homes, but if the church came to their rescue they would be reared in an institution [Keith-Lucas 1991].

Yet the ideal of the church was still the family, and agencies became acutely aware that institutions, even with small groups of children, could not simulate a family. As one staff member put it, "whoever heard of a family where the parents took weekends off, or quit and the neighbors moved in, and children came and went?" [Keith-Lucas 1991]. Also, as government services began to take a major role in child welfare services, church child care institutions experienced major shifts in the population they served and the nature of their services.

First, children were no longer staying all of their childhood in the "children's home." Children were placed for short periods of time and then, presumably, either returned home or were placed in some other family setting. Consequently, they had less opportunity to develop a loyalty to the church institution, and whatever they made of their lives was less clearly attributable to the church's intervention. As Alan Keith-Lucas noted in 1958, "It will become harder and harder to point to a model citizen and say, 'He was raised in our Church Home'" [see Keith-Lucas 1962: 17]. The orphanage football teams that had been the source of so much pride were gone. Children were incorporated into public schools and sports teams so they would be prepared to return to life in the community. It was harder for the agency—and supporting churches—to clearly identify the outcome of their giving.

Second, the children who did enter institutional care were seriously disturbed, difficult to manage, and in need of professional services. Children who could be served primarily by a loving, consistent environment were being placed in family foster care. Those who came into institutional care needed a trained staff of houseparents—the forerunners of today's child care workers—not the matrons who had formerly filled this role. The church had previously employed older women, widowed or otherwise without means of financial support, to serve as matrons. Thus, the agency provided support both for the women and for the children in their care. One woman often oversaw 30 to 40 children [Keith-Lucas 1962]. The primary qualifications for the position of matron were piety, good moral character, and housekeeping skills. Now group care became a setting for helping troubled children, not simply a means of providing custodial oversight.

In response to these changes, church agencies developed a number of workshops, including the Chapel Workshops at the University of North

Carolina that began in 1945 and continued for nearly 40 years. These workshops provided education and training experiences for child care staff members from every state in the nation and several foreign countries, 80% of them from church-related agencies. In 1954, church agencies asked the university to offer on-site consultation and training for child care agencies. In 1968, the name Group Child Care Consultant Services (GCCCS) was adopted and a certificate training program was implemented. GCCCS emphasized the significant role of the child care worker, the need to work with the child's entire family, and the necessity of defining the goals for a child's placement, developing what would later be called a permanency plan [Keith-Lucas, personal correspondence, March 4, 1992].

With the development of the milieu as a treatment modality came the realization that living groups should be limited to units small enough to simulate family living. At the same time, agencies were beginning to address the need for services to the families to whom children would be returning. Professional social workers were needed to provide these services. At a time when the church could take less pride in the outcome of its work with children, the cost of services was thus expanding exponentially, requiring more professional staff members, better training for nonprofessional staff members, and greater numbers of staff members to serve fewer children.

Finally, the identity of the agency began to shift from the status of being "church-sponsored" to that of being "church-related." Although this shift was hardly noticed at the time, it was a minor deviation from the previous path that has resulted over time in a major change of course. The agency no longer belonged to the church; instead it was related to it [Keith-Lucas 1962: 22]. That relationship could be maintained as exclusive, with the church as the only or the major source of resources for the agency, or, as was the case for many agencies, it could be supplemented by other support resources, including government funding and foundation grants. For some agencies, this was the beginning of the move toward only nominal relationship with the founding group and its religious mission. For others, it was the beginning of mounting tensions resulting from the attempt to relate to supportive systems that had different and at times even conflicting values and objectives.

Government-Church Agency Relations

Government funding for church agencies was not a new phenomenon, however. The practice of public support for private institutions was well established by the nineteenth century [Bremner (1) 1970: 662]. For example, the New York City Orphanage received its first government appropriation in 1806; government grants were also made to the Roman Catholic Orphan Asylum in New York City [Lundberg 1947]. The practice of government subsidy for church agencies spread in a rather unintentional and haphazard manner. "Payments, in the form of either lump sums or per capita grants, seemed to make available the specialized treatment needed while requiring little effort on the part of the authorities and making minimal demands on the taxpayers" [Tiffin 1982: 192]. In some respects, the motivation for governments to fund church agencies has not changed over time.

Then, as now, this arrangement did not go unchallenged. In many states attempts were made to prohibit government allowances to religious organizations. New York's state legislature was specifically forbidden to authorize payments to children's agencies. This policy was successfully circumvented, but aid was also dispensed by municipal and county bodies. By 1904, over 50% of the maintenance of New York's children's institutions was provided in the form of government subsidies. Nationwide, government subsidies constituted 21.7% of the total budget of children's institutions; the majority of these were church agencies [Tiffin 1982]. The policy of subsidizing church agencies was based on the assumption that private institutions invariably can manage with much less cost than public institutions.

Reform in services and funding came at the turn of the century. In his 1900 book, *Care of Destitute, Neglected and Delinquent Children,* reformer Homer Folks argued that children permanently removed from their families should be maintained by the state; private organizations, he suggested, were best suited to the care and protection of children in need of temporary aid and to the rehabilitation of families. Many would still agree with him today. He maintained that government subsidies had created increases in the number of children being raised in institutions because institutions were tempted to keep children in order to receive the funds attached to them. This limited the funds available for public agencies, which were subsequently forced to make do on inadequate budgets. At the first National Conference of Catholic Charities in 1910, David Tilley, President of the Vincent de Paul Society of Boston, argued that withdrawal of state aid from church agencies would be in the best interests of the agencies themselves, because public grants discouraged people from giving. Even when the state subsidy was very small, it created the impression that the state was supporting the agency so donations were not needed [Tiffin 1982].

Regulation of church agencies by government policy became another hot issue. At the White House Conference of 1909, the question of regulation of private charities was debated extensively. Those in favor of state supervision stressed three main benefits to be achieved: eradication of abuses, uniformity of methods, and improved direction of child-caring as a whole. Others argued that it was the responsibility of government to ensure that funds received from public sources or private donations were properly and economically used. Even more important, state supervision could determine that children in care were not exploited or ill treated. Even though only a minority of agencies were guilty of abuse, regulation would provide interchange among professionals and agencies and raise the standards of child care. A state supervisory body could provide linkage and professional discourse that would help agencies learn from each other's experiences and mistakes [Tiffin 1982]. Some leaders of church agencies–including David Tilley, who had gone on record as opposed to government subsidies–agreed, and tried to persuade others to join in the drive toward government regulation. Some, however, saw government regulation as a threat to their autonomy and an unwarranted interference [Tiffin 1982].

> At the same time some agencies were fighting against govern-
> ment regulation, they were also fighting to retain their govern-
> ment funding. Perhaps one of the best examples of the defense of
> subsidies is that of Illinois. Here, since 1879, the legislature had
> authorized per capita grants to the state's two Protestant and two
> Catholic industrial training schools. Between 1882 and 1917, nine

attempts were made by various county and state authorities to nullify the practice, generally on the question of the validity of aid to sectarian organizations. ...These challenges were consistently defeated. The courts regularly brought down a decision that, in religious institutions, it was "contrary to fact and reason to say that paying less than the actual cost of clothing, medical care and attention, education and training...is aiding the institution where such things are furnished." ...Rather than restricting the incidence of subsidies in Illinois, the publicity and an increase in per capita grants from 1911 onward led to the formation of 14 more training schools before 1920. Expenditures increased from approximately $62,000 in 1910 to $271,000 in 1920. [Tiffin 1982: 203]

The issues of government regulation and government subsidy were necessarily intertwined. Agencies saw supervision and regulation by government as interference with the religious liberty the U. S. Constitution guarantees. Nevertheless, the reformers made headway. It is estimated that by 1923, between 18% and 21% of the nation's dependent and neglected children were being cared for by government agencies, compared with 10% at the turn of the century [Tiffin 1982]; obviously, however, most children were still cared for by private, usually church, agencies. Government supervision and regulation developed only gradually, until by 1929, the majority of states had passed legislation regulating the activities of children's institutions and placing agencies [Tiffin 1982]. The welfare systems of 29 states included the issuance of licenses, although only 13 required regular certification of all children's agencies. Reporting at intervals to the respective government regulatory body was compulsory in 22 states [Tiffin 1982].

In the mid-1960s, the "war on poverty" by the federal government brought with it federal subsidies for not-for-profit agencies that would develop and deliver a variety of social services. Some have subsequently argued that private service providers precluded rational public policy and planning because of their influence over the purchase of services; because they were able to respond to the offer of federal matching dollars with their own budgets, public services did not develop as intended [Kamerman and

Kahn 1989]. The debate over government funding of church agency programs continues, although the issues have shifted somewhat. It now seems that the lack of comprehensive planning and service provision by public agencies is more at issue than the quality of the services provided by the church agencies. For churches and their agencies, the issue of government oversight and control continues to create debate.

The Secularization of Church Agencies

Since the turn of the century, the process that perhaps most commonly characterizes many church agencies has been a slow secularization and alteration of the mission that served as the original impetus for their creation.

Notes

1. Iowa Congregationalist minister Charles O. Brown evidently first used the term "social gospel" in 1886, in response to Henry George's book *Progress and Poverty* [Leonard 1988].

2. In 1910, Roman Catholics operated 24.4% of the U.S. institutions caring for children, caring for 45% of the nation's dependent children; Protestants operated 23.7%, caring for 15.1%; Jews operated 2.2%, caring for 4.5%. The remainder of the children were cared for by other private organizations (39.7%, caring for 24.2%) and public institutions (10%, caring for 11.3%) [Tiffin 1982; numbers do not add up to 100% because of rounding].

3. Morton [1988] researched the history of five sectarian maternity homes in Cleveland from 1913 to 1973. He found that although the agencies conformed to some professional and secular standards that developed over this period, they retained their 19th-century religious commitments and mission for at least 60 years. After 1973, however, the agencies either closed or made significant changes; she concluded that "although institutions may have great staying power, they are not immortal" [Morton 1988: 78].

PART II

CURRENT AND FUTURE DIRECTIONS FOR THE CHURCH'S FAMILY MINISTRIES

CHAPTER 4

The Work of the Church Agency Today

The Covenant Children's Home and Family Services, of Princeton, Illinois, is owned and operated by the Central Conference of the Evangelical Covenant Church of Illinois. It provides residential treatment for 52 youths, 12 to 18 years old, most of whom have been physically, emotionally, or sexually abused. In addition to the residential program, the agency offers counseling services to the community at large, including individual and family therapy. A homemaker program provides professional services, including instruction in budgeting, parenting, and family living skills, in the homes of community families. The agency also has a family foster care and adoption program that includes counseling and other services to women with unwanted pregnancies.

Church Agencies in the '90s

Covenant Children's Home and Family Services is characteristic of many church child welfare agencies today. As discussed in chapter 1, they range in the strength of their affiliation with supporting churches from receiving a name and token support from a denomination to receiving virtually all their financial support, identity, and mission from a church or other Christian organization.

Historically, church agencies have been the primary resource in this country for residential care, as well as for other child welfare services. Residential care continues to figure prominently in the work of church agencies, but churches and church agencies offer an array of services to children and their families:

- community programs of family support—preschool child care and Head Start programs, after-school care, and parent respite programs for children with and without special needs;

- family information and resource services—parent and family education programs; drop-in centers; telephone hot lines, which offer help in a crisis, and warm lines, which offer information and support to parents; family information, toy, and parent education libraries; and support groups for families with various needs;

- family and adolescent recreation and activity programs;

- job placement services;

- volunteer support programs, such as adopt-a-foster grandparent, parent aides, and peer outreach volunteers;

- professional crisis intervention—family counseling, family therapy, and family preservation services;

- emergency assistance;

- out-of-home treatment and respite care—crisis care for children and families with special needs, foster homes, therapeutic foster homes, group homes, residential care and residential treatment services, independent living programs for older teens; and

• crisis pregnancy and adoption services.

Church agencies offer programs in response to the values and beliefs of the church community that shape the agency's context. In addition, agencies exist as part of a larger societal system of human service organizations.

The Human Services Context for the Church Agency

Three aspects of the current human services system in the United States are having a significant impact on church agencies' programs of services for children and their families: (1) primary emphasis by public child welfare services on protecting children from abuse and neglect, (2) changes in the level and nature of government funding for human services, and (3) current professional thought. Each of these elements has interacted with the others.

Public Agencies' Emphasis on Protection

Programs for assessing risk and protecting children from physical abuse, sexual abuse, and neglect have come to dominate public child welfare. In many communities, child protective services are taking all the resources in public child welfare budgets because of increasingly limited funding for child and family services, the burgeoning number of child abuse and neglect reports, and the media visibility given some tragic cases. In many American communities, children can gain access to help from public agencies only through the doors of child protective services; families who have not reached this level of crisis do not receive services [Kamerman and Kahn 1989, Kahn and Kamerman 1990].

At the same time, however, other serious social problems that dramatically affect children and their families have been emerging—striking increases in drug addiction, homelessness, and HIV/AIDS, and growing numbers of deinstitutionalized or not-institutionalized young developmentally disabled and mentally ill persons, some of whom are now becoming parents [Kamerman and Kahn 1989]. No increase in public child welfare resources has accompanied these emerging problems. As a consequence of the increasingly narrow focus by public agencies on protecting children from abuse and neglect, many of these other very difficult family situations are falling on the shoulders of private social service agencies—unless the families affected become abusive or neglectful, at which point government agencies are mandated to respond. Many public agencies simply have no resources with which to respond to the cries for help from troubled families who have multiple problems, but who do not appear to be in danger of abusing or neglecting their children.

Public agencies are not typically designed to provide preventive services, but private agencies are not usually designed to provide comprehensive services. Consequently, private agencies find themselves operating as one piece of what should be a mosaic of services. Overall coordination of services to children and their families with complex and multiple needs is inadequate or wholly lacking [Lourie and Katz-Leavy 1991]. The work of private child welfare agencies, both sectarian and nonsectarian, is rendered less effective when the foundation of public response to child welfare needs is inadequate and uncoordinated.

The Level and Nature of Government Funding

Needs have been increasing without any accompanying increase in federal government funding for services. The inadequacy of federal funding and federal involvement has created major problems in almost every community and with every issue facing the field of child welfare. It is difficult even to know what the needs are and what services are being offered, much less to evaluate those services. The federal government dismantled its child welfare statistical activities in the 1970s, so there are now no national data regarding the services offered, the interventions employed, or even the characteristics of providers. Similarly, no government agency is systematically accumulating data about the characteristics and numbers of children being served [Kamerman and Kahn 1989].

Not only the level of government funding, but also the current government process for funding services is having dramatic effects on church agencies. Government agencies are turning to private agencies to provide client services through grants, contracts, and fee-for-service agreements. In some states, the public agencies themselves are offering few or no intervention services, focusing instead on assessment, case management, and referral to a network of private not-for-profit and proprietary agencies and facilities. Consequently, church agencies are offered government funding for providing certain child and family service programs. The funding requires them to be responsive to those needs of children and their families that government funding sources perceive as most salient, especially protecting children from abuse and neglect. Also, if they want to be funded, their programs of service must fit government funding guidelines.

Current Professional Thought in Child Welfare

Professional thought is congruent with public interest in protecting children from abuse and neglect. More broadly, however, professionals have increasingly emphasized children's need for permanence in a family home, preferably that of their own biological family. Permanency planning has become an indispensable and dominant part of the services for every child and family who come into the care of a child welfare agency.

> Permanency planning is the systematic process of carrying out, within a brief, time-limited period, a set of goal-directed activities designed to help children live in families that offer continuity of relationships with nurturing parents or caretakers and the opportunity to establish a lifetime relationship. [Maluccio and Fein 1983]

Child welfare professionals emphasize services for preventing children's placement outside the home whenever possible. When placement is unavoidable, services are supposed to intensify, with the objective of reunifying and stabilizing the family or of finding another permanent family home for the child. As a consequence, two major types of services have become increasingly important in professional thought: family support and family preservation.

Community-based family support programs (day care, respite care, family drop-in centers, emergency financial assistance, information and referral) and educational programs (parent education, play groups, parent-child activities that focus on child development and promote healthy family relationships, warm lines and hot lines for parents with problems) [Weissbourd and Kagan 1989] prevent child abuse and neglect by strengthening parental skills and by developing needed family resources. Family preservation programs provide intensive and extensive services to a family in their home when removal of a child to foster or residential care seems imminent, in order to avoid separating the child from the family whenever possible. A professional provides up to 20 hours of service to the family per week for a limited period of time. This may include parent education, family therapy, material assistance, transportation and other concrete services, and whatever else may be needed that is at all feasible to help mitigate the family crisis and strengthen the family's ability to meet the needs of its members and the demands of its environment.[1]

Both family support services and family preservation services give primary attention in their objectives and evaluation to the prevention of child abuse and neglect. They also respond to the current funding climate of child welfare services: program evaluation studies point out the significant cost-effectiveness of these programs when contrasted with expensive out-of-home care for abused and neglected children [Children's Defense Fund 1991, Kinney et al. 1991].

How Church Agencies Function in This Context

Few church agencies have experienced dramatic growth in their funding bases; in terms of real income, giving to all religious organizations has increased less than 1% a year over the past 30 years [Jacquet 1985]. The cost of services that can respond effectively to the complex needs of children and families in care, however, has markedly increased. The funding resources of government grants and contracts, therefore, have been especially appealing to church agencies. In fact, many agencies have seen major areas of growth in their budgets and programming coming from grants and fees for services from these public sources. This growth often reflects the public sector's primary focus on protection of children from abuse and neglect. Family foster care and residential care, services the church has historically provided, have thus found new funding from the government sector.

Family support services and family preservation programs also have an intrinsic appeal for church agencies. Professional agency staff members are influenced by the professional literature and research supporting these programs; moreover, family support services require much smaller funding bases than residential care and treatment services. Church agencies are also particularly well suited to the community-based approach of these programs because of their relationship with communities through local congregations. Meeting the primary need for community and responding to human isolation are, after all, what church parish programs can do well. Churches of every major Christian tradition have developed small-scale community programs based on the voluntary efforts of parishioners [Burke 1989]—programs such as parent-child play groups, friendship groups, self-help groups, recreational groups, and family life education groups. All of these represent the capacity to create community and supportive relationships in the place of human social isolation. Thus family support programs suggest an exciting new avenue for linkage and mutual support between agencies and the churches and Christian organizations that support them.

These features of the current human service context in the United States interact with the organizational characteristics of the church agency and the social systems that support it to create the milieu in which church agencies are currently serving children and their families. To what extent does the church as an institution give shape to the agencies that serve children and their families in its name? Keith-Lucas and Sanford [1977] suggested that church-related agencies often have four responsibilities to their sponsoring church groups that influence agency services and that may be more or less significant for any given agency: (1) to carry out the church's mission and beliefs in a practical way; (2) to serve families in the church or denomination; (3) to evangelize, often understood as treating people in a loving way so they will be able to understand and accept a gospel of love; and (4) to implement beliefs on which the church or denomination places particular emphasis and to which it may require the adherence of staff members or clients, such as abstinence from alcohol (some Baptist denominations) or pacifism (Quakers).

To evaluate the nature and scope of the influence of churches and church organizations on church agencies, I surveyed a group of executive directors of agencies that met two criteria: they held membership in the National Association of Homes for Children, a major professional organization for residential child care agencies, and their names indicated some past or present affiliation with a church or religious group. From the resulting pool of 128 agencies, 79 administrators responded, a return rate of 62% [Garland 1992].

The clearest impact of the church context on these agencies appeared to be in organizational mission and goals. Over two-thirds of the respondents indicated that religious affiliation had a major impact on agency mission and goals; over half indicated that it had at least some impact on the nature of the services their agencies provided; and only a handful (6%) indicated there was no impact. An agency's services usually directly reflect its mission and goals, and thus are influenced by the religious context in which services are offered. Respondents were asked to name programs or services their agencies offered that, in their assessment, developed because of their religious context. Respondents most frequently named traditional church child welfare services, such as family foster care, counseling, residential treatment, maternity care and adoption, and the operation of residential group homes, emergency shelters, and homes for developmentally disabled adults. But these 79 agencies also offered an array of community-based prevention and family support programs:

- pregnancy counseling;
- family preservation services;
- transitional housing for homeless families;
- independent living and transitional housing programs for older adolescents aging out of residential and foster care;
- information and referral services;
- in-home services for single parents of infants and toddlers;
- pregnancy prevention programs;

- parent education and other family life education programs offered through and for church congregations, as well as with client groups;

- continuing education and support services for professional church leaders (such as pastors and Christian educators);

- emergency receiving homes for children whose families are in crisis;

- weekday child care consultation to churches; and

- a volunteer speakers' bureau to address church groups on child and family issues.

They reported using volunteers to provide a number of services for their clients, such as activity groups, special outings and parties, summer camps, after-school programs for children at risk of delinquency or abuse, and a project matching church women with pregnant adolescents for friendship and support.

Respondents were asked to share their dreams for the future of their agencies' relationships with churches and/or religious organizations. The responses centered on programs they would like to develop or discontinue and ways to strengthen or weaken ties with churches and religious organizations. By far the most frequent response expressed a desire to increase the support, particularly financial support, of churches and denominations for the work of their agencies. The next most frequent response indicated a desire to develop or expand the services of the agency to programs in church congregations and local communities, emphasizing family life education and other preventive and developmental services. Other interests these agency administrators frequently mentioned included developing family counseling and crisis intervention centers in local communities; developing or expanding pregnancy, maternity, and adoption programs; and expanding the use of volunteers in their agencies. Programs that agencies were already planning for the future included family foster care and group care, day care for low-income families, family treatment services, emergency shelters, involving churches in political advocacy, developing denomination-wide Children's Day celebrations in the congregations, and serving developmentally disabled persons and their families.

The religious groups that support these agencies do contribute to shaping their services. Their governing boards represent the churches and bodies that support them and to whom they must answer for the use of that support. Although many of these agencies offer the child welfare services church agencies traditionally offer (emergency shelter, residential child care, family foster care, maternity and adoption services, group homes), many also offer or are planning to offer a wide range of community services, often housed and cosponsored by the churches and religious organizations that support them. These services include family life education and other prevention-oriented family services in congregations and communities, community-based crisis services, involving church volunteers in service and in child advocacy, and even influencing the worship of church congregations (as in the development of Children's Day services). Obviously, most agency administrators see the relationship with supporting religious groups as one to be strengthened, not diminished.

Residential services continue to be the heart of these 79 agencies; other services are often expansions of this basic program. These residential programs are responding to the current professional emphasis on working with families to serve children, sometimes in home-based services, but perhaps especially when children are in out-of-home care. In the next two sections, we will look into the array of family-centered residential services and how these services actually work with families. We will then examine ways in which volunteers and congregations can be involved in helping the agency to fulfill its Christian mission of both providing quality services to clients and leading and guiding the church in service. In the next chapter, we will look at ways the agency can further expand services into the community by consultation and through services and programs offered jointly with congregations.

The Array of Family-Centered Residential Services

Residential services, particularly residential treatment, are necessary components of a comprehensive array of child welfare services. Unfortunately, all out-of-home child welfare services, including residential services, suffered denigration as an unintended effect of Public Law 96-272, the Adoption Assistance and Child Welfare Reform Act of 1980. This bill was enacted in response to the discovery that large numbers of children were adrift in the foster care system, moving from home to home with no permanent family ties. The Adoption Assistance and Child Welfare Reform Act emphasized children's need for permanence, called for the delivery of in-home services to prevent placement, and expanded subsidized adoption programs. It also called for avoiding placement in out-of-home care—family foster care and residential care—except as part of a child's overall permanency plan.

Indeed, before 1980, many children were in residential care who could have been better served by intensive services to their families to avoid out-of-home placement, or who needed to be released for adoption. The goals and focus of residential care have changed a great deal as a result of Public Law 96-272 and of current professional thought about the needs of children. Residential care is no longer seen as an acceptable substitute for a family. Instead, it is considered a means of intervening in the lives of children and their families in ways that will allow reunification, or that will clarify the family situation so that other permanent family living arrangements can be made. It can provide respite care for families (such as families of children with special needs) who need additional support to keep the child at home with them as the primary providers. Residential care can also serve as a "safe place" where children can emotionally prepare for placement in an adoptive home.

Residential Treatment Programs

Many residential programs offer intensive services to children whose serious problems require placement outside the home—severe emotional disturbance (often related to child abuse and/or sexual abuse), or behavior that is potentially or actually destructive to self or others and that parents cannot control (such as chemical dependence or abuse, sexual abuse of younger children, and physical violence towards self or others). Programs may specialize in services for children with special needs, such as those with drug addictions or those who have been sexually abused. Professional staff members work with the family as well as the child, and aim to resolve the problems to the point that the child can be returned home successfully or can be placed in another permanent setting (kinship care, adoption, or occasionally, long-term family foster care).

Support Programs for Families in Crisis or with Special Needs

Residential care facilities also offer an array of out-of-home services to support families in crisis or with special needs. Some agencies provide crisis care for homeless runaways or children who must be removed from their homes because of imminent danger (abuse or neglect), receiving children 24 hours a day from referring authorities or from parents in desperate situations.

In a quite different program, agencies offer respite care for children with special needs, such as developmental and/or physical disabilities, to provide families with needed respite and support so they can continue to offer ongoing care for their family member. These programs may offer seasonal camps and weekend programs for clients, sometimes including whole families.

Transitional Care

Other programs provide transitional care during a period when decisions are being made about the best plan for a child and family or when preparations are being made for a child to return home or to move to a new permanent care arrangement. Family clarification programs offer residential care for children and intensive family services designed to help the family resolve problems and decide whether to move toward reunification or toward alternative family care arrangements for a child. The environment of the residential care program, more structured and less emotionally intense than that of a foster home, may be particularly helpful to a child whose family is in emotional upheaval and who cannot cope with the demands of family living. Agencies also offer care programs designed to prepare children for permanent foster care or adoption. Many children are not able to move immediately from one family to another, however loving the new family may be. Many family situations from which children have been removed can be considered "emotionally toxic." One does not give a poisoned child a feast; one tries first to eliminate the poison [Keith-Lucas 1987].

Children who have come from turbulent family situations may find comfort and support in the rules and routines of group living as they work to develop the greater self-control that may be necessary to live successfully in a future foster or adoptive home. The services offered and the milieu itself can help the child work through and begin to resolve past losses and anticipate and prepare for the new living situation [Zuckerman 1983]. In group care, children can find relief from the demands of family life. This can be a time for parents and children to make long-lasting decisions free from the complications of a rival set of parents (such as foster parents) and with the support of other children and families facing similar problems. Parents may feel less threatened by competent professional staff members than by competent foster parents, who are more likely to be perceived by parents as replacing them in the affections of the child. Short-term residential care can also be more appropriate than foster care during a family crisis or transition in care, since children already in crisis are not asked to adjust to the nuances of family living that by definition exist in all families, including foster families. It can allow an older child to develop needed independence without breaking family ties.

The clarification period, limited to a maximum of one year, is used by parents and children to develop or test their ability and willingness to live as a family. For some children and families, this work results in the conclusion that the child will not be able to return home, so an alternative living plan is necessary. At the conclusion of the family clarification period, children who cannot return home may enter one of three residential care tracks: supplementary parenting, plan clarification, and independent living.

Supplementary Parenting

Children in this track continue to relate to their parents as their family, much as children do in boarding school. The family ties are too significant and positive for child and family to rupture these ties and place the child with an adoptive family. Sometimes, long-term foster care can provide the most appropriate placement for children in this situation. Other children, however, need the structured care that a group setting can offer, without the emotional stress of seeming competition between foster and biological families.

In supplementary parenting programs, staff members work to nurture ties between parents and their children. Parents are consistently and frequently involved in the child's life and take part in all major decisions about the child, but they cannot assume full-time parental responsibilities because of their own circumstances or limitations, because of the child's special needs, or because of a combination of these elements. This type of program can preserve a child's family ties even if she or he cannot live with the parents. Current thought in reunification services recognizes the importance of maintaining a child's connection with the family even when she or he may never be able to live at home permanently [see, for example, Maluccio et al. 1990].

Thus, on occasion, the group care setting may also be a long-term placement of choice, allowing individuals to continue to be family for each other in a situation where that would otherwise not be possible. For example, group care may preserve the bonds of a large sibling group (such as five or more children) who want and need to live together as a family, when foster care would necessarily mean further family dismemberment. In this case, sibling relationships are considered the most significant ties the children have, justifying a residential placement where these ties can be nurtured.

Plan Clarification

Children in plan clarification are those whose parents are no longer a resource and for whom permanency must be found elsewhere—often, but not always, by adoption. It may be more helpful for the child to remain in residential care during the transitional period than to be placed in a foster home, especially if the period between the decision to pursue adoption and the placement in an adoptive family will be relatively short and the time can be used productively to prepare the child for living with an adoptive family.

Independent Living

Some older adolescents or young adults and their families may develop a plan of continued placement with the agency until the adolescent is old enough to live independently. Agencies offer transitional and independent living programs for adolescents who are beyond the age when adoption is a viable possibility. These programs prepare them for the relative independence of young adulthood; they often live in a small group home or a transitional living apartment in the community that is not readily identified as connected to an agency. These programs are also being offered for young adolescent mothers and their children. Young people who are not prepared to be completely responsible for themselves can benefit from a sheltered environment where they receive nurture and structure as they learn to provide for their own needs, and in some cases, the needs of their children.

Working with Families in Residential Services

Each of these programs demands that the agency have specialized structures and professional skills and knowledge specific to its focus. For example, agencies with respite care programs have or should have structures conducive to providing repetitive short-term care for special-needs children and their families. The agencies should have professional staff knowledgeable and skillful in working with this population. Treatment programs require the structures and skills to establish a therapeutic milieu for residents and their families, to defuse volatile situations, and to physically manage adolescents who are potentially violent toward others or themselves.

These programs have a common focus on the family. The child's context is the family; services to a child must begin, therefore, with that context. Helping professionals are at least one ecological level removed from the child, and when they move into a relationship with the child as an individual apart from the family context, they violate the child's ecology [Combrinck-Graham 1989]. At times, this violation is essential because of extreme circumstances, but it should never be seen as the answer to the perceived problem. For example, establishing a trusting, safe relationship with a child who has been the victim of incest may be necessary to collect vital information and to demonstrate to the child what a safe, trustworthy adult is like. But the professional relationship can never substitute for a safe, trustworthy family. Treatment must seek the development of wholesome familial relationships and the protection and support of those relationships as primary.

Even work with older adolescents in transitional and independent living programs looks to the family as the context for understanding and helping the child. Rarely do young adults who age out of a residential program go off to live alone and lose contact with their families. Whether or not they actually live in the family home, they usually maintain contact with family members. These relationships frequently have a significant impact on the young person's adjustment to life outside the agency's supervision.

In fact, several studies of residential treatment programs report that the environment to which children return after residential care is a powerful factor in determining their long-term adjustment, regardless of their progress in the program [Whittaker 1988]. In other words, the quality of the individual treatment provided to children is less important than the quality of work with the family in determining how children will fare once they are released from the agency's residential care. The implication is that professionals need to invest as much in families and their support networks as they do in the children they care for—or more. If the residential treatment center is to be viewed as a temporary support for families in crisis or a long-term support for families with special needs, rather than as a substitute for families that have failed, it must engage families as full and equal partners in the helping process [Whittaker 1988].

The question is, what can we do with families? Many of the families who have children in residential care programs have been through counseling or family therapy at some point, often extensively and with multiple agencies. If professional dreams came true, all the families seen in residential care would either have been through a home-based intensive services program, with placement for the child as a short-term part of that plan, or placement would have been a response to a situation that could not be handled by intensive home-based services alone. The placement would then be part of a larger, ongoing treatment picture "in which the extended family, direct family therapy, intense in-home services, and other community resources are marshaled to sustain children and families" [Itzkowitz 1989: 395]. This definition of the role of residential care suggests its major contemporary challenge.

When parents and professionals place children in residential care, they often feel defeated. The agency must fight the risk of parents walking away from the perceived source of their trouble, limiting or even ceasing contact with the child, and, consequently, exacerbating everyone's feelings of failure. The family may continue physical contact but withdraw emotionally, simply "going through the motions" of being a family to the child, all the while having abandoned any hope of change in the family situation. Children thus emotionally or physically abandoned to residential care are at risk not only of losing their families, but also of being unable to form attachments with anyone else because they have no way to resolve the family's difficulties. They become either pseudoattached and clinging or very distant and aloof, pushing people away [Itzkowitz 1989].

The family services provided by the residential program, therefore, must be different from those that have already been tried. If family therapy did not work with the child at home, it is even less likely to work with the child out of the home. Because the family's hope and motivation for change may be at an even lower ebb than before placement, services must actively engage parents in the lives of their children in ways that emphasize strength and engender hope. Residential treatment requires more family work than other forms of treatment, not less.

The following section suggests programs that can help the agency move to a family focus in its residential care of children, and that recognize and strengthen parents' roles as the primary caregivers for their children. In these programs, the term "parents" refers to the permanent caregiving adults with whom it is planned that a child will be living or relating in the future—biological, adoptive, or long-term foster parents; grandparents or other adult relatives; or adult siblings. Some children in residential care came from and will return to caregivers who are not their biological parents. A program's scope includes all caregivers to whom children are attached and who can be the permanent, nurturing families to which they return.

Programs and Processes that Support and Nurture Families

Clearly, if professional staff members are going to involve family members in the agency's work with the child, the agency and family need to be geographically accessible to one another. Most of these programs require that the agency be in close proximity to the family home, or at least within a feasible distance for frequent travel, with the resources for the family to come and go. The agency almost always needs some kind of leverage to keep families involved when they might find it easier to withdraw. Ideally, contracts should specify the involvement required of the family in order for services to be offered and continued, and consequences for a family's failure to involve itself in the treatment plan should be clarified at the outset of services. If these basic conditions for service cannot be met, the agency colludes with the family in taking responsibility for a child without an active plan for return to the family or an alternative appropriate placement.

Flexible Respite Care and Family Reunification

Programs have to be flexible in relation to the many kinds of families with whom they work. For example, Astrachan and Harris [1983] suggest a weekend-only residential program that offers weekend respite for families dealing with troubling children. A concomitant program offers special educational resources not available in community schools in the format of a five-day residential week. Children in this program go home on the weekends.

When children have been in residential care, weekend-long home visits may be initially unmanageable for their families, because weekends are often relatively unstructured blocks of time. Instead, some children may adjust to the return home best by spending one or more weekday overnights in the parents' home (with the daytime hours in school or day treatment), returning to the agency for the other days of the week, and reserving the weekend for treatment services for the child and respite for the family. Such flexible care can be considered a normal part of the residential service continuum rather than a service only for those with special needs. This will not work, however, if it requires a school transfer.

Susan, an emotionally troubled 14-year-old, had been in and out of residential care and foster homes since she was five. She was initially placed in a foster home as a preschooler because her mother had repeatedly left her home alone without supervision. When she returned home at age eight, she was sexually abused by her mother's boyfriend. After Susan's second stay in family foster care her mother agreed to relinquish her for adoption, but the adoption was disrupted; the adoptive parents could not manage Susan's alternating moods of clinging, regressive behavior and angry rebellion. At age 10, Susan was placed in a church-sponsored residential care facility to prepare her for another adoptive placement, while the state special-needs adoption program sought an appropriate home. Because she had no regular contact with the biological family, except for infrequent calls from a 22-year-old sister, she was linked with the McDonald family, a couple with three teenagers of their own. They were members of a congregation that provided some financial and volunteer support for the agency. The McDonalds volunteered to be a "visiting home," befriending Susan and providing support during this interim period. Initially, they visited her at the agency and took her on family outings. As their relationship with Susan developed, she began spending one weekend each month with the McDonalds.

In 10 months, no adoptive home had been located for Susan, and the McDonalds began to talk about adopting her themselves. The home study and other necessary processes were begun, and Susan moved into the McDonald home. The situation rapidly deteriorated, however. Conflict with the teenage McDonald children erupted when Susan transferred to the school they attended;

they were embarrassed by her behavior around their friends. The adoptive parents maintained a rather permissive and open relationship with their children, with a good deal of discussion and negotiation concerning family decisions and discipline. Susan, however, defiantly broke rules, refused to compromise with others, and generally floundered in the unstructured environment so unlike the placements she had previously experienced. Exasperated, the McDonalds were ready to return Susan to the agency. Susan, angry and devastated, vowed she never wanted to live in a family again.

When the staff discussed the various alternatives available to Susan and the McDonalds, they decided to delay any decision until the end of the school year, only eight weeks away. In the interim, Susan would remain in the home of the McDonalds from after school on Monday until she left for school on Friday, spending the weekends at the agency. In this way she could stay in the school, where she was doing well, despite the embarrassment she caused her new siblings. The entire family was given counseling on managing sibling conflicts. Compromises were reached and clear rules established. The unstructured time of weekend family activities, which appeared to be creating the most stress for everyone, would be a time of respite for both Susan and the family.

Susan found her weekend returns to the agency and her relationships with other residents and child care staff members comforting. The time with the family was much less intense during the busy weekdays, and tensions eased. All agreed to continue the respite arrangement over the summer months, accompanied by Susan's involvement in a community activities program that provided structure for her weekdays. In addition, the adoptive parents agreed to, and encouraged, Susan's contact with her biological sister. They also told her that she could continue to use her own surname, which was a symbolic link with her sister and a critical part of her identity.[2] Though this may not be an ideal permanent arrangement, the respite program has averted yet another adoption disruption for Susan, and will be phased out only gradually as she and the McDonalds feel ready to take on additional time together.

Other parents sometimes find that the support of flexible respite services provides enough relief from the demands and stressors of an emotionally disturbed child returning from residential care to enable them to tackle reunification. Ongoing respite, emergency, and aftercare services enable these parents to consider reunification sooner than if they were expected to resume total responsibility for their child all at once [Astrachan and Harris 1983].

Incorporating the Family into the Residential Setting

The families of children in care often have to make major changes in the way they function as families when they prepare for their children to return home permanently. Agencies have therefore included parents in programming, encouraging parents to visit their children at the agency and encouraging children to make weekend home visits, and, foremost, involving parents in therapy to correct family dysfunctions. Often it is a social worker who conducts the parent education and family therapy, usually in weekly sessions.

This structure for family intervention presents some major strategic problems, however. How can the social worker help a family to develop new patterns of relating to one another, in an hour or two per week and often less, when the family does not have an ongoing life together in which to try out and establish the new patterns? Many of the problems that originally necessitated out-of-home care do not reside solely either within the parents or within the child, but instead in their interactions with one another in daily living. Since child welfare service systems increasingly offer intensive services designed to keep children in their own homes whenever possible, when a child reaches residential care, the family situation has already been deemed too volatile for parent and child to continue to live together. Often these families have already been involved in and "failed" at family therapy.

When a situation requires that a child be removed to a protective setting, therapeutic efforts must shift gears. This does not necessarily mean an intensification of efforts, but rather a different focus of efforts and a different modality of intervention. Staff involvement with the family has to be extended beyond the limitations of therapeutic sessions, so that intervention occurs as families are observed and guided through daily activities and the transitions in family organization that take place in daily events.

Ravnsborg [1982] and Cooklin et al. [1983] have developed programs in which whole families live in an agency or residential facility. Because of constraints on facilities and budgets and other family commitments of clients, however, admission of an entire family into a residential facility is often not feasible or desirable. Some families of children in care have experienced significant upheavals in employment and living arrangements, and even changes in family membership, such as divorce. Intervention should reinforce rather than challenge the stability of the family home and the fabric of the social network. Cooklin et al. [1983: 461] report that the requirement for full-time attendance by families "meant that initial engagement was often difficult and sometimes failed altogether. Many admissions have now become much briefer, and some families will have attended for as little as a day or half a day per week."

A modified approach in which parents are involved in significant ways in the daily lives of their children but maintain a separate residence thus holds more promise with the majority of families and for agencies with limited resources. Webster et al. [1979], Martone et al. [1989], and Peterson and Brown [1982] pioneered this approach in residential child care, and Johnston and Gabor [1981] developed a model for family foster care in which foster parents are trained as parent counselors and assume a primary role in family intervention.

In a residential facility, this model may be applied in a variety of ways. For example, one or two weeknights each week, parents and siblings of a child in placement may join the residential unit in preparing, eating, and cleaning up the evening meal; completing school homework; and enjoying recreational activities. "Food represents nurturance and thus meals are key times for group care staff to involve parents in providing a nurturing environment" [Kagan and Schlosberg 1989: 127].

During these times, parents are responsible for their children, but child care staff back them up with support and guidance. For example, a child care worker may suggest that a parent use recently learned parent-child communication skills, and may provide on-the-spot coaching in using the skills when a child is trying to explain a school paper to a parent. Staff members can coach both parents and children in using what they have learned in parent education and family living groups. This kind of involvement provides time for child care staff to work directly with parents in learning and reinforcing new skills, and to model various communication, discipline, and behavior-shaping skills. Established roles for parents in the living group provide ways for parents to experiment with, develop, and be reinforced for new patterns of family living in the relative safety of the residential setting, before the child returns home.

The residential milieu also exposes parents to a variety of models of family interaction as they observe child care workers and other families interacting in various relationships and contexts. For most families in our society, opportunities for learning family interaction skills have been severely limited; the only models are families of origin or television actors. Particularly for parents who were raised in troubled families and who may be relatively isolated, without much social support in their parenting roles, the residential milieu may be a significant and safe context for learning new ways to relate to their children. This kind of work with the family resembles family preservation services, but it takes place in the protected and structured context of the agency and, ideally, with families who have already received or been evaluated for such intensive in-home services but for whom out-of-home placement was deemed necessary.

Family time in the agency should be adapted to each family's needs. It should not be an additional demand that places the family under stress. For example, instead of the family having to prepare a meal or to purchase fast food before rushing to the agency for an evening meeting, the family participates in preparing and eating the meal at the agency. Siblings may bring their homework. Parents may even be invited to bring ironing or mending, craft projects, or other activities that are (or could be) part of the family's normal evening routine. Watching favorite television shows together is an opportunity for informal discussion of the use and misuse of television and its influence on children and families.

Simms and Bolden [1991] have developed an innovative family reunification program for children in family foster care that involves both biological and foster families in a two-hour weekly visiting program. The model might also work well for children in residential care. During the first hour of the weekly program, the children and their biological families participate in a group activity facilitated by the art therapist. Professional staff members assist, observing and working with parents and children. Parents who choose not to take part in the activity can sit with their children in small areas close by and read or listen to music with them. The atmosphere is homey, with comfortable furniture, books, puzzles, and games. A small outside playground can also be available.

During these visits, short (20-minute) individual family therapy sessions are conducted with each family by a staff social worker in a private setting away from the rest of the group. Foster parents meet together in a support group during these visits, in a conference room separate from the visiting area. After the foster parents take the children home, the biological parents meet for the second hour in a group with the social worker.

The program aims to provide a nurturing, educational environment for visiting among biological parents, foster parents, and children; to help biological parents maintain their relationships with their children and improve their parenting skills; to provide educational and supportive services for foster parents; to continue to provide services after reunification to help families function appropriately; and to collect data for professional decisions about reunification. Although Simms and Bolden's program was limited in scope, the positive response from biological and foster parents, including very high attendance rates, suggest this model as a promising program component for serving children and their families in the family foster care system. Similar structured programs that combine family visits, parent education and support, and therapeutic intervention with families also hold much promise for residential care programs.

Parent Education Programs

Increasingly, residential treatment programs do not view parent education as a valuable "extra" program, but as an indispensable part of the basic service contract with families. Families may be required to attend in order to receive other agency services, including residential services for their child.

A short introductory program of one to three sessions can familiarize parents with the philosophy and programs of the agency and help them to understand their role as members of the family service team. A basic parenting course can follow, to cover building child/adolescent self-esteem, parent-child communication, discipline, and so on. A number of prepackaged programs could be used in this basic course. Care should be taken, however, that parent workbooks and videotapes reflect families and problems that are relevant for the group participants. For example, parents will probably not identify with the example of an upper-middle-class teenager who cannot remember to take out the trash when their own children are openly defiant, chemically dependent, or threatening them with personal violence.

The basic course should be offered at varying times to make it convenient for parents, especially fathers, who are notoriously difficult to keep involved. Child care for other siblings should be provided. Sibling activity groups may be planned for these times, but both residents and their siblings may also be included in some parent sessions, such as those on family decision making and communication.

Incentives related to the groups' purposes and the needs of the participants, as well as recognition for participation, encourage attendance and involvement. These may include reimbursement for transportation expenses and/or child care for poor families, gift books or tapes on the topic of parenting, family games or passes to a local movie theater for the whole family, other family recreational resources, and/or certificates of course completion.

Targeted Parent Education Programs

Targeted parent education programs follow the basic parent education model, but are developed around the known special needs of a particular population group (parents of children with a history of substance abuse or parents of children with mental illness or emotional disturbance, for example) and/or developed from the felt needs of parents involved with the agency at any particular time. The programs should be short term in order to encourage maximum participation, although they may be continued for another short term if the group so decides. The group can emphasize a sharing of the expertise parents have developed in their work with their own children, as well as expertise that the staff can bring to the group.

Family Treatment Teams

The parents of clients are members of the treatment team and included in case management and planning sessions with the clinical and child care staff. Holding these sessions in the home of the family is convenient for the parents, contributes support and communicates sensitivity to families, and yields valuable assessment data for the agency staff and other human service professionals involved with the family. Coordinating the work of the child care staff with the parents is particularly significant [Garland 1987]. Beverly James [1989] suggests the active involvement of parents in any individual treatment provided to the child.

Parent-Child Care Staff Communication and Coordination

Whenever possible, parents should be encouraged to retain normal parental functions such as transporting and accompanying their children to special events, purchasing clothing and other items, and working with the child care staff to provide appropriate discipline (both positive encouragement and the correction of misbehavior). This kind of involvement requires frequent, consistent communication between parents and staff members, by phone as well as in scheduled meetings. It empowers parents to continue to influence their children's lives and avoids miscommunication, the use of children as primary communication channels between the agency and the home, and the possibility that children may set staff and parents against one another.

Ongoing Parent Support Groups

Parents of children with special needs may find particular help from involvement in support groups sensitive to the needs of parents of troubled and troubling children. Self-help groups, such as the Families as Allies group in Kentucky, which serves the families of emotionally troubled children, have developed in many communities. Parents Anonymous (for abusive or potentially abusive families) [Lieber 1983] or other relevant self-help group chapters can be established for current and former clients' parents. Agency staff members may provide facilitation for such groups [Pancoast et al. 1983; Powell 1987].

Sibling and Family Groups

Time-limited educational and treatment groups may include several whole families, with the assumption that entire family systems are affected by and affect the family processes and issues that led to placement. In a multiple family group, a number of objectives can be addressed simultaneously: changes in family processes (communication, problem solving, expression of feelings and needs), learning from other families who offer a variety of models and styles, and appreciating that other families struggle with similar problems. Highly interactive, activity-oriented programming can be integrated with discussion of these experiences and their application in ongoing family life. These programs can be the heart of recreational, positive experiences for family members and an extension of life in the residential unit and in the family home.

Family Retreats and Family Camping

Parents can be involved with their children and other families in weekend retreats in a variety of settings, similar to wilderness camping treatment programs for adolescents [Marx 1988]. These may include camping, wilderness experiences, or simply a weekend in a recreational setting away from the home environment. Programming can emphasize developing new family skills, family problem-solving and decision-making, family self-reliance, and finding pleasure in shared activities.

Family Network Intervention

Other persons may be brought in to create an altered home environment for a child in residential care, such as influential members of the extended family, other adults living in the same household, neighbors, friends, and community members (perhaps even including a child's most significant peers) who are important in the family's life. The network can be convened in the family home, in a community setting such as a church or school, or if a community location is not possible, in the agency [e.g., Attneave 1976; Collins and Pancoast 1976; James 1989].

This approach to family services derives from using ecology as a metaphor for the relationship between a family and its environment [Hartman and Laird 1983]. It views families as permeable systems in reciprocal interaction with their physical and social environments. This ecological context is seen as having a direct impact on the relationships within the family system. Families are embedded in a physical and social ecology just as significant in their functioning as the family is significant in the functioning of a child. Aspects of the family's social ecology include:

- the child's peer group in neighborhood and school;

- the family's relationships with kin, neighbors, friends, and work colleagues;

- the involvement of professionals (physicians, teachers, public assistance caseworkers); and

- representatives of other formal social systems (the landlord, school bus driver, corner grocery store owner).

Similarly, the family is embedded in a physical environment that gives shape to its life together and to which the professional has to give attention:

- the arrangement of the family home's space for shared activities and privacy;

- the safety of the neighborhood and its resources for children to play or spend time with peers and for parents to meet and talk with their peers;

- the distance to services and the availability of transportation;

- the distance to work and the time used in commuting; and

- weather, climate, and air quality (especially in the case of the asthmatic child or parent).

Finally, the agency itself becomes a part of the family's ecological system, not only for the child in care but for the family members, as they encounter receptionists, child care workers, cooks, and other residents and their families.

Church agencies have access to what can be key resources for developing more nourishing, supportive social ecologies for many children and their families—individual volunteers and groups of volunteers and congregations located in the family's own community. These resources can be particularly important for families who have social relationships that stress rather than support family functioning, as well as for isolated families who have withered or nonexistent social networks.

Involving Volunteers and Community Groups

Research suggests a significant correlation between a strong social network and effective parenting. In an early study, Young [1964] found that 95% of severely abusive families had no significant relationships with others in the community or neighborhood. Vogel and Bell [1960] discovered that families with emotionally disturbed children often had relationships with neighbors that were either minimal or hostile. Colletta and Gregg [1981] found that an active support system was positively related to a mother's mental health and negatively related to the frequency of restrictive, demanding, and rejecting interactions with children. Mothers with high levels of support were more affectionate, closer, and more positive with their children, and those with low levels of support were more hostile, indifferent, and rejecting. Zelkowitz [1987] found that children of poor, depressed mothers behaved in less aggressive and more socially acceptable ways when they felt cared for by other significant adults in their lives. Dunst et al. [1988] report research demonstrating the significant relationship between informal social support and "good" parenting of children who are retarded, handicapped, or developmentally at risk.[3]

The influences of a network extend beyond support for positive parenting behavior by adults, however, and affect children directly. Not only do parents need a network of relationships with other adults in order to be good parents, but children also need a network of adults to whom to relate. These other adults may include parents of peers, neighbors, activity leaders for church and community children's programs, friends, and relatives. These relationships offer children a number of important resources.

First, they provide security. An informal network of adult friends and extended family members gives a child a sense of rootedness and belonging; it takes some of the power out of a child's dependency on the heartbeat or the goodwill of a parent. Second, a network provides children with respite from parents. Staying with a trusted adult friend or family member for a few hours, days—or longer—may be an acceptable alternative to running away or even emergency shelter for a child when parents are incapacitated or unable to cope with the intensity of family relationships. Third, adult network members provide alternative life models, offering balance and alternatives to parents' values, views, and blind spots. Children can survive and even thrive in difficult home situations if they have adult allies elsewhere [Garbarino 1979]. Other adults in a child's life may identify and encourage skills and gifts in ways that the parent does not or cannot. The affirmation of a coach or another admired adult for resisting peer pressure to use drugs or to cut school, for example, may be more valuable to a child than anything the parent might do or say.

Finally, social networks help children to develop an identity rooted in mutuality and significance in the lives of others. An informal network not only offers role models, caregiving, and security, but also encourages children to give in return. As children learn to share with others beyond their own family unit in meaningful ways—tutoring a younger child, or running errands for an elderly neighbor—they develop a sense of themselves as functional members of the social network. For example, Covenant Children's Home and Family Services of Illinois, a residential treatment facility for adolescents, arranges for residents to visit and develop friendships with elderly nursing home residents. One adolescent presented a Chicago Bears cap from his own sports hat collection to an elderly man, a fellow Bears fan.

Networks can be sources of difficulty as well as solutions to problems. Not all network relationships are supportive; social networks are not equivalent to social support [Gottlieb 1981]. Children may be abused instead of nurtured by extended family members, peers, or neighbors. Peer networks may encourage drug use or delinquent behaviors, and some network members can be threats to a child's development rather than resources.

Children need a network of positive relationships with loving, supportive adults. Yet most children do not experience such relationships. In a study of the social maps of children approaching adolescence, Garbarino and others [1978] found that many children do not have supportive adults, other than their parents, in their lives. Urban children named an average of 2.3 adults among the 10 people they knew best and saw at least once a month. Rural children named 1.5 adults, and suburban children 1.0. In fact, 60% of the suburban children reported no such relationship with an adult. The number of adults in a child's life also decreases with the age of the child. The researchers concluded that "the results reinforce the widely held concern over age segregation in American life as a developmental and historical trend" [Garbarino et al. 1978: 426].

In the 15 years since that study, this trend does not appear to have reversed itself. In addition, we might hypothesize that those children who are most troubled by family problems, peer pressures, and emotional difficulties are least likely to have supportive adult friends. A research study with 16-year-old boys in Norway supports this hypothesis: Cochran and Hogskolesenteret [1987] found that the larger the number of non-kin adults in a boy's social network, the better the boy's school performance, attendance record, and social behavior.

Church agencies can use the resources of supporting congregations to create support for families and children who have withered or dysfunctional social support networks. Programs for strengthening families by involving others as supportive network members include educating potentially supportive persons regarding the needs and the roles they can play in the lives of children in care and their families, and providing structures that allow relationships to develop and grow, with professional support and consultation when needed.

Building Social Support Networks

Sometimes a family's social network already contains persons who could play a supportive, nourishing role in the family system. Professional staff members help them envision that role and provide support and consultation. Neighbors, relatives, and others involved in the family network sessions described above may be significant "volunteers" for working in a different way with a child and family.

> Mark, age 12, had been placed in a residential facility by his mother because of intense conflict between them. Mark's father and mother had divorced six years earlier and the father subsequently had no contact with the family. Mark's mother had difficulty supporting Mark and his younger brother on her wages as a waitress. The younger brother was developmentally disabled and required constant care; he attended a special school and after-school program while the mother worked. A year before placement, Mark's grades had dropped, and he had begun a pattern of truancy and running the streets. His mother was fearful that he would become involved with the drug traffic in their impoverished neighborhood. Her attempts to control Mark, however, only resulted in shouting matches.
>
> A two-month period of residential care initiated by the mother was used to sort out their relationship and restore the mother to her role as parent. Mark's grades improved, and he was willing to live with the behavior contracts they established so that he could come home. In assessing the family's social supports, the social worker learned that Mark admired his uncle, age 25, his father's younger brother who lived in the same community. The uncle valued his relationship with Mark, but the relationship with Mark's mother was somewhat strained. Several sessions were spent with the uncle and Mark's mother in determining how they might best be helpful to Mark. Mark's mother worked on separating her feelings about her ex-husband from her relationship with Mark's uncle. With her agreement and apprecia-

tion, the uncle began to take a more active role in Mark's life, enrolling him in a sports program and accompanying him to practice, and having Mark spend alternate Saturdays with him. Mark flourished in this strengthened relationship, and the behavior contracts held; aftercare services were uneventful, and professional services were terminated.

Working with friends and family members is in some respects like working with "natural helpers," those central persons in informal social networks who are especially skillful at maintaining interpersonal relationships, accessing resources, and helping others with problems. A professional can offer advice in an informal consultative relationship, suggesting additional resources and approaches to helping that may be outside the natural helper's experience and thus enrich the impact of the natural helper. The professional should resist any pressure to organize a program or assign a formal role to the natural helper. It is the informal quality of the relationship that is often of great significance in the lives of clients with impoverished informal relationships [Pancoast 1990b].

Unfortunately, not every family has a young uncle waiting in the wings to provide support and a positive role model. When such resources cannot be identified in the family's current social network, the agency has to create them. Church congregations, especially those located in the communities where client families live, can be an invaluable resource for families in our care [Garland 1990b]. Rarely, however, do volunteers spontaneously call a church agency to ask if they can become a supportive friend to a child or family who needs such a relationship. Instead, church programs, sermons, and reading materials must point out the importance of social networks in the lives of all children and families. For example, one parent education program for church members includes a unit on appreciating and assessing parents' and children's social networks [Garland et al. 1991].

Second, such caregiving to families and children ought to be described as ministry, as "caring for the least of these," in ways that no professional service can duplicate. Friends, grandparents, and neighbors cannot be purchased with any government or charity dollars. Stories of social support from the Bible may provide useful illustrations and scriptural grounding important in communicating with some congregations:

> The young boy Timothy learned to be faithful from the example of his grandmother, who evidently played a key role in his becoming a missionary. (2 Tim. 1:5; 3:16)

> The prophet Samuel visited Jesse, seeking the next king of Israel among his sons. Jesse assembled his boys for Samuel's inspection but did not even think to include David, his youngest son. It took the special vision of someone outside the family—and then only by special revelation from God—to recognize qualities in the young David that his father had missed. Samuel called for David and named him the new king. (1 Sam. 16:1-13)

> As a young child and growing adolescent, Jesus experienced the recognition of his special gifts by other significant adults besides his parents (Luke 2:25-38). The teachers in the temple were "amazed at his understanding" and talked and shared with him (Luke 2:46-47). He found favor in their eyes even when his own parents did not understand. (Luke 2:47-52)

Few children in agency care, however, are in the same category as the boys Timothy, Samuel, and Jesus. These children have serious emotional, social, and developmental disabilities. As one agency director said, "These kids are costly; they not only require staff-intensive services and are hard on facilities, but also they are costly in community relations" [Baker 1991]. Outside the agency, they are often in the eye of the storm in school, community youth programs, and neighborhoods. Churches need to hear these children's stories, too.

Volunteers working with the children in the care of church agencies need determination, toughness, compassion, humor, healthy self-esteem, and sometimes a vision from God of a child's hidden gifts and possibilities. They also need a healthy, supportive system that affirms their caring, especially when affirmation is not readily forthcoming from the child or the child's family. They need their work framed as ministry, as a response to God's call to service and thus not dependent on reciprocity from those whom they serve. The agency staff can provide some of that support and encouragement, remembering that the care and feeding of church members in ministry is just as much a significant part of the agency's responsibility as professional services to children and their families. Pastors and church congregations can also be encouraged to recognize, celebrate, and support the work of these volunteers.

Structures and Supports for Involving Volunteers and Congregations

Many volunteers do not have the personality, commitment, and resources to provide a foster or adoptive home for a child. They may not be able to provide friendship to a child and family who have special needs. Some children and families who need social support are those with whom it is most difficult to develop enduring informal relationships; their great needs and their poor interpersonal skills drain and wither relationships with others. It takes a high level of professional skill and interpersonal sensitivity to assess the potential of volunteers, to coach and develop their ministry skills, and to match them with the kind of client need that they can appropriately and successfully meet. In some respects, assessing the skills and capabilities of volunteers, establishing a place of service for them, and providing continuing support and consultation is even more difficult than supervising professionals. Because volunteers are not paid, they are difficult to dismiss if their work is not what was envisioned. Professionals working with volunteers have to proceed with considerable deliberation and preparation, carefully attending to client confidentiality and self-determination, the meaning and perceptions of the work in the mind of clients and volunteers, and the need for relationships to develop and be nurtured over time.

Work with volunteers is professional practice requiring professional training and expertise.[4] Working with volunteers is time-consuming. Training and consulting with them often require spending hours of professional time in activities other than direct practice with the client family.

Some volunteers may not have direct contact with a child; they may bake birthday cakes or sew teddy bears for children in the care of the agency. Others may initially fill structured, time-limited roles with a child, such as tutoring one evening per week or teaching a sport or craft. Parents may appreciate a volunteer working with them on GED or literacy studies, providing transportation and company to visit an incarcerated spouse, helping with a physically disabled child's exercises, or sharing a craft or leisure activity. The possibilities are limited only by the creativity of the professional and the needs and resources of clients and volunteers.

Over time, it may be desirable for some of these relationships to become more extensive, so that the volunteer becomes a more significant and central figure in the family support network. Volunteers may also begin by offering befriending relationships and visiting homes to clients and their families. The volunteer can be a critical resource in providing care for children who have no family to whom they can return, and who may not be adoptable or currently appropriate for foster home placement. Volunteers can provide homes for these children to spend an evening or weekend away from the residential facility.

> The Methodist Children's Home of Ruston, Louisiana, trains and certifies families and individuals to serve as Visiting Resources for the adolescents in their residential program. Visiting Resources must complete the training, a background check, and a home study to qualify for certification. In the first two years of the program, the agency trained 21 families and individuals, certifying 18 of them. At the time of writing, 18 children had visited in 10 homes.

> First priority is given to approvable family members and relatives, who, while unable to accept custody of the child, may offer a consistent family relationship. If such family members or relatives are not available, friends or others with whom the child has a previous positive relationship are encouraged to serve as Visiting Resources. Only when such resources are not available are volunteers sought to fulfill the need of a child for a family relationship outside the agency.

> The first meeting between an unrelated Visiting Resource and an

adolescent is usually brief and structured, often in the office of the child's social worker. Later, the volunteer is allowed to take the child off campus for a few hours. Only after some bonding has taken place and willingness is mutual is the volunteer allowed to bring the child home for an overnight visit.

This kind of relationship may be enduring, but not necessarily intensive. For example, the Covenant Children's Home and Family Services of Princeton, Illinois, arranges for volunteers to serve as pen pals for the adolescents in its residential treatment facility. These programs are not intended to take the place of family relationships, but they can enrich children's lives with social support.

Over time, a few of these volunteers may come to consider family foster care or even adoption for them and the child to whom they have become attached. Although this is not initially a stated goal, several of the Visiting Resource families who have served with the Methodist Children's Home of Ruston, Louisiana, have subsequently decided to offer their homes for family foster care. For other children, friendship that will last into the adult years after release from agency care meets a critical need. In a research study of the experiences of youths being launched into adulthood from family foster care, most youths (89%) reported continuing contact as young adults with foster home or group home parents. A striking 15% reported having no psychological parent, however; they had no parental figure to whom they could turn for advice or emotional support as they faced the demands of young adulthood [Barth 1990]. One suspects that the percentage of youths without psychological parents who are launched into adulthood from a residential child care facility is even higher.

Family Foster Care and Therapeutic Foster Care

Recruitment of foster parents can be a critical service of the church agency. An unintended and undesirable effect of the Adoption Assistance and Child Welfare Act of 1980 (P.L. 96-272) and the valuing of permanent homes as the appropriate goal for children in care has been a devaluing of family foster care [Kamerman and Kahn 1989]. Nevertheless, many children do need family foster care as the service of choice [Fanshel and Shinn 1978]. In fact, the number of children in family foster care has risen sharply, in response to a multitude of social problems.

Other factors have joined the devaluation of family foster care to create a real crisis in the recruitment of foster care parents. Most foster parents in the past were husband and wife families in which the woman was not employed outside the home. With increased participation by women in the work force, fewer families are able to take on the responsibilities of family foster care; stipends have in no way kept pace with what women (and men) can earn in the labor market, so few can choose family foster care as a career path. In addition, most children entering family foster care today need far more from foster parents than good custodial care. In a reversal of recent trends, many more very young children with special needs are in need of foster care.

Many of these preschool children were born HIV positive, exposed to alcohol and other drugs, and/or with multiple handicaps; others have been physically and/or sexually abused. Difficult and unmanageable adolescents also need out-of-home care. Estimates suggest that half the children in foster care are age 13 and older [Children's Defense Fund 1991, Kamerman and Kahn 1989]. In addition, many children need active support by foster parents in retaining significant relationships with biological families and in working toward reunification, which means that many foster parents must work with biological families as well as caring for children in their own home. As a consequence of all these elements, many adults who might have considered providing family foster care in the past cannot commit themselves to the complexity of the demands of foster care today.

Recruitment of qualified foster parents, therefore, has become a major source of concern in many public agencies. Churches and religious organizations increasingly serve as vital sources for recruitment. Many foster parents recruited from churches bring a special strength to their work from their sense of Christian calling and commitment. It is reported that some people who become foster parents because of religious motivation refuse to accept stipends [Kamerman and Kahn 1989].

Religious fervor can, of course, lead people to volunteer as foster parents, or in other roles related to the agency, who have neither the personal strength, knowledge of their own strengths and limitations, or skills for the demanding work of loving a child in crisis, and, perhaps even harder, the child's family. Although foster parents may find it more difficult to nurture and support the biological parents than to provide care for the child, this may be the more important part of their work—teaching parenting skills, affirming the parent-child relationship, offering a listening ear. The agency has the sensitive task of screening volunteers and finding the most effective ways their need to serve can be addressed. Often, this may be in roles other than that of foster care providers.

Churches can serve as strong support networks for families providing foster care or adoptive homes for children with special needs. An agency professional can work with the adoptive parents' or foster parents' church, helping the church to become a system of support and an extended family for the parents and child. The development of such a support system does not often happen naturally. It requires the subtle, highly intricate work of a professional who knows how to intervene in and strengthen natural systems of support. It may require recruitment, education, and ongoing consultation with concerned persons in the church community—the pastor, the youth minister, the Sunday School teachers, the church basketball coach, and individuals who are willing to provide respite care for the foster parents.

Moved by their own commitment to Christian service, a young couple considered volunteering to provide foster care for two severely physically and developmentally disabled adolescents. During the time they were exploring the decision with the agency staff, they also shared what they were considering with their congregation. The congregation agreed to form a mission group to support them in their work, committing itself to provide respite care and to find ways to include the foster children and foster parents in community life. The agency staff trained volunteers to take turns working with these severely developmentally disabled children during the Sunday School and church hours, freeing the parents to be in class and worship with their peers. Some of these volunteers were also trained to provide an evening of respite care each week. When the foster mother learned that she was pregnant, the couple decided that they could no longer continue providing foster care for both children; one child did remain in the home, however, and the congregational and volunteer support continued.

Foster parents need respite resources for children and adolescents, as well as quality day care for preschool children. Foster care providers who work outside the home need after-school programs. Church agencies and their supporting congregations can often provide a range of services and supports that enable families to provide foster care.

The Center for Family Life in Sunset Park, a poor and working-class neighborhood of Brooklyn, New York, was founded by the Sisters of the Good Shepherd. It provides a comprehensive array of family support services at no cost to the recipients, including counseling services and therapy groups, 24-hour crisis services, family life education, women's support groups, therapeutic activity groups for children and teens, a foster grandparents program, wide-ranging after-school programs and teen evening centers, summer day camps, pre-employment and job placement services, emergency food assistance, and an advocacy clinic to help families in crisis negotiate resources from public service agencies. The Center's fundamental purpose is to sustain children in their own homes.

The Center licenses satellite family foster homes that provide care for neighborhood children in instances of serious crisis. The matching of biological and foster families in the same neighborhood reduces the trauma of separation—children do not have to be removed from their own neighborhood, school, and friends—and facilitates intensive family reunification services. All of the services and auxiliary resources of the center's prevention programs can be used by both biological parents and foster parents, as well as the children themselves, during and after discharge from foster care. Services for each family are coordinated by a single social worker, who serves biological parents, foster parents, and the child. Biological parents are strongly encouraged to maintain as active a role as possible in the lives of their children. During the three years from 1988 to 1991, 73 children were admitted to the program; of these, 44 were discharged. Only one child required readmission to foster care. The program has reached the conclusion that "in every instance so far we have found the best possible opportunities for family work, and the most humane arrangements, through this neighborhood-based design." [McMahon et al. 1991]

Many children today need therapeutic foster homes, in which foster parents are considered agency employees and paid a salary, trained much more extensively than foster parents in general, provided with ongoing supervision, and given access to professional respite care and professional consultation 24 hours a day. It is unfortunate that such support is not available to all foster parents; the concept of foster treatment homes implies that "traditional" family foster care is trouble-free and does not require these kinds of supports [see Lowe 1991].

There are currently between 250 and 500 therapeutic foster care programs in the United States, serving children with retardation, moderately and severely disturbed and disturbing behavior, and delinquent behavior. Only about one third of the children in therapeutic foster homes are placed there immediately after removal from their biological families. Another third come from family foster care, while the remainder have experienced multiple out-of-home placements, such as residential care, group home care, and detention–most of them more restrictive than family foster care. It is not known how many of these programs are connected to church agencies, but more are administered by voluntary programs than by state agencies [Snodgrass and Bryant 1989].[5]

Even in these more intensive treatment settings, children and parents need the social support that a church community can provide. Training and consultation for key support figures are one necessary component of therapeutic foster care. Although these supportive neighbors are not paid salaries, they may be reinforced in their caregiving by professional consultation and other services that the agency can provide, thus strengthening rather than depleting the church's resources for ministry.

In the case of one church that offered respite care and support to the foster home for developmentally disabled adolescents, the agency loaned training materials for volunteers and educational materials for use in the program and with other developmentally disabled members of the community, provided professional training and consultation to church volunteers and staff members, and generated publicity for the church's ministry with the families of developmentally disabled persons. The church experienced an influx of families who valued educational experiences for their developmentally disabled family members, support for themselves, and inclusion in a community sensitive to their life situations. Several of these families became contributing members of the congregation. Perhaps just as important, the volunteers and their church, as a corporate entity, developed a role of service clearly expressing and deepening their understanding of Christian ministry.

In-Home Crisis Programs

Child welfare agencies are increasingly offering in-home crisis intervention programs such as family preservation. These programs aim to prevent out-of-home placement by intervening for a short term with many hours of professional involvement. A social worker may be in the home with a family for 20 hours a week, providing family life education services and family therapy and making community connections and referrals [Whittaker et al. 1988]. One such program, the Seattle-based Homebuilders, has reported a phenomenal success rate—88% of the families served were still intact one year after termination of services. At the time of referral, these families were on the brink of having one or more children placed outside the family. Social workers in these programs typically carry small caseloads, often only two families at a time, providing eight to 25 hours a week of direct services to each family for a period of time ranging from four weeks to three months [Whittaker et al. 1988].

Some church agencies are beginning to offer intensive home-based services as part of their continuum of care. One key element in home-based services is involving and supporting the family's social network. If a child has to be removed from a family, placement with someone in the family's social network disrupts as few social ties as possible. Even when the child is moved to a group or foster home setting, work with the social network can sustain and strengthen social ties that are a vital preparation for the child's return [Klefbeck et al. 1991].

Church agencies can bring resources to these programs that are not available to the social worker from a public agency. Church members can be involved directly as volunteers with the family in crisis—providing transportation, offering friendship to parents and children, providing respite care, and offering volunteer professional consultation with church members who are lawyers, physicians, car mechanics, and others, as needed. A Texas child protection agency, for example, established a program in which church groups "adopted" a child protection worker [Duncan et al. 1988]. The worker called on the designated group for many supports, both material and social. The evaluation of the program indicated that the social workers did not understand the church networks well enough to avail themselves of intangible resources like befriending and other forms of social support—a major drawback. Church agencies may be able to develop these relationships more effectively if their staff members understand the church community and its strengths and limitations.

These program initiatives require agency staff members to spend enormous amounts of time with church groups and individual church staff members and volunteers, as well as with clients. This time is not readily recorded as units of service, and is not likely to be third party reimbursable. For this very reason, church agencies may be able to take the initiative in these programs and develop demonstration projects that would not be possible for state agencies.

Conclusions

This chapter began with a description of the context and current configuration of services in today's church child care agency. Although residential care and family foster care continue to be two of the staple programs of church agencies, the focus of these programs is no longer "substitute" child care. Instead, these services are part of a continuum of care to support families in distress because of internal and external demands that exceed their resources. Although the child may be a central focus in these services, the closeup lens has been replaced by a wide angle lens that takes in the child's family and the family's environment. This widened focus has led to innovative ways of broadening services beyond professional family therapy and a therapeutic milieu for the child. The new framework for services includes social support—and the church's formal and informal ministries—as potential resources for effective intervention.

This move from the agency to the community to provide effective services for clients leads church agencies to find ways to involve congregations in the work of the agency and vice versa. If congregations can be resources in supporting the families the church agency serves, the agency can likewise be a resource for the congregation's prevention and support services with its own families and others in its community.

Notes

1. For a further description of family preservation programs, see Kagan and Schlosberg 1989; Kinney et al. 1991; Pooley and Littell 1986; and Whittaker 1988. Wasik et al. [1990] offer a useful guide for developing home visiting programs.

2. For a description of a family preservation program targeting special-needs adoptive families, including short-term respite care to avert a permanent disruption or dissolution, see Groze and Gruenewald 1991.

3. See also Beavers et al. 1986; Garbarino and Sherman 1980; Grey et al. 1979; Hetherington et al. 1976; Kazak 1986; Reis et al. 1986; Trute and Hauch 1988; and Turner and Avison 1985.

4. For resources, see Bowman 1990; Hoch and Hemmens 1987; National Crime Prevention Council 1990; and Wilson 1983.

5. Hawkins and Breiling, in *Therapeutic Foster Care: Critical Issues* [1989], offer general guidelines for comparing therapeutic foster care programs to other child welfare services, for training and supervising therapeutic foster parents and staff, for involving biological parents, and for conducting research and disseminating therapeutic foster care program models.

CHAPTER 5

The Agency and Its Professional Services in Congregational Life

To THE EXTENT THAT THE ROLE of the child welfare agency is to lead the church in responding to the needs of children and families, specialized professional services supported financially by the church may be highly significant, but not the centerpiece of the agency's services. When professional services directed to families and children are the primary focus of the agency, the essential role of the church is to serve as a financial resource for the agency, so that in return, the church may claim the ministry of the agency as its own. The church, in effect, purchases professional services as a means of fulfilling Christians' responsibility to care for hurting neighbors. It is only a small step, then, to allowing this exchange to become a rationale for church members being personally uninvolved in service to others. They have purchased a substitute, sometimes because professionals have not encouraged personal involvement, believing that "laypersons," by definition, do not have the professional skills to do what needs to be done for children and families in crisis. The agency relates to the church primarily as a funding source, a resource to be mined to support the work of the agency.

Professional services to clients and professional services that engage members of congregations personally need to be balanced with one another if the agency is not to drift further from its identity as a church agency and the church is not to drift further from a sense of personal responsibility for neighbors in pain. The discipline for church members of financially supporting the agency's professional services ought to be accompanied by the discipline of personal caring. To give financially to programs for children and families is a significant way churches can minister, but many churches and denominations are also developing resources and programs through which churches and their members can minister directly to children and families, building on the church's own characteristics as a voluntary association and its valuing of service as a principle responsibility for all Christians.

The compelling need to involve laypersons in the services of the agency distinguishes the church-related child welfare agency from other agencies perhaps more clearly than any other characteristic of this setting for child welfare services. It also suggests an important niche church-related agencies can fill in the array of a community's child welfare services.

In a sense, professional agency staff members have been commissioned as leaders of the church's ministry with children and their families. The last chapter described ways congregations can become involved in the work of an agency. The current nationwide focus on community-based preventive services, however, highlights ways for congregations to minister significantly within their own community contexts. Just as congregations have supported child welfare agencies, so agencies can support congregations in ministry to their communities. For some, this may mean agencies funding programs in churches. For most agencies, however, this support is given in the form of consultation by agency professionals who understand the church, can assess the resources and needs in a particular congregation and community, and can provide professional expertise in planning, developing, administering, and evaluating family service programs. This chapter describes this kind of professional practice with congregations.

These suggestions for turning the church agency toward congregation- and community-based services grow from the confluence of two streams of thought: the role in child welfare of the church as a voluntary organization with religious and theological foundations, and the growing attention child welfare professionals are giving to prevention and family support services. In the last century, child welfare services were performed by volunteers, many of them churchwomen who were concerned about orphans and built homes to take them in and friendly visitors who became advocates for children against physical abuse by families and grinding labor in mines and factories. With the growth of the professions came the growth of professionalized services for children. Gradually, professionals replaced volunteers in providing direct care for children in crisis.

Our understanding of how best to serve children in crisis has come almost full circle, however. We are realizing now that as much as children and families in crisis need professional services, they also need volunteers—friends who can detect early signs of neglect or abuse; neighbors who can provide family support in times of crisis; loving foster, adoptive, and respite families; and adults who can provide friendship, support, and mentoring for teenage, single, high-risk parents. Highly specialized treatment services will still be necessary; volunteer and natural helping relationships cannot substitute for professional intervention, but neither can professional intervention substitute for family and social support.

Thus, the continuum of child welfare services perceived as needed by communities has grown from highly specialized treatment for individual children to family therapy, and then to family preservation and placement prevention programs. Now it stretches all the way to community programs that involve natural helpers and social networks—the people in our churches—in providing nurturing environments for children and their families. The burgeoning development of grassroots family resource centers demonstrates this trend [Levine 1988]. This seems to be a niche that church agencies are particularly suited to filling in the social service continuum.

Family resource centers have emphasized the need for interaction and coordination between primary services and specialized services. Primary services are the organized community activities that support child development and family functioning—toddler play groups and after-school programs, youth volunteer activities, telephone warm lines and mentoring programs, parent support and education programs—as well as the community resources such as parks and libraries. Anyone in the community can use these services, without having to certify need or eligibility. They are part of the familiar social world of families, and thus can provide assistance in ways that do not stigmatize families and children and serve as an excellent early warning system to identify problems. Specialized secondary and tertiary services address the special needs of children through child welfare, mental health, juvenile justice, and substance abuse programs [Wynn and Costello 1990]. If specialized services and the professionals who staff them work in concert with the role and presence of primary services, children and their families can be served effectively in the context of the community. Professionals in church-related child welfare agencies stand on the interface between the primary services of church congregations and the specialized services of child welfare agencies.

The Congregation as a Base for Community Services

In the United States, more individuals belong to congregations than to any other kind of voluntary association; 60% of the population are church members, and 40% of adults report attending a church or synagogue during a typical week. There are 337,000 congregations in the United States, with a total of 141 million members. Each week, over 65 million adults attend church [Carroll et al. 1986, Jacquet 1985].

The needs of the families in their midst and in their communities are a major concern for most churches. The recent development of family ministry courses and degree programs in seminaries, the establishment of denominational family ministry departments, and the flood of popular and professional church literature regarding the family stand as evidence of the strength of concern, from the level of the individual congregation to the highest levels of denominational government. These churches can benefit from the involvement of professionals who understand and are sensitive to their values and identity as people of faith and can direct them with productive family support services and programs. The possibilities for family support services are many. Almost 20 years ago, Sister Mary Vincentia Joseph noted that "within church-related social service systems, the parish church is, by its very nature, an ideal community structure, close to individual and family life-cycle events...and is a natural social structure for community organization and action" [Joseph 1975: 45].

Too often, however, the efforts of professionals to work within church structures have met with frustration and disappointment. Congregations have been enthusiastically urged into action and then written off as irrelevant, at best, or damaging, at worst, because they failed to perform as envisioned. "But the initial failure may lie not with the congregation but with those who have urged the congregation on without a sensitive understanding of its inner life and resources, or of its possibilities, as well as the limits placed on the congregation by the context in which God has called it into being" [Carroll et al. 1986: 7]. The church is not a community mental health center or a family service agency. A congregation must be understood in its ecological context in a particular community, in its historical context of identity and values as a community of faith, and in its development as a social system with roles and processes that have changed over time.

The Role of the Church in the Community

Churches, as congregations of people and as physical structures, have particular functions in the ecology of the community. "By the presence of their buildings, their steeples and stained glass, and in the regular gatherings of members for public worship, congregations provide symbols and occasions for transcendence of everyday life and for grounding that life in faith and hope" [Carroll et al. 1986: 7]. Authors Jackson Carroll, Carl Dudley, and William McKinney have provided an excellent resource for congregational studies, on which this chapter relies heavily. They suggest that the church congregation serves six functions for the larger community.

First, it draws community residents out of their isolation and differences into relationships with one another that may become mutually supportive.

> One young mother of two children, describing a period of family crisis when her husband was seriously ill but desperately continuing to work every day to support his family, said, "We have no social life except for our church. But church folks have been so good to ask after us, to pray for us, and to do what they can to help. I just hope I get the chance to give back some of the caring I've received."

Second, congregations provide programs that promote community solidarity and continuity. Although congregations often provide these services on their own, they also join with other congregations in their denomination or ecumenically in their community to serve this function:

> An urban community was devastated by a tornado. The churches in the community joined forces in responding to the critical physical needs of their members and other community residents. An ecumenical community ministry was born, with a part-time director and a staff funded by contributing churches. The ministry has continued in the 15 years that have passed since that time, turning its attention to other pressing human needs, offering emergency financial and food assistance, counseling, adult and child day care, meals for homebound senior citizens, after-school care for children previously without supervision, and other services. In addition, however, the community ministry has become a rallying point for community solidarity. It sponsors gatherings to discuss political issues that affect the community, often inviting elected officials to speak to residents. It sponsors social events and community festivals. It also organized and facilitated a community pride and beautification project that has

altered the area's earlier assessment of itself as a declining community. [Bailey 1991]

Third, congregations socialize children and newcomers. In some communities, the activities the congregation sponsors for children and adolescents become the focal point for a significant peer group, often the only peer group, other than the one in school, that can challenge the influence of gangs and informal adolescent cliques.

Churches also provide one of the most powerful means for newcomers to meet other community residents. Any given congregation may or may not fulfill a particular function in its community. Some congregations have relatively closed boundaries that make it difficult for newcomers to move into the inner circle. Even so, many congregations do fulfill this socialization function. Helping professionals, whatever their personal faith or church relatedness, frequently look to church programs and groups as a possible resource for clients who are isolated and in need of social support.

Fourth, churches sustain persons in need. Congregations address the whole range of personal and family needs, from financial and material support to emotional and physical caregiving. In addition, needs are met both through formal programs, often with paid staff, and through informal support networks. For example, many churches, or the community ministries in which they participate, have emergency assistance programs that provide short-term financial assistance to families in crisis. These programs have a range of volunteers and paid staff members. Their screening and record-keeping systems range from a shoebox with handwritten index cards of names and addresses to sophisticated computer systems linked with other community agencies.

But churches do not limit their financial and other assistance to these formal programs. Needs are often communicated through the social network, so that a child in the youth group who wants to go to camp but whose family does not have money for the registration fee learns that a scholarship is available, provided informally by someone who heard of the need. A teenager in conflict with his single mother, who believes he is out of control and wants to place him in a residential child care program, is offered the chance to stay with a church family temporarily while the mother and the teen sort out their relationship with one another under the guidance of a professional counselor.

Fifth, churches provide rites of passage to mark significant life transitions. Even people who are not members often look to the church for the significant life transitions of weddings and funerals. Churches that do not practice infant baptism have found other ways to ritually celebrate the addition of family members, such as baby dedication services or, alternatively, parent dedication services. Some churches have developed rituals for adoption, divorce, young persons leaving home, children returning from foster care, and other transitions, both common and unusual, that families face [Laird 1990].

Sixth, congregations both support and challenge community values and institutions. Sermons and Sunday school discussions often address current community issues in light of Christian teachings and beliefs. Denominational statements and policies express positions on a wide range of current subjects, from gender roles to government action on military spending or environmental protection. Churches also mediate between the private lives of individuals and families and the large social institutions of a community, thus protecting persons from having to deal with these institutions alone. The church is one of the few societal institutions that can serve in this way [Himes 1985; Roozen et al. 1984]. For example, pastors and their churches have been known to take on the policies of industries that were creating unsafe working conditions.

Denominations vary in the extent to which congregations consider it appropriate to take sides formally on political issues. Baptist churches historically have tended to fall toward the end of the continuum that loudly supports the separation of church and state and eschews the taking of political sides. Nevertheless, pastors preach about the issues; sermons commonly reveal stands concerning abortion, government spending on defense, ecological responsibility, and local laws governing the sale of alcohol. And although the congregation as a group may not make a public statement, a regular weeknight church supper and prayer meeting around the tables may include letter-writing materials and addresses. Members are encouraged during the meeting to write congressional representatives or other public figures, speaking their mind on some matter that is of concern to the community.

In fulfilling these functions, congregations often touch the lives of children and their families who cannot be reached by other family service agencies. Church members will often attend family life education seminars and programs offered by their church when they would never consider seeking such resources for family living from community agencies, and certainly not from the outpatient educational programs of a psychiatric hospital or community mental health center.

Through informal social networks, these families can often reach many more families. Community members who do not belong to the congregation may be incorporated into a family support service offered by a church more easily than one offered by a social service agency. Congregations serve more children and youths, and certainly more parents, than any other institution in our nation except the public schools [Clark et al. 1990]. More preschool children are cared for by churches than by any other system in the United States. Thus, the church's programs are also readily accessible to these children and their families, who may or may not be members of the church [Freeman 1986]. Day care has increasingly become a key resource in preventing at-risk children—those whose families are in crisis and only marginally able to care for them—from entering out-of-home care.

In addition to child care, day care programs can include a number of supportive service components for families: parent education and support groups, emergency caregiving, family counseling, baby-sitting, resource centers, and Parents Anonymous and other self-help groups. Because child care services are inherently long-term, they have the potential to provide ongoing support for families.

Christian Values and Beliefs about Family Life

Access to children and families who can benefit from family life education services does not in itself justify their provision by the church. To proceed only with that justification risks mistaking the church for a satellite family service center or community mental health center rather than an entity with a unique mission and role in the lives of families. Practice in the church, as in the agency itself, should be firmly grounded in a theological and Biblical understanding of the nature of family relationships and the role of the church in nurturing health in these relationships. The following paragraphs sketch the outlines of such an understanding.[1]

For Christians, family relationships serve as the most challenging and constant source of discipline in Christian living. Although the difficulties may be great, the Christian disciplines of love, commitment, self-giving, and forgiveness can be practiced nowhere so readily as in family relationships. These relationships have value in addition to the meaning they have for the individuals involved; Christian family life is to be a demonstration of discipleship to those with whom Christians live and to the world. They will know "that you are my disciples, if you love one another," said Jesus (John 13:35). A Christian's relationships, including family relationships, are to be a witness of God's covenantal love. Thus, the New Testament expresses concern that nothing be awry in the family life of a Christian (see 1 Thess. 4:3–8; 1 Tim. 3:5, 5:4–8, 12, 14; Titus 2:4–5). The Bible frequently describes the relationship between God and God's people with images from family life; God is bridegroom, forgiving husband (Hosea), nursing mother, and loving father. God is seen in the love and loyalty and acts of devotion that one expects in a family—the response of a parent to a child who says, "I'm hungry" (Luke 11:11-13).

Although individual churches may not have overtly identified family life education as a means of spiritual education and discipline for their members, many have implicitly done so by seeking professionals and media resources that they assume share their values and beliefs about family life. Despite the vast resources of family professionals and the excellent media resources available in many communities, churches often prefer to use resources and leadership from within their own ranks. As an example, James Dobson's Focus on the Family organization, which publishes overtly Christian family resources targeted to churches, has met with an unparalleled reception from many churches because it is identifiably Christian and speaks to practical family matters. This organization has made available for rental family life education films and videotapes that have now been used in over 38,600 congregational worship services and programs [Matthew Plummer, personal correspondence October 24, 1991]. Similarly, a parent education program [Crase 1986] published by the Southern Baptist Convention, based clearly and overtly on Biblical principles for family living, has sold over 120,000 copies in three years, primarily within Southern Baptist churches [_The Family Touch_ 1990]. Whether or not the professional agrees with all the premises of any particular program, the overwhelming success of these organizations suggests a widespread hunger for the kind of resources they provide.

The professional may well want to use the variety of excellent media resources available in conducting family life education and support programs, whether they are overtly Christian or not. They should be examined and interpreted from the cultural and religious context of the faith community, however, if they are to be congruent with the church's objectives for the program. If beginning and ending with prayer is the only way in which a family life education program in the church differs from one provided in a community mental health center, one might as well pour salsa over a chicken pot pie and call it Mexican food. Instead, the professional should lead church members in examining the values and principles of living implicit throughout programs and media resources in the light of Christian values and beliefs. This makes the service more effective in achieving the church's underlying objectives of spiritual discernment and growth; it also communicates sensitivity to, and valuing of, the church's mission, and thus strengthens the relationship between agency and congregation.

Understanding Church Congregations

Congregations are certainly not all the same. They vary in the extent to which they fulfill the six functions Carroll, Dudley, and Mckinney have described, summarized above. Some churches are small, with only one full- or part-time staff member, serving a handful of families in the immediate neighborhood. Megachurches, by contrast, draw members from all over a metropolitan area, requiring acres of parking lots and an array of professional staff members. For example, Pleasant Grove Missionary Baptist Church in Houston numbers 6,500 members; West Angeles

Church of God in Christ in Los Angeles numbers 7,001 [Religious News Service: 1992].

Churches differ widely, of course, according to denominational affiliation, but churches within the same denomination also differ widely in the extent to which their denominational identity is central to their self-identity. A congregation's identity, history, values, culture, and relationship with its community have a significant influence on the kinds of support it can offer its own families and other families in the community. No program is appropriate for every church. Not every church is suited to providing a day care center, for example, or has the resources to do so. Effective family support services in a church must be tailored to fit the congregation's character, resources, goals, mission, and values.

Carroll and his associates [1986] describe four dimensions that can organize the life of a particular congregation:

1. Congregational identity—that persistent set of beliefs, values, patterns, symbols, stories, and styles that makes a congregation distinctively itself. Like family identity, congregational identity is rarely verbalized, even by members to each other. Instead, it can be distilled from gossip, unwritten rules, and tacit signs and symbols.

2. Social context—the setting, local and global, in which a congregation finds itself and to which it responds. The context includes institutions and social groups, as well as the social, political, and economic forces operative in the setting.

3. Process—the underlying flow and dynamics of a congregation that knit together its common life and affect its morale and climate. Process includes how leadership is exercised and shared, decisions are made, communication occurs, problems are solved, and conflicts are managed.

4. Program—those organizational structures, plans, and activities through which a congregation expresses its mission and ministry both to its own members and to those outside the membership. This is the face most often visible in the church's representation of itself to itself and to the outside world.

These dimensions constantly interact with and shape one another. Carroll et al. [1986: 19] describe the rich variety of church congregations in theological terms:

> In the Incarnation, God became present to the world in human form, in a particular place, at a particular historical moment, in a particular society and culture. While, in effect, this limited who could hear the Word and how they would hear it through available language and cultural forms, this very particularity made the Word hearable and seeable. And while the Resurrection was, in one sense, a freeing of the Word from those particularities so that it could become fully universal, it was, in another sense, a freeing of the Word so that it could become particular again and again, in different times and places, under different social and cultural forms, and be given voice in a multitude of languages. It is our conviction that local congregations are one of the ways in which the Word continues to become flesh. But if this is true, then congregations need to be helped to discern the intention and tendency of Jesus' ministry in which they are called to participate, to examine their present life in terms of that intention, and also to find ways of becoming truly indigenous in the social and cultural setting where they find themselves called to serve.

An accurate assessment of a congregation's potential for developing prevention and family support programs takes into account the complexities and multiple dimensions of each congregation. An assessment sensitive to the nature of a congregation will look at the extent to which the congregation is captive to past patterns and programs that are out of touch with congregational development and current context. It will also look at the extent to which the congregation has been responsive to its community context, becoming more complex and diverse in the process, and perhaps consequently in need of reaffirming or redefining its identity and historical continuity as a community of faith. Finally, it will look for opportunities for the congregation to become more effective in pursuing its own mission and responding to its particular community. The most effective congregational assessment will involve the church members themselves in the process of defining their church along these dimensions.

Congregational Identity

A congregation's identity is, in essence, its culture. Congregational identity includes history, heritage, worldview, symbols, rituals, demography, character, context, process, and program [Carroll et al. 1986].

History

A congregation's history includes both its understanding of its past and its expectations of the future. There may not be one simple history, but rather multiple histories, depending on the number of groups and sub-groups within the congregation, that are congruent with one another to varying degrees. A history includes the critical turning points and events in the congregation's development and the stories of its members, past and present. Written records may provide some data relevant to a church's history. Guided interviews with representatives from different groups within the church can also be a rich mine of data. Appendix 2 contains suggestions for learning about the history of a congregation as well as suggestions for other aspects of a congregational assessment.

Heritage

The congregation's heritage includes its foundation on Christian thought and practice, its theology, its inheritance as a Christian church, and the meaning of its membership in or independence from one (or more) denominations. Although many churches stand alone as independent organizations, most affiliate with, or belong to, a denomination. Denominations are organizations of congregations that share certain beliefs and practices and cooperate in sponsoring missions, colleges and universities, agencies, publishing houses, and other endeavors. Denominations are organized into overlapping levels, such as local, state, and national bodies. Some congregations may be allied with more than one denomination; dually allied, for example, with the American Baptist and the Southern Baptist denominations. In some denominational traditions (such as the Baptist) congregations retain autonomy and can choose whether or not to affiliate with the denominational body. In other traditions (such as the

Episcopal), the property, policies, programs, and personnel of the local congregation are controlled to a greater or lesser extent by the parent denomination.

Congregations and/or their denominations may (or may not) also participate in ecumenical organizations, through whose goals and activities participants can transcend theological, ecclesiastical, and historical differences. Ecumenical activities take place at several levels. At the local level, community ministries involve congregations of various denominations that are located in the same neighborhood. Ecumenical organizations exist at the metropolitan, regional, state, and national levels. Finally, the World Council of Churches is composed of worldwide denominational organizations, although not all denominations choose to participate, just as not all churches participate in community ecumenical activities. Agency professionals may find themselves working with churches individually or through these various cooperative organizations.

Instruments are available for evaluating the beliefs and theological positions, both implicit and explicit, of church members [Carroll et al. 1986, Roozen et al. 1984]. The congregation's relationship to its heritage can also be determined in part by studying the themes and interests reflected in sermons, liturgies, teaching, and written documents. A particularly significant aspect of the church's relationship with its heritage is its definition of and commitment to its mission.

Worldview

Closely related to a church's heritage is its current perspective on its place in the world. Congregations work out together a worldview that reflects the negotiations among members of their various explanations of the events in their lives as individuals and as a congregation. Usually, the development of a worldview continues as an ongoing process; members may find the congregation's worldview to be highly congruent or highly dissonant in relation to their own. A congregation's worldview includes its understanding of who God is, what purpose and meaning life has, why tragedies and crises occur, how contemporary Christians should live and care for others in the community and the world, what the meaning of poverty and suffering is, what role government should play in providing for the needs of citizens, and other questions. The different aspects of a congregation's worldview may best be determined by interviewing various members. Roozen et al. [1984: 32–36] have developed a classification system for congregations, based on the dominant way any given congregation defines its relationship to its community; they call this aspect of a congregation's worldview its "mission orientation." Their classification system consists of four categories:

- Activist: a congregation that perceives the here and now of the world as the main arena of God's redemptive activity and consequently considers achievement of a more just and humane society through social action a high priority;

- Civic: a congregation that concerns itself with public life but is relatively affirming of dominant social structures, giving high priority to educational programs that prepare individuals to play important roles in the social order;

- Sanctuary: a congregation primarily focused on a world to come, when the cares of this world will be surmounted, and emphasizing providing people with opportunities to withdraw from the trials of daily life into a company of committed fellow believers; and

- Evangelistic: a congregation with a focus on a world to come, similar to the sanctuary-oriented congregation, but which is also concerned with the deterioration of traditional standards of personal morality and encourages its members to participate in public life in order to share the message of salvation, not necessarily to bring about social reform or change.

It might seem that churches that are more theologically liberal would be more active on social issues than evangelistic churches, which emphasize personal salvation. Research has indicated, however, that this is not necessarily the case. Most activist congregations are actually motivated by moderate and evangelical theological roots, not by liberal theological perspectives; they embrace both the importance of personal salvation and a passion for social justice [Dudley and Johnson 1991]. For example, one large congregation located in the inner city of a major metropolitan area emphasizes personal evangelism and concludes passionate preaching with long altar calls. It follows Sunday worship with weekday programs, including respite care for children, and, on another day, persons with Alzheimer's disease; a free dental clinic; a shelter for homeless families; emergency assistance and financial counseling; tutoring for neighborhood children; and various support, educational, and activity groups for children and adults who live in the low-income neighborhood immediately surrounding the church. Agency professionals, therefore, should not shy away from theologically conservative churches, presuming them to be uninterested in the needs of children and their families; these churches may be strong allies in service.

Symbols

Congregational life is rich in symbols, objects that carry meaning greater than their apparent worth to one outside the culture or community.

Carroll et al. [1986] suggest four categories of symbols. Transcendent symbols communicate the congregation's Christian traditions and the community's ultimate identity; the cross, the sacraments, stained glass pictures, and banners are transcendent symbols. Even hymns sung by the congregation are highly symbolic; Clark [1991] has called them the Protestant equivalent of Orthodox icons. Symbols of love indicate the solidarity members have with one another. Food is often used as a symbol of love (regular church suppers, "dinner on the grounds," coffee and cookies after worship), and the Eucharist itself is sometimes called a _love feast_. Symbols of power assure that what the congregation does has consequence; the pledging of resources, mission reports, attendance figures, numbers of baptisms, the offering, and accounting for money show the congregation its own power. Finally, symbols of justice indicate the congregation's identity with matters of justice. Posters, special offerings, programs, and mission action groups and organizations often symbolize a congregation's concern with justice. Since a congregation's symbols indicate its most foundational values, understanding the meaning of these symbols is often critical to the success or failure of programs and services.

The greater the diversity within the congregation, however, the more likely that symbols of value for some segments of the congregation are not necessarily symbols for the values of all. For example, a church budget may well represent the values of a significant segment of the congregation, but prompt head-shaking and frustration for others. A bumper sticker on the back of the church bus may be applauded by some and infuriate others. Congregational discussions around the use of certain symbols may well indicate significant diversity within a congregation:

> During a business meeting of a church that had many international families as members, a young adult moved that the United States flag, usually placed in the front corner of the sanctuary opposite a Christian flag,[2] be removed. He suggested that the international members of the congregation might find the flag disconcerting; they should be able to worship and be a part of the community without being confronted with American patriotism. He suggested that the flag was hindering the church's ministry with international families. Several older members of the congregation, some of them war veterans, sprang to their feet in protest. A heated discussion followed; the issue was not resolved.

Rituals

In addition to rites of passage that signal the developmental transitions of individuals and their family units, churches also engage in rites of intensification. These rituals intensify a group's commitment to shared beliefs and meanings, such as special days and seasons and standard worship patterns. These rituals may connect a church with the great traditions of the faith (baptism, Eucharist, foot washing), yet may also reflect its own unique past and current identity (songs that are sung at certain times, established prayers and greetings, the order of worship).

Demography

Helping professionals are on familiar territory when it comes to assessing a congregation's demography. These are characteristics we are accustomed to assessing in a community—age, gender, marital status, race, ethnicity, and socioeconomic characteristics. Demography also includes the relationship of the congregation to its community. A map of the community with pins indicating the homes of members will portray the spread of membership throughout a metropolitan area or a concentration in a few neighborhoods.

Some churches draw their members primarily from the immediate geographic community. Other churches, some deliberately placed close to expressway systems, may draw members from all over a metropolitan community, or from various pockets within that community. On the one hand, these large "magnet" churches drawing members from a wide area may have little commitment to their immediate neighborhoods. On the other hand, they are more likely than neighborhood churches, particularly neighborhood churches located in poor communities, to have the kinds of facilities, financial resources, and professional staff that can develop and sustain service programs.

Character

A congregation's character involves a more subtle dimension of congregational life. It includes the congregation's values, behavioral tone, ethos, and corporate integrity. For example, some churches in Kentucky wonder if they should accept gifts from money made on the growing of tobacco; others grow tobacco on the church grounds to supplement the church budget. Some church congregations struggle with problems such as these; others simply dismiss them as "the way things are."

Context

Most simply put, a congregation's context is the demography and social networks of the community or communities and the larger church structures (e.g., denominations, ecumenical organizations) with which it interacts. The documents of local government and private community groups, such as a community mental health center's needs assessment, provide some information about the community. Census data, walks through the community, and interviews with community residents provide more information.

The orientation of congregational members to their local community and the context of the wider world is also important. A local orientation may be indicated by membership in community organizations and neighborhood social networks. A wider orientation may be indicated by wider social networks and membership in professional and specialized voluntary organizations. Carroll et al. suggest that an evaluation of the congregation's context can include the messages people wear on T-shirts, the topics friends and acquaintances discuss as they gather for church programs, and the turnout at community events. The extent to which members of the congregation belong to the various social groups in the community, the role of the pastor and church members in the community, and the community's role in the church also indicate the congregation's orientation toward its community context.

Third, context includes the social issues, both local and global, that confront a congregation in its community. Every congregation is confronted with many possible directions for ministry. The extent to which a congregation has been concerned about children and families, when confronted with so many other pressing concerns, suggests something about the church's understanding of its context for mission.

Finally, the resources of a congregation's community give shape to the identity and possibilities of a congregation. In resource-diminished communities, such as inner-city poor neighborhoods, the church may struggle to survive and have little to invest beyond meeting its own needs as an organization. These churches will need help with funding for personnel, program supplies, and building expenses if they are to develop new ministries to serve children and families [Friedrich 1990]. Many affluent churches, however, engage themselves much less in social ministries than congregations with more limited resources, with the exception of those whose strong, prophetic leadership pulls them toward higher levels of social activism [Mock et al. 1991].

Process

A congregation's processes are the many ways it goes about its life together—the way it plans and evaluates its work, the roles and tasks of the congregation, the patterns of authority and leadership, the way it manages diversity and conflict, and the way it makes decisions and solves problems. In addition, a congregation's processes include its church polity, which often develops in response to its denominational identification.

Generally, there are three main types of church polity: hierarchy, a combination of hierarchy and local autonomy, and local autonomy [Moberg 1984]. In the hierarchical form of government, a group of superiors in a central church government appoints the church leader (pastor or priest), who continues to be subject to discipline from these superiors. As an officer in this central hierarchy, the church leader is constrained by the central church government, but also freed from dependence on a local congregation. The congregation may protest the actions of the church leader, but may not have the authority to initiate action against that leader. Hierarchical structures characterize Roman Catholic, Episcopal, and Lutheran churches. By contrast, in a locally autonomous church structure, as typified by Baptist churches, the congregation has the power both to choose and to exercise control over its church leader and its church organization. The central church organization retains minimal power, leaving the church leader dependent on the members of the congregation for financial and programmatic support.

Some churches, such as the Presbyterian and Methodist, combine these forms of polity, placing major control in the hands of a central body that endorses and therefore enhances the authority of the church leader. The congregation, however, is controlled by an indigenous board of elders that requests the appointment of a particular church leader and has considerable control over the life of the church community.

A church's polity affects the role it plays in family services and the choices the agency professional must make. For example, a hierarchical polity allows the church leader to use the power of a secure office to take a stand on social issues and to develop services, such as supportive care for teen parents or a recreation program for neighborhood adolescents. Sometimes, the church leader may choose to use this power even though the congregation does not wholeheartedly support the direction the leader chooses. The national church offices of hierarchical denominations often produce social justice materials, develop policy statements, and call on congregations to address these social problems.

Locally autonomous churches, however, may be particularly able to develop creative services to meet particular local needs. They may offer service programs or engage in advocacy activities that would not be condoned by a central governing body. For example, a church in an inner-city community with a high rate of teen pregnancy may open a multiservice center for community teenagers. The center may provide health services, including contraception, despite opposition by the national denominational body to contraceptive services for adolescents.

Denominational polity is significantly tempered by the leadership styles and values of pastors and others who have power in a congregation. Some pastors govern churches with almost total power and control. Others operate with democratic, shared decision-making styles. As to relationship to the denomination, some congregations choose to ignore the policies and positions of higher levels of church government and work informally out of a different value base. In a church, as in any organization, the formal position statements and processes may be quite different from the values that actually pilot the organization and from the informal processes through which it operates. Even in democratically oriented congregations, however, the pastor is usually a primary shaper of the involvement of the church in social services and the gatekeeper to the church community. The support and involvement of the pastor in any family support programs the congregation is considering are therefore critical.

Finally, church processes must be placed in the context of the church's historical development. Moberg [1984] posits that churches have life cycles just as families do. As a church develops, it creates or takes on formal structures. If it is a member of a denomination, it often mirrors the structures of the denomination. Over time, the collective excitement and the informal processes of a new congregation evolve into a formal organization with a creed and behavioral norms. Leadership becomes less charismatic and more bureaucratic and rational. Rapid growth requires new committees, boards, and executives. Formalism takes over. Conflict and consciousness of distinctiveness from the outside world are replaced with toleration. The church may become unresponsive to the personal and social needs of its members. At this point, the church may become inactive, or new leadership may emerge that reevaluates the church's mission and carries it into another cycle of development [Moberg 1984].

Program

Program, the final dimension of congregational assessment, is also the most readily accessible dimension. Program includes the organizational structures, plans, and activities through which a congregation expresses its mission and ministry both to itself—its own members—and to those outside.

Program gives concrete expression to the beliefs and norms of members present and past; it carries the values to which members commit financial resources and energies. Program is the plan of action, what a congregation does [Carroll et al. 1986: 12]. It includes the various worship services, committees, and ongoing and short-term educational and service programs and projects.

Balancing the Assessment

Different church consultants have emphasized one or more of these dimensions. Carroll et al. stress the importance of keeping them in balance, not allowing the most visible information about a congregation to hold sway as the most important. From a different perspective, Schaller [1983: 163] has suggested that the internal dynamics of congregational life are far more important than the community context. When Schaller worked with African American churches in Ohio, he realized that "the history of a particular congregation, the impact of the minister's personality and leadership, race, social class, and other internal considerations, were far more important than the community context in shaping the life of a particular congregation." The community context was an influential factor in the life of a new congregation, but as years passed, the impact of internal factors began to exceed the context in shaping the church community. Schaller ranks the following factors in order of their usefulness for understanding a congregation:

1. Size, as measured by the average attendance at worship and by membership attendance patterns

2. The ideological-behavioral dichotomy (Some congregations emphasize the second of Jesus' two great commandments—love your
neighbor as yourself; others emphasize the first commandment—
love God with all your heart, soul, and strength. They thus tend to
emphasize either service or worship.)

3. The internal dynamics

4. The tenure of today's members

5. The contemporary role of the church and the goals evolving out of
that role

6. The age of the church and the length of time it has been meeting in
the present building

7. The age distribution of the members

8. The community context

9. The polity

10. The tenure of the current pastor and of the past five pastors

Summary

Obviously, agency staffs and congregations do not always comprehen-
sively examine all the dimensions of congregational life when considering
the implementation or reshaping of a family support program. The extent
of the congregational assessment is determined by the size and complexity
of the congregation, the congregation's interest in an overall planning and
evaluation process, the agency's willingness or ability to invest professional staff time in facilitating the congregation's study, and the nature of
the project being considered. For example, a one-day parent education
seminar may demand only the briefest of congregational assessments—
the ages of parents and children in the congregation and community who
will be participating, the values and beliefs of the church community
related to parenting, the concerns that brought the congregation to a
decision to offer the workshop now, and the common worries and stres-

sors facing children and families in the community. By contrast, the church considering the development of a family resource center with an array of family support programs will need to conduct a thorough assessment.

Appendix 2 suggests tools that may be used separately or in conjunction with one another in designing a congregational assessment appropriate to the goals and context of an agency professional and a particular congregation. The assessment process should be tailored to the particular concerns and objectives, as well as the context and resources, of a particular congregation. Agency professionals can be helpful consultants not only in shepherding the assessment but also in determining its nature and extent.

Churches can conduct assessments without a professional facilitator. Certainly, the more the church is invested in the process, the more likely it is to use the findings in shaping its programs. A professional facilitator, however, can often suggest approaches, follow up curious findings, and point out issues that congregation members may be unaware of because they do not have expertise in the assessment of social systems.

Working with Church Congregations

Agency professionals can use the findings of the assessment process to shape their roles as facilitators in churches' development of useful family support programs. Their primary roles are consultation and working with volunteers.

Consultation

Agency staff members may consult informally with churches by volunteering, or they may develop contracts with churches as independent professional practitioners or agency representatives. Such contracts may or may not involve financial reimbursement. The agencies by which they are employed are often oriented primarily to the provision of direct services to children and their families—the missionary function described in chapter 4. Churches contact staff members because they know them as experts in these services. In turn, staff members provide their services to congregations because they see these services as an expression of their personal calling as Christians, and sometimes, in the instances that involve financial reimbursement, as a way to supplement their salaries.

Agencies that identify work with and through churches as a primary focus of their mission, however, often make church consultation a formal part of their programs. Two rationales for the agency may be involved. First, agencies may believe that working in local communities is the most effective way for them to accomplish their goal of serving children and their families, and that churches are ideal community sites. Others, however, also recognize their function as spiritual guides, with responsibility for encouraging and empowering the service of Christians.

When the consultation agreement is between the agency and the church, the agency identifies the consultation as part (or all) of its professional staff's responsibility. The agency thus is responsible for providing its staff with time and resources for the consultation. Agency-church consultation has included such projects as developing networks of child advocates in congregations (Deaconess Children's Services in Washington), programs for adolescents in impoverished communities (Barnardo's Church and Community Project in Glasgow, Scotland), parent education programs (The Children's Home, Inc., in Winston-Salem, North Carolina), pre-school child care and after-school activity programs (ChildServ in Illinois), and the development of African American adoptive homes for African American children on the adoption waiting lists of public agencies (One Church, One Child in Illinois). Some of these agencies have also worked with churches to develop child abuse prevention programs, teen pregnancy prevention and teen parent programs, and programs as alternatives to youth gangs.

The Church/Community Consultation Services of ChildServ, an agency affiliated with the Northern Illinois Conference of the United Methodist Church, serve as a model of agency consultation services. The agency works with local churches to develop ministries to children and to involve members in meeting the needs of children and families through service and advocacy. The agency offers consultation to congregations free of charge, so that all congregations can make use of its services, regardless of their resources. Nevertheless, having professionals in local churches provide consultation that is sensitive to the needs of the community and the interests of the church raises awareness—and support—for the agency. Church members now have faces and personal relationships to identify with the agency; consequently, churches may choose to support the agency financially.

Some congregations call on consultants to help them study particular family issues, to develop family service programs, or to become active as advocates for families in the arena of social policies and public legislation [Johnson and Long 1983]. Often, but not always, congregations follow these interests progressively: They begin by studying issues, such as the factors that lead to teen pregnancy and the stressors teen parents and their children face. Their study motivates them to do something about the identified problems, so they explore various approaches to action. The congregation develops a family support program that offers respite care, parent education, and support groups for teen parents. In the course of providing this service, they become sensitized to broader social issues; they may take on the local school board, advocating greater access to family planning information in the schools and more supportive policies and programs for teen parents. The objectives of the consultation thus must be clear to both congregation and consultant: Do members want to learn more, provide service, advocate for social change—or all three?

Consultants from ChildServ in Illinois help churches identify the needs of children in their communities, determine what resources they have to respond to those needs, decide where to focus their effort, develop a program, and evaluate it. A program development consultation of this kind involves the consultant in the work of the congregation for nine to 18 months. The agency also offers technical assistance to congregations with ongoing programs. The focus of this assistance may be on training volunteers and staff members or developing a budget. As part of their agency responsibilities, agency staff members also deliver sermons and facilitate church meetings about issues concerning children [Friedrich 1990].

The Consultation Contract
Everyone who will be involved in the consultation project or in imple-

menting any programs or services being considered should be included in the consultation contract, which may be anything from a verbal agreement in an informal conversation to a formal written document. If the church is considering an after-school activities program with a hired staff supplemented by volunteers, contract formation will involve the staff, potential volunteers, representatives of the parents and/or children the program will serve, representatives of the church finance committee, and teachers in the Sunday school who will share space and supplies with the weekday program. In addition, the pastor, the governing board or congregational planning committee, and perhaps a denominational executive in the local judicature may be included in developing a contract between agency and congregation. Some or all of these people may then continue to serve as members of a planning committee or task force.[3]

What do the congregation, the staff, the consultant, and the agency expect of themselves and one another? The consultant may apprise the congregation and church staff members of the ways the consultant and the agency can and cannot work with them, and perhaps provide examples of what other congregations have done. Initially, the expectations of congregation and consultant may differ considerably, so a period of discussion and negotiation is often necessary before a contract can be formalized.

Some agencies charge congregations consultation fees; others do not. The church should have control of the consultation, and the right to say yes or no to initiating proposed programs, or even to continuing the consultation process. If a bishop or other denominational officer has assigned a consultant to a congregation, or paid the fee for the consultation, claiming this right may be difficult [Schaller 1983]. Care should be taken, therefore, that the contract is clear about the church's prerogative to make decisions about its own life as a community.

As a consequence of the contract and the congregational assessment, a considerable body of data may be collected for planning a family service program. Schaller [1983] suggests that these data be presented in written form to those most directly involved, with additional copies. He suggests that 50 copies be presented by the consultant to the congregation, since it is hard to lose or keep secret 50 copies of a rather lengthy document. This provides the planning group with precise information to which they can refer when memories are limited or selective. It also prevents some possible misunderstandings, because everyone receives the same information, which is often not the case in verbal reports. In addition, putting the findings of a congregational assessment on paper provides a powerful impetus for doing something about whatever the congregation has learned about itself and the needs in its community.

Relating to the Congregation and Staff

Clearly, the initial and continuing congregational assessment process will provide the agency staff with useful information about the congregation, such as its values, its styles of decision making, and where power is vested for approving and implementing new programs. The assessment of the congregation, however, needs to be accompanied by the consultant's self-knowledge, a critical factor in the work between agency and congregation. The value system, assumptions, beliefs, prejudices, understanding of contemporary reality, academic preparation, theological stance, age, biases, life experiences, denominational background, and other baggage carried by the consultant constitute the most important single dynamic or variable in determining what happens in a parish consultation [Schaller 1983: 161].

If consultants identify conflicts of their own values and beliefs with those of the congregation in the initial stages of the work together, they can deal with these conflicts professionally. Otherwise, progress may be undermined by the consultant's own frustration or ambivalence growing out of unidentified dissonance between consultant and congregation. Congregational consultants often face conflicts between their own professional and religious values and those of the congregation and/or its leadership, as the following example illustrates:

> A very large church with a sizable budget and a large staff is located on the edge of an impoverished community where large numbers of single working mothers desperately need quality child day care for preschoolers. The church, however, describes the target of its ministry as young couples and their children.

Church leaders have stated that churches should not support day care centers, because women ought not to be employed, but should stay at home and care for their children. The church asked a denominational agency serving children and their families to help them establish a parent education program and a weekday morning play group program for children and their mothers in its well-furnished family life center.

The agency staff was in conflict about how to respond. On the one hand, the staff was outraged at the church's refusal to use its considerable resources to care for the families in their community who had the greatest need. On the other hand, working with the church to pursue its stated objectives might well establish an agency-congregation relationship that could be used to shape and even alter the church's response to the poor single-parent families in its neighborhood.

Such dilemmas are not unusual in church-agency consultation, and are certainly as demanding and difficult as the ethical dilemmas of confidentiality and client self-determination that often rear their heads in direct practice with client families. When value conflicts between congregations and professionals develop, it helps to view the church as a client with a value system different from the professional's. Professionals strive to find common ground for a contract with clients whose values may differ from their own; they can do the same with congregations. And, just as with other clients, the target of change may include the values at issue. Consultation can require the same care in building a professional relationship of mutual trust and respect as one would give to building a relationship with a client. Nevertheless, there will also be occasions when the agency refuses to provide consultation to a church because of insurmountable differences that make a contract impossible, or because the relationship may be too costly when weighed against other significant agency relationships. For example, investing significant agency resources in one congregation may siphon resources from other possible liaisons that would be more central to the mission and goals of the agency.

In her or his relationship with a congregation, the consultant should use the language of the church and limit or avoid the use of professional jargon. In many respects, the church community is quite similar to an ethnic group, and resembles or actually is a subculture, with its own language and life-ways that have to be understood and adjusted to if professional practice is to be effective. This takes time and a commitment to learning the language and ways of this cultural milieu.

The professional will interpret statistics and data as they apply to the lives of the people in the congregation. In addition to talking about poverty in the nation, for example, the consultant talks about poverty and its consequences in the county and community in which the church is located. In addition to talking about national teen pregnancy rates, the consultant extrapolates the number of teenagers that a church can expect statistically to become pregnant in its congregation. The consultant can find out about drug use, suicide rates, or other pertinent data in the schools the church members' children attend.

When presenting needs and issues to churches, the consultant must be specific. Time-limited projects will probably receive a more positive response than ongoing ones, at least initially. The consultant explains exactly what is needed from church members, what they will be expected to do, and what they can expect in return.

Recruiting, Training, and Working with Volunteers

In an institutional model of organizations, structures are created and staff members are hired to fill particular positions, in which they are expected to move the organization toward established goals. Often, in this model, a volunteer is viewed as an unpaid staff member, someone who fills a slot because there is not enough money to hire staff for a particular function.

An organismic model of organizations, however, suggests beginning with persons—their resources, values, interests, and motivation—and developing structures to support their work. Instead of beginning with an organizational need (vacant positions, community needs, and organizational objectives to meet those needs), one begins with the sense of calling and mission that motivates persons to serve. This model is congruent with the spiritual guide function of the church agency, in that it recognizes and calls out the gifts and possibilities in the congregation and does not concentrate solely on organizational goals and objectives [e.g., Hessel 1982; Tillapaugh 1982]. From their experience in working with volunteers, Hunt and Paschall [1984] suggest that volunteers be encouraged to develop their own objectives; their service should belong to them, not just fill unmet agency needs for paid staff members.

Few church-based child and family service programs can embrace one or the other of these models of organization—institutional or organismic—exclusively. The nature of the program and the gifts and motivation of the volunteers suggest that one or the other model may predominate, but that both structures and individuals receive significant attention. An after-school activities program, for example, may operate predominantly from an institutional model. A certain number of experienced adult volunteers must provide supervision and leadership for groups of children. An adopt-a-grandparent program, however, may pair adults in the church community with single teen parents, focusing primarily on the volunteers' gifts and motivation in matching them with families.

The trend has been toward an organismic model for describing the roles of volunteers. There is a shrinking pool of people who have time to devote to unpaid staff positions in organizations. Women, who in decades past formed the army of volunteers that staffed church programs, have moved into paid employment in growing numbers. To volunteer, many must fit their service into snatches of time between work and family responsibilities. Others whom the agency considers as volunteers may not even think of what they do as volunteer work; the agency simply provides them with resources and consultation while they care for friends and neighbors as a part of their everyday living and as members of a particular community or social network.

It is important to recognize that an emphasis on the development of parish community work should not devalue the distinctive contribution of individual Christians in community life. A problem in many parishes is that the varied ministries of individuals are not affirmed or recognized as such. Schemes are developed to involve people in the life of the Church that may, in fact, serve to divorce them from the social worlds into which God has called them [Burke 1989: 4].

Much work with laypersons in congregational family service programs thus ought to support caregivers in the interpersonal roles they already play in their social networks. Second, laypersons may be involved in reciprocal support networks, as in the development of parent co-ops for sharing child care responsibilities among parents or parent support groups for families with special needs. Third, laypersons may be formally identified as volunteers and enlisted to reach out with support and caregiving to families who may not be able to reciprocate that care and support, at least in the short term. As volunteers, they may be involved in befriending an isolated, depressed parent living in the community who has come to the attention of a public agency as abusive. Or they may provide adult friendship to adolescents at risk for school failure, drug use, or gang involvement. It is hoped that some reward is forthcoming for the volunteer, however—the sense of doing something worthwhile, the growing warmth of the relationship, or perhaps even a positive change in the client system. Some such relationships develop over time from created support to become a part of both the volunteer's and the client's natural support system. In other words, a relationship develops that is more extensive and long-lasting than that described in the initial program goals.

Professionals will be most effective in recruiting for volunteer positions if they communicate the assumption that the people they are trying to recruit are the kind of people who want to help. When we describe potential volunteers to themselves as "the kind of people who are willing to give of themselves," they are more likely actually to do so. This type of "attribution effect" has been shown in several studies [e.g., Grusec and Redler 1980; Grusec et al. 1978]. Calling people caring is more effective in eliciting caring, self-giving behavior than telling people that they ought to care.

Volunteers are a precious agency resource; they should be involved in service programs that are sensitive to their gifts and nurture their continuing involvement and the involvement of others they may recruit. This approach to working with volunteers suggests several principles for professional practice:

Use volunteers in roles that cannot be effectively filled by paid staff.
Volunteers can provide friendship, support, and even family care, roles that a paid professional cannot fill in a client's life. The definitive charac-

teristic of a professional-client relationship is that it includes a formal contract for services and is not an ongoing primary relationship. A person can be paid to answer the phone or seal envelopes, but not to be a friend. Therefore, volunteers who can befriend and support clients in informal ways are a precious resource for professionals to protect.

Match volunteers' capabilities with appropriate tasks.
A young adult may feel frightened by and not want to work personally with street kids, but she may find a very fulfilling ministry role in developing a computer support system for the teen activity program that serves neighborhood adolescents. Over time, she may also agree to provide one-on-one computer tutoring for those adolescents who indicate a particular interest. Wollman [1985] suggests that volunteers begin with small assignments with a high probability of success. Volunteers who experience their actions having some intended effect are even more willing to continue to give of themselves, sometimes in tasks that may not seem to have much impact, at least in the short term.

Be flexible.
When there are no financial resources to purchase clerical and other support services, volunteers may have to be used as substitutes for paid staff. Clearly, the first principle above is not inviolable. Volunteers may be needed and will serve willingly in the office work of a family service agency. Residential care programs often use volunteers to supplement the staff or to allow a more efficient and a greater range of use of existing staff [Mykytiuk 1989]. Most family support programs, with average annual budgets of only $7000, also rely at least to some degree on volunteer staffing [Jacobs 1988]. Priorities for using volunteers, however, should not be sacrificed. It may be best for paid staff to seal envelopes and answer the phone in order to keep the volunteer working with clients. The agency's paid staff can empower the volunteers, and not just vice versa.

Plan for the appropriate involvement of clients.
Explicitly identifying those who can and cannot be served by the program will also facilitate the use of volunteers. Clients will not automatically appear because a program that they "ought" to want to use is launched,

and volunteer programs cannot serve all the needs that might present themselves. Developing channels through which clients who can be effectively served may reach the program often requires professional attention to relationships with key community agencies and persons who can link those in need with the service.

Carefully define a client population and design a program specifically tailored to its needs. No aspect of the program is more important than finding and attracting participants who are likely to benefit. If insufficient attention is given to promotion and recruitment of appropriate clients, successes will be rare and volunteers will soon feel they are failing and leave the program [Johns 1988: 58].

The agency professional can meet with a family applying for services in order to clarify what can be expected from the program, "selling" those who fit on the opportunity of participating, and carefully referring others to appropriate community services [Johns 1988].

Help volunteers set realistic goals and boundaries.
Volunteers often need a professional consultant to help them in setting goals *with* clients rather than for them, so that clients will not consider the volunteers' efforts to be irrelevant or even undesirable. It is essential to state the parameters of the volunteers' assistance and the extent to which they can and cannot offer material assistance, such as gifts of money or groceries. It should also be clear that volunteers should not be asked to work with clients who are hostile or to work in potentially violent situations, unless they understand and accept what they should do if violence seems possible. The agency should be sure that its liability insurance coverage is adequate to cover the volunteers who serve in its name.

Evaluate the processes and outcomes of the volunteers' work.
Evaluation includes measures of changes in the clients and/or target systems of the program. In addition, however, it includes changes in the volunteers themselves, particularly if the focus of the program is the spiritual guidance and growth of volunteers as well as intervention in the lives of children and their families. The attitudes, motivations, and beliefs of the volunteers may all be relevant to the evaluation process, which

provides valuable feedback not only to the program, but also to the volunteers themselves.

Encourage clients to serve in turn.

The ultimate impoverishment is receiving with nothing to give back. Many services of the church are—and ought to be—free. Nevertheless, clients may be invited to serve others as they have been served, either in the church's programs or through their own social networks, or perhaps even within their own families. In other words, services given freely are not cheap; they are an investment in the lives of clients.

Provide volunteers with support.

Reimbursement for expenses makes it possible for some persons to involve themselves who would not otherwise have the resources to do so. Even financially sufficient volunteers, however, experience supports such as reimbursements for expenses, access to materials and photocopying, and secretarial help as recognition of the importance of their work. Training, information, and ongoing consultation are also requisite forms of support [see Pancoast 1990b and Bowman 1990].

There is almost always an element of risk involved for volunteers. Their values may be re-ordered because of their service. Their involvement in caregiving takes time away from other social relationships and commitments. They may feel psychologically burdened or even physically threatened as a consequence of responding to the needs of others. For all these reasons, volunteers need a community of support made up of people with similar commitments who are trying to live out their own understanding of the gospel in visible commitments to ministry and social justice. In addition to group support, an informal self-help group that meets over coffee can provide opportunity for reflection on volunteers' experiences in the context of their original goals and motivations. As they tell the stories of their work, of successes and disappointments and unanticipated learning, they can progress in their own spiritual journeys and become more effective and sensitive caregivers. Evans et al. [1987] call this process "transformative education." Involving persons in ministry and social justice issues in ways that immerse them in a social environment different from their own encourages risk-taking, offers community support, encourages reflection, and provides stories of the efforts of others that parallel their own deepened commitments and involvement over time.

Training and consultation by professionals should be congruent with the volunteer's role with the client; volunteers are not junior helping professionals. In fact, training can inadvertently make natural helpers who have been giving support to others for years feel less confident of their innate abilities. Overformalized training may turn friendships into volunteer-client relationships, which is in most cases a big step backward. Volunteers may quietly decide that they have been "doing things all wrong." Consequently, formerly effective natural helpers may either back away from giving help or adopt ways that seem more professional but are less successful because they are artificial, not the normal way friends relate to one another [Pancoast 1990b].

Recognize and reinforce volunteers' service.
The manner of recognition should match the profile of the service. Churches typically recognize volunteers who fill organizational positions (deacons, Sunday school teachers) by publishing their names in the church newsletter or having them stand in a church meeting to receive words of appreciation. Sometimes, such formal recognition may be valued and reinforce the esteem of volunteers serving in less conspicuous ways, but often this is not the case. The friendly visitor who has unobtrusively moved toward a family at risk to offer friendship and support may consider formal recognition embarrassing, and perhaps even damaging to the work that has been done. Recognition might better be offered in a handwritten note from the agency consultant or pastor, with a small symbolic gift, or by being the consultant's guest for lunch. These efforts should always be framed as "tokens of appreciation," recognizing that the volunteer did not undertake the work in order to be praised by others.

Even the term *volunteer* is inappropriate in many roles, because of the connotation of organizational position. The man who notices a troubled young boy growing up in the home of a single mother and develops a relationship with him, taking him to ball games, teaching him to fish, and helping him paint his mother's home, is hardly a volunteer. The mother who struggles to help her developmentally disabled child develop social skills is in one sense involved in ministry; she may benefit from the support and informal consultation of a professional, but she is not a volunteer. Calling the Christian who is involved in a deliberate caring effort a *minister* may be an effective and powerful way of describing the role.

Provide ways for volunteers to talk about their work.
An informal support group can be a significant resource for volunteers and ministers. Offer informational sessions tailored to meet their needs, embellished with a shared meal or refreshments and time for socializing with the consultant and with others engaged in similar ministries. The consultant will also want to meet with individuals singly on occasion, to review their work and discuss whether or not they want to continue and what supports might be effective.

Social support from staff members and other volunteers often makes all the difference in keeping volunteers (and staff members!) energized, committed, and hopeful about their work. This support includes not only support in the work, but also opportunities to be playful with one another—the same thing we want for the families with whom we work. Wendy Forman and Laura Slap, psychologists who are active in the self-giving work of building peace and social justice, describe what gives them support:

> The major factor that has prevented our burning out is the invention and existence of Hedonists for Social Responsibility (HSR).... Unlike other peace groups, there are no meetings, no dues, no newsletters, and no fund-raisers. Most HSR events are fairly spontaneous and tend to resemble parties or vacations. Dancing and music, while not part of the original group charter, are strongly encouraged. It is useful (for summer meetings) to find someone who has a swimming pool or access to a beach or lake; a sprinkler on the lawn will do in a pinch. We are hoping that other people will follow our lead and start their own chapters. [Forman and Slap 1985: 67-68]

Strengthening the bonds of friendship and building a foundation of good memories as a working group may help all concerned weather the often difficult and demanding work with children and their families in crisis.

Gain the active support of the pastor.
The attitude of the pastor can make or break any program of the church. The pastor's involvement in the work of the program and words from the pulpit and in other spoken and written messages to the congregation provide ongoing congregational visibility and ownership.

If the agency has provided staff members to develop and coordinate a volunteer program for a congregation on a time-limited basis, the contract between agency and congregation should include arrangements for the church to take over responsibility for program coordination and oversight. Although some small programs can continue solely by key volunteers assuming administrative responsibility, most programs, even of quite modest scope, need to have the congregation's pastor and/or other paid church staff actively invested in them.

Some Cautionary Words

Volunteers have not participated in the learning processes of professional education. They may not have wrestled with values and ethical matters such as confidentiality and self-determination. Second, volunteers may see themselves as rescuers, as the only ones who really care about a child or a parent. They may take on too much responsibility and encourage too much dependency. They may be reluctant to set boundaries or limit the scope of what they do. They may experience significant role strains in their own lives, become unable to carry out their own family or employment responsibilities, and even relinquish the social lives that provide them with sustenance and support. Finally, volunteers may not be as conscious as professionals of their own psychology and how its workings influence their relationships with others.

Volunteers often become so invested in a relationship that they begin to take responsibility for the direction of clients' lives. If the client continues to have difficulties and does not make what the volunteer considers positive choices, the volunteer may feel this as an accusation that his or her care is somehow inadequate. If this feeling is experienced repeatedly, the volunteer may even come to believe that the client is purposely undermining the helping effort and denying the volunteer an opportunity to feel good. This predicament is made even more difficult if the self-interests and self-esteem of the volunteer are considered taboo topics, and the volunteer denies any agenda other than giving care [Coyne et al. 1988, Powell et al. 1988]. Consultants should be particularly watchful for these developments, and if possible, provide empathic, supportive guidance before they become problems for either volunteers or clients. This guidance must be offered in the spirit of consultation, however, and not as supervision, since the volunteer by definition is not a staff member.

Examples of Church-Based Services and Programs

The programs and approaches to congregational family support services that are described in this section suggest the kinds of services that can be offered by churches; their inclusion here is not necessarily an endorsement of any particular program or a judgment about its effectiveness. As Mon Cochran [1991] has said, "Adapt the idea; don't adopt the model." Some programs have been concerned with evaluating the outcomes of their services on clients, and to a lesser extent, on the church congregation itself. Many have not.

Pooley and Littell [1986: 223] reviewed 25 impact studies of family resource programs, and reached the following conclusions about such programs:

1. Parenting skills and parent-child interactions can be enhanced by programs that provide support and education to parents in the early child-rearing years.

2. Parent support and education programs can also have a range of positive effects on parents' knowledge, attitudes, and behaviors and on their use of social network support and community resources.

3. There is some evidence to suggest that family resource programs can produce lasting changes in family functioning and economic circumstances.

It appears that the specific program structure and content of education programs is less significant than the relationships between parents that these programs foster, but without continued evaluation, one cannot validate this. Large, carefully controlled, and well-funded programs tend to invest in careful impact evaluation. Family resource programs, however, tend to be small, based in the community, and partly or completely staffed by volunteers. Although these programs may not be able to invest in sophisticated evaluation studies, they can be consistent in gathering outcome data that contribute to professional understanding when combined with studies of programs in different contexts and with different population groups. Enabling programs to develop unobtrusive but relevant processes for gathering consistent data about their outcomes is a significant role for the professional staff member and/or consultant.

Child Care Services

One of the most critical needs of families, particularly low-income families, is affordable, high-quality child day care. Currently, churches are a principal provider of child day care—one church in three houses a program. Churches house at least one-third of the day care programs in the United States; in 1986, 2.3 million children received day care from our nation's churches [Freeman 1986]. Some programs provide day care for working parents; others provide respite care for parents who are not employed outside the home.

> The Soulard Family Center in the inner city of St. Louis, Missouri, provides drop-in child care services for children and personal support services for their parents. No fee is charged, but for every three times a child is left at the center, the parents are required to participate in an enrichment or support activity for parents that is offered by the center. ["Preventing Abuse before It Starts" 1990]

Church-related child welfare agencies can help churches shape these ministries to serve those with the greatest need. For example, sliding fee scales can help poor families obtain child care they could not afford to purchase in the private for-profit sector. Many churches offer Mother's Day Out and other respite programs that can be modified to serve, in addition to those parents who seek out such support, isolated parents, who are at risk for abusing and neglecting their children, or parents whose children have special needs and for whom respite care would be a critical support.

Volunteer and paid staff members in such programs require training in the skills and sensitivity necessary to reach out to these parents and children with encouragement and nurture. Child care services can be combined with parent education and support groups, with family visiting by a volunteer trained in befriending and supporting isolated parents who may lack skill in developing and maintaining social relationships, and with the crisis intervention services of a professional social worker.

Home Support

One church in the Chicago area brings baskets of baby items to new mothers in the hospital who have been identified by the social services staff as high risk, such as single teenage parents. The baskets include coupons for one evening of in-home child care by one of the women in the church, a monthly visit in which the church woman involves mother and baby in game-like activities that support the baby's development, and carefully chosen on-loan toys.

There are many ways churches provide support for vulnerable families, such as teen parents, and families in crisis.

The First United Methodist Church of Wilmington, Illinois, developed Family Care to provide short-term support for families at times of intense stress. Volunteers may provide transportation for a family with a chronically ill child who needs medical treatment, run errands or cook meals, or provide short-term child care. Families with new babies routinely receive a home-cooked meal along with coupons for Family Care services. The church also provides Parents' Day Out. Volunteer coordinators plan activities for children and manage the program, which is offered one day each week. Parents work on a rotating basis alongside volunteers. Additional meetings provide parent support and enrichment activities. [Friedrich 1990]

First Presbyterian Church of Lexington, North Carolina, developed yet another model. A church discussion group identified child abuse and neglect as a significant problem in their county, and led to the development of the Davidson County Parent Aide Board. In partnership with the Baptist Children's Homes of North Carolina, Inc., the Philpott Parent Aide Program was established. Volunteers are recruited from area churches of all denominations by means of bulletin inserts and presentations to church groups. They complete a 16-hour training program and are then assigned to work with families referred to the program by various human services agencies. The volunteer visits in the family's home twice weekly for a total of four to six hours a week over a maximum of 18 weeks. Volunteers agree to be available to the family 24 hours a day by phone, although calls for help are infrequent. As one volunteer commented, "I don't think we've had one call after midnight. They are sensitive. It is like taking care of another part of your family. It really becomes your extended family" [Stephens 1990: 8a].

Volunteers seek to build parental self-confidence and self-esteem; strengthen parenting skills in problem-solving, communication, and discipline; increase parents' knowledge of child development; expand social contacts and reduce isolation; and help parents gain access to other community resources. In its first year of service, volunteers served 28 families involving 62 children. (For more information, the address of the Philpott Parent Aide Program is listed in Appendix 3.)

In a similar program in Texas, one volunteer reported that she "drank more coffee than I ever imagined I could consume" while she regularly took an isolated and psychologically trapped young mother out for a chat at a nearby restaurant [Johns 1988: 12]. In this case, the most significant ingredient in effective support was the slow, nonspecific process of relationship building.

Johns [1988: 12] reports on one of the successful relationships between a volunteer team and a family consisting of a paraplegic and severely depressed father, a troublemaking six-year-old boy with learning disabilities stemming from a previously undiagnosed hearing loss, an exhausted and frustrated mother, and a nine-year-old boy whose behavior was beginning to reflect the family's crises.

With the help of other church members, the team fixed up the house, arranged for physical therapy and daytime help for the father, found a hearing aid for the youngest and arranged to get him into special education, sent both children to camp (a pleasure for them and a respite for the parents), and supplied books and educational games for the youngsters. Other activities were even more important. Volunteers played games with the children and took them for outings. The couples spent numerous weekend evenings playing cards or Scrabble. The women went window-shopping or lunched together. A special friend recorded the father's comments about being a paraplegic as a guide for other paraplegics. The father was helped to go to a ball game with the two boys. And hours were spent just talking about feelings, fears, hurts, hopes, and how to work through the family's many problems. Friendship and just-for-fun activities were reintroduced to this distressed family, enabling them to explore the world beyond their own front door once again.

Teams in this program participated in a 15-hour training program and consulted an hour each week with a professional program director hired by the council of churches in their metropolitan area.

A survey of 191 parent aide programs designed to prevent abuse and neglect compared those programs using volunteers with those employing a staff to provide support services to parents in their homes [American Association of Retired Persons 1987]. Of the families served by these programs, 61% were single mothers, 6% were single fathers, 27% had both biological parents, and 3% were foster parents. These percentages did not vary significantly between the paid-staff and volunteer-staffed programs. Most typically, families served were isolated, with inadequate support systems and "inexperienced" or "immature" parents. The two types of programs did differ significantly in the nature of services they provided parents. Volunteer-staffed programs were more likely to offer companionship and role modeling, whereas paid-staff programs were more likely to offer home management services, help in finding community services and resources, and help with daily activities.

Telephone Warm Lines

Other churches have developed telephone reassurance networks of latch-key children and senior citizens. The "phone friends" talk to one another each afternoon after school and meet some days of the week at the church for special activities. Another program has used a telephone warm line to support parents.

Four churches in Austin, Texas, established the Parents' Warm Line of Austin, a phone-in support, parenting information, referral, and peer counseling service for parents [Johns 1988]. Volunteers answer phones either in the city crisis hotline office or by call-forwarding to their own homes. The warm line was originally developed as the churches' response to child abuse and neglect; almost 20% of the calls received through the phone line deal with these threats. Most typical are "the tearful calls from single parents who feel hopeless and exhausted, from mothers of preschoolers who feel isolated and trapped, and from parents of 2-year-olds or teenagers who feel that yesterday's delight of their life has suddenly turned into an uncontrollable enemy" [Johns 1988: 9].

The most commonly sought referral has been a parent support group or parent-child play group. Less common, but more serious, are the calls from angry, panicky, or grimly controlled parents, such as the 25-year-old mother of five who said without emotion, "Where can I find a cheap baby-sitter right now? I can't stay around these kids another minute. I don't need help, I don't want to talk, I've just got to escape" [Johns 1988: 9].

Parent-to-Parent Programs

Parents of emotionally disturbed, physically ill, and developmentally handicapped children and adult children often gain enormous support and new skills and information that help them cope with their family's situation simply by meeting and spending time with other parents who face similar challenges. This network of support, when coupled with the professional services of family counseling and respite care available from the church-related agency, enables some families to continue caregiving who would otherwise be forced to consider placement outside the home for their child with special needs.

Adopt-a-Social-Worker Ministries

In Corpus Christi, Texas, Metro Ministries, an agency composed of 88 congregations, implemented the Adopt-a-Child-Abuse-Caseworker Ministry. Over 100 congregations participate in a similar ministry, "Adopt a Social Worker," which was developed by Covenant to Care in Hartford, Connecticut. The ministry was designed to give caseworkers more time to work directly with abused and neglected children. A caseworker is paired with a congregation and a covenant is made based on the kinds of unmet needs the caseworker encounters in families and the resources the church states it might be able to supply. The interface between client needs and church resources has provided a variety of material supports—food, clothing, prescription medicines, furniture, medical examinations, school supplies, legal assistance, bus tickets, cleaning supplies, and a dress for an adolescent's high school prom. Congregations have also provided tutoring, transportation, and respite child care. In addition, the congregation offers emotional support and recognition for the social worker, meeting a need that often goes unmet for professionals who provide protective services in pubic agencies. Evaluation indicates that the needs of both clients and social workers are being met by these programs, and participating congregations feel personally involved in caring for families in crisis. Although the congregations are primarily empowering the professionals to do their work more effectively, they in turn are being empowered to care personally for families.

Prison Family Ministries

Some church volunteers, by means of church ministries, provide friendship, transportation, emotional support, linkage with other resources, and advocacy in behalf of families of incarcerated parents and youths [Ferguson 1992, Garland 1985]. This can be particularly critical support for dependent children whose mothers are imprisoned. Churches that have been involved in providing worship services and visiting in jails and prisons often welcome consultation designed to extend their ministry to the families outside.

Mentor Programs

Operation Getting It Together (OGIT) serves low-income and minority persons in Sonoma County, California. It is sponsored by 14 local churches representing seven denominations, and has its headquarters in a United Methodist church. The Youth Outreach Program of OGIT carefully screens, trains, and supervises high school juniors, seniors, and college students, called "youth outreach workers," who are teamed with no more than two children considered at risk for school failure and/or delinquency. Outreach workers provide friendship, guidance, and positive role modeling; help with school; and share worthwhile experiences in the larger geographical area. The outreach workers must submit brief written monthly progress reports, attend quarterly training workshops, and commit themselves to at least five hours a week with their assigned youngster for a minimum of one year. They receive a modest monthly expense allowance to pay for activities and transportation, and a $300 annual community service scholarship; some receive school credit for their involvement in the program.

OGIT also has a Family Nurture Program, which provides "family strengthening services"—professional family guidance, encouragement, crisis intervention, and advocacy—in the homes of juvenile clients. These services are available 24 hours a day, seven days a week. The agency's Legal Aid Program provides legal assistance and representation. The program has resulted in 85% of the 90 juvenile clients served in the past year being able to avoid school suspension, 95% being able to avoid school expulsion, 95% being promoted to the next school grade level, 90% avoiding negative contact with juvenile authorities, 86% improving communication with other family members, and 89% being able to avoid use of alcohol and illegal drugs [Schilling 1992].

Programs have also developed that pair "parent mentors" with parents and families considered at risk: teen parents, single mothers, and parents of children having problems in school.

A child came home from the day care center at Bridge Street African Methodist Episcopal Church in Brooklyn, New York, and told her mom, "They are giving away grandmothers at Bridge Street and I want one." A parent from another family participating in this program said of the grandparent mentor, "When I began seeing her at her home, I saw her long gray hair and her happy face, and I suddenly realized that she was a real grandmother to me. I felt then that I could talk to her and trust her." [National Crime Prevention Council 1990: 7]

Mentor programs do not differ appreciably from the home support programs described above, except that mentoring does not always take place in the setting of the family home. Mentors may serve as tutors in an after-school program or as supportive friends in a youth activities program or parent support group without ever visiting the family home. Many home support programs that use volunteers, however, are indeed developing a mentoring relationship between the volunteer and the parent. Withey et al. [1980] suggest that mentors working with parents can serve as (1) teachers of child rearing, household management, how to have access to resources, and what it means to be a responsible adult; (2) sponsors, in that they help parents obtain services; (3) guides, giving emotional support in times of stress; and (4) models of how to solve problems and enhance the quality of life for themselves and their children.

Youth Activity Programs

Churches frequently provide recreation and activity programs for children and youths: after-school and weekend recreation, camps and retreats, clubs and organizations, and sports leagues. These programs can be instrumental in building healthy self-esteem and shaping the value systems of children and youths.

Community Development Ministries

Some church leaders have considered their role to be one of community development and social change. The Voice of Calvary Ministries in Jackson and Menhall, Mississippi, with the leadership of John Perkins, has pioneered efforts in community development and racial reconciliation through church programs and ministries with the rural poor of Mississippi. Perkins argues that African American churches have too often been release valves for the frustration and oppression that African Americans have experienced rather than forces for change. The Voice of Calvary Ministries have focused on social concerns as an integral part of evangelism. They offer the following programs in their community that directly touch the lives of poor children and their families:

- day care center and preschool program;

- tutoring program to supplement public education;

- housing co-op to build duplexes with government loans and rent them at low rates;

- playground and gym to meet the recreational needs of youths;

- feeding program, cooperative food store, and cooperative farm to combat poor nutrition;

- health center (developed before health services were forced to integrate racially);

- summer enrichment program to prepare high school students for college; and

- leadership development program to prepare future African American leaders for Christian community development. [Perkins 1982]

Conclusions

Parents are the primary persons who can prevent the need for child welfare services in the lives of children. By supporting parents' positive influence and persistent efforts to care for and guide their children, congregational family support services can create conditions that avert the need for direct professional services to children. Many parents, both those who are clients in our agencies and those who involve themselves in church congregations, become better "preventers" when they have access to services that help them to be good parents. These services may include counseling, family life or parent education, child care, drop-in centers, emergency financial assistance, respite care, and supportive friendships.

> What is most striking about parents today is how isolated many of them are from other families and from each other, and how hungry they are for new ways of making contact. ...Isolation among parents helps create isolated kids—or more specifically, kids isolated from the adult world, more vulnerable to their peers. Why are parents so isolated? ...longer commutes; both parents working ever longer hours, the new urban form; the fading of older networks—coffee klatches, churches, neighborhood schools. In the workplace, parents seldom discuss parenting because parenthood is too often considered a career hindrance. ...As lonely parents fear their environment and doubt their own competence, community—the real preventer of child abuse and other violence—diminishes." [Louv 1991: 6]

Consequently, community-based family support services, as described in this chapter, are receiving increasing attention from the helping professions [Kamerman and Kahn 1989]. The term *family support* has recently begun to be used more in relation to families with very young children (usually preschool) and in relation to high-risk, vulnerable families, especially those with very young and immature parents. The common features that church-based programs share with other community family support programs are their local base, broad access, nonbureaucratized organization, and an emphasis on help with parenting.

Unfortunately, the research seems to suggest that many family support programs, as helpful as they may be to many parents, are least likely to be successful with poor, high-risk families [Dumas and Wahler 1983; Tracy and Whittaker 1987]. Since drop-in centers are voluntary, many who could profit are not there; lonely, isolated people appear to benefit least from programs that are designed specifically to meet their needs [Wandersman 1987]. If, however, these programs become mainly parenting education resources for cases reported to the child abuse/neglect services, they cannot be expected also to be attractive drop-in centers for the average young parents in the community [Kamerman and Kahn 1989: 248]. In short, there is no program panacea. Just as volunteers can play a critical role in supporting and intervening in some families, so the professional services described in the previous chapter are also essential in meeting the needs of other children and their families.

Notes

1. A more thorough introduction to a theology of family might include Anderson and Guernsey 1985; Friedman 1985; Garland and Garland 1989; Garland and Pancoast 1990; Greeley 1980; Guernsey 1982; National Conference of Catholic Bishops 1988; Olson and Leonard 1990; McGinnis and McGinnis 1981; Schillebeeckx 1965; and Sheek 1985.

2. Charles Overton, a New York Sunday-school superintendent, designed a flag in 1897 that has subsequently been adopted by a number of Protestant denominations as the Christian flag. It has a white field, and the top inner quarter, which attaches to the flagpole, bears a red Latin cross.

3. Johnson and Long [1983] offer an excellent guide for forming and facilitating social ministry committees and task forces.

CHAPTER 6

Beyond Agency and Congregation: Advocacy for Children and Families

" AND LOOK OUT FOR ONE ANOTHER'S INTERESTS, NOT JUST FOR YOUR OWN. THE ATTITUDE YOU SHOULD HAVE IS THE ONE CHRIST JESUS HAD."
(Philippians 2:4-5)

Caring for children and their families who are at risk of or in the midst of family crisis is becoming a larger and larger task. They are no longer a minority of families in unusual circumstances. Prevention is coming to mean attention to the needs of all children.

This spreading concern for children is only partly due to new perspectives on the needs of children and families embedded in the larger community and societal context. Much more significantly, and with much more sinister implications, we are realizing that more and more children and their families are at risk for a variety of miseries—poverty, child abuse, neglect, leaving school illiterate and unemployable, pregnancies at too early an age, single parenthood, drug abuse, and crime.

The Need for Advocacy

For the past 20 years, the diversity of family structures—never-married parents and children, divorced parents and children, blended families—has been hailed by many family experts as indicating that families have more choices. For example, rising divorce rates have meant that partners who are physically and/or emotionally abused have been able to choose divorce over remaining in a destructive relationship. Fewer women have been forced to stay in abusive marriages because there was no other option for financial survival for themselves and their children. The growing acceptance of single parenthood has meant that young people ill prepared to begin a marriage have been able to choose to remain single and raise children without adding to that stressor a too-early marriage. These family structures, though different and perhaps stressful, have been considered no less functional inherently than the nuclear family.

Indeed, freedom from rigid societal constraints on family life has ended some suffering. But the rising rates of divorce and single parenthood (and the many other changes in the American family that they represent) mean far more than that safety hatches now exist for those experiencing destructive marriages or unplanned pregnancies or wanting to live an alternative lifestyle. Much more significantly, many experts in family studies are saying that the family is in trouble, that the parent-child relationship is in trouble, and that our culture is not supporting parents in the basic tasks and responsibilities of child rearing. Four systems largely determine the growth and development of the child in our culture: health care, the family, the school, and day care. In the past 30 years of monitoring the indicators of child well-being, never have the indicators looked so negative across all four systems essential to the growth of the child [Zigler 1990]. The research of the Children's Defense Fund reveals grim statistics.

Health Care

Although the United States remains the world's wealthiest nation, its infant mortality rate ranks twentieth in the world, worse than the rates in Singapore and Hong Kong. One in six children has no medical insurance of any kind. As an example of our poor health care for children, 44% of the 15-year-olds living in low-income families have untreated dental cavities [Children's Defense Fund 1991].

Family

Family systems lack the assistance they need to fulfill their role in the development of children. Reports of child abuse and neglect rose 147% in the 10 years from 1979 to 1989; 2.4 million children were reported abused or neglected in 1989 alone. Some of the increase in reports may be attributable to greater public awareness, and thus greater willingness to speak out when abuse is suspected. Research indicates, however, that poverty, lack of medical care, homelessness, domestic violence, and substance abuse are directly related to increases in child mistreatment, and these social indicators have risen dramatically in the last 10 years.

Despite the growth of family preservation and other programs to prevent out-of-home care, 360,000 American children are living in placements away from their families, a 29% increase since 1986. Children are entering the child welfare system at younger ages, staying longer, and re-entering more often. The funds for caring for these children are inadequate; in some communities, foster parents are paid less each week for caring for a child than a kennel operator receives for boarding a dog [Children's Defense Fund 1991].

Education

Almost 29% of the students who enter ninth grade fail to graduate four years later; almost 15% fail to obtain a diploma or equivalency certificate by age 22. Among 17-year-olds who are still in school, only half can use decimals, fractions, and percents to compute; fewer than half can understand, summarize, and explain the kind of material found in encyclopedias or high school textbooks. About 465,000 violent crimes and 2.5 million thefts occur in or around schools in one year's time. The 500,000 homeless children on any given day in our country typically receive neither health care nor education. And homelessness is increasing: in the two-year period 1990 to 1992, requests for shelter for homeless families with children increased 37% [Children's Defense Fund 1991].

Child Care

For many families, economic survival depends on both spouses working outside the home. Over half of all children under age six now have mothers in the work force. In 1989, the House Select Committee on Children, Youth, and Families reported that in two-parent homes, 60% of the employed mothers had husbands who earned less than $20,000 annually. Good day care is expensive, however, and a two-tiered child-care system has emerged. The affluent are finding very good care. But single parents working full time at the minimum wage would have to pay an average of 50–78% of their income for child care by a licensed facility for one child alone . Consequently, thousands of children are receiving care that is compromising their development [Children's Defense Fund 1991].

These statistics describe costly shortsightedness. Every dollar spent on prenatal care saves more than three dollars in costs for remedial care in the first year of life. Every dollar invested in childhood immunization programs saves an average of $10 in later medical costs [Children's Defense Fund 1991]. Comprehensive family support programs to keep children in school, to help parents encourage the social and intellectual development of their children, and to increase the level of employment of the parents themselves cost far less than care for families after they break down. The most effective and efficient programs are those that support parents, helping them to do a better job with their children. For example, family preservation services for families at high risk of having children placed in out-of-home care cost an average of $4,500 per family, compared with costs of $10,000 per child for foster care or $42,000 per child for residential group care [Children's Defense Fund 1991]. The safety net of social supports that is supposed to protect families and their members from catastrophe is developing larger and larger holes, however, and the smallest members of society—the children—are those most likely to slip through.

We have heard much in recent years of society's safety net...but it is clear today that the safety net, given current trends, cannot hold. I have therefore come to think of the overall environmental pattern in this way: visualize, above the safety net, a great network, a supportive and intricate web. This web is far more important than the safety net, yet we pay much less attention to it, to patching and respecting it. It is a wonderfully intricate and liberating web, and not easily described or quantified or fixed through fad legislation. One strand, the most important, is made of parents, another is the school system, another is the work place and how it treats parents, another is the neighborhood, another is how the city is shaped. As a boy, I sensed that I could get much of what I needed from the web: neighbors to watch out for me on the street, schools that cared, an understandable community in which to prove myself. Once the web begins to unravel, the smallest bodies fall through first—and that is what is happening today. [Louv 1991: 6]

It is not just the children of the poor who are falling through the net. Many middle class families have no medical insurance; some are one paycheck away from homelessness. Parents of all classes worry about teen pregnancy, the prevalence of drugs in youth peer groups, and whether or not their children's education will be adequate in coming decades. In short, parents feel powerless and afraid. In a study of middle class parents in Baltimore, Barbara Whitehead was surprised to discover what worried these parents the most. It was not the shortage of day care, or how much they were earning, or what the government was doing, or the state of the economy, or the quality of the public schools. They worried most that their children would vanish off the streets, kidnapped by a "crazy" or a "pervert." In fact, incidents of abduction and molestation are relatively rare; most of the parents interviewed had never experienced or witnessed such a crime. Their fears symbolize the root fears of parents, as well as the literal fears they expressed. They know the danger of crime, but they also recognize a larger and more insidious danger: the danger of our cultural assault on children.

> This assault comes in the form of an increasingly aggressive consumer economy that grabs even the very youngest children with alluring promises of popularity and success, if only they will buy the right brand of sneakers and stone-washed jeans. It comes in the form of a precocious peer culture, where girls want to be thin at age nine and seductive at eleven; where children talk about "doing it together" at age twelve; and where sexually transmitted diseases, drugs, pregnancy, and the threat of AIDS are all part of teen life in America. It comes in the form of a hands-off, me-first adult society, where children are the exclusive "problem" of parents rather than a responsibility we all share—a society that is increasingly unwilling to make the sacrifices necessary to foster good outcomes for children. In such an unfriendly culture, parents today are both frightened and angry at their growing helplessness to protect their children, not just against "crazies" and "perverts," but against a society that peddles greed, sex, and violence every day of the year. [Whitehead 1991: 15]

It is not just parents who are afraid; children are afraid too. Cecile Adams tells the following story:

> Jennifer sat two seats over from me on a plane going to Milwaukee. Sometime during the flight, Jennifer's mother, who sat next to me, excused herself and went several rows back to talk with friends.

> After a few moments of silence, Jennifer said to me, "What's your name?" Cecile," I answered. A few more moments of silence went by as Jennifer continued to color in her coloring book. Then, very matter-of-factly, Jennifer asked, "Would you watch me?" Surprised, I replied, "Yes...what do you want me to watch you do?" "I want you to watch me so that no one gets me," she said. I raised my feet and planted them firmly on the dividing wall in front of

me. Smiling, I said, "They'll have to get by me before they get to you." She returned my smile and continued coloring. In a few minutes, Jennifer handed me a neatly colored page from her coloring book. At the top, she had printed "To: Cecel From, Jennie." It was, I think, a thank-you note, a way of letting me know that she felt more secure because I was willing to "watch her."

Jennifer is in the third grade. She is polite, alert, and expresses herself well. Apparently, she is able to ask for what she needs. But why would she feel the need to ask for security from a stranger at 35,000 feet, in an enclosed, well-functioning plane with her mother within hearing distance? Does she know about hijacking? Has she ever been accosted or abused? Has someone overzealously cautioned her about strangers? The reality is that I do not know the answers to any of those questions. I do know, though, how sad and angry I am about living in a world where children must ask for security. [Adams 1990: 7]

At first, the concerns and fears of middle-class parents and their children (including Jennie) seem to be of a different character than the hard experiences of poor children and their families. The fears of a homeless boy that if he goes to school this morning, he may not know where to find his mother this afternoon seem to eclipse Jennie's innocent request. Yet although they are very different, all these worries and fears are threads of the same cloth, interwoven in the attitudes and values of our culture about children. The only security most children receive comes from their parents. Parents know and children sense that parents are all that stands between a child and homelessness, poverty, and a myriad of other specters. The wealthiest nation in the world has allowed "the least of these" to receive the least of the nation's resources and supports. Children are the poorest population group in the United States; 20% of all children live below the poverty line [Children's Defense Fund 1991]. One indicator of the lack of value placed on children is what advocates have learned—that the best way to plead the cause of children is to tell decision makers that progressive family support programs, such as family preservation, will cost less than the alternatives (foster care and residential care programs) in the short term. The value to which we can appeal most effectively is not the importance of children, but how the nation can save money.

A Definition of Advocacy

One of the responsibilities of the church agency is to lead the church in advocacy, in speaking out against the oppression of dependent children whose needs are not being addressed effectively. At times, that means involving the agency and its supporting religious organizations in political advocacy in ways that public agencies find difficult or impossible. When presented with the shocking facts about the effects of our society's policies on the health, education, and care of children, many churches respond with, "We had no idea." When presented with the powerlessness and vulnerability parents feel, many churches respond with empathy and resonance; they may not have verbalized these feelings, but they ring true to their own experience.

Too often, however, the response of church congregations (and the professionals in church agencies) resonates with the same helplessness parents express. Churches and helping professionals often feel powerless and hopeless when confronted with overwhelmingly negative realities. To know how bad things are does not move people to action; first, professionals and church congregations have to learn that they and their agencies can make a difference—that change is indeed "within our reach" [Schorr 1988].

When challenged with possibilities for action, many church congregations contain groups that willingly involve themselves; they want to work in behalf of children. They may differ politically and theologically from one another and from other congregations in their denomination, but they can be brought together in their belief that children should be a priority and that the Bible provides Christians with a mandate to be advocates for children. Many denominations have successfully launched coordinated child advocacy efforts. The United Methodist Women's Campaign for Children, the United Methodist Church Child Advocacy Network, the Presbyterian Church (USA) Five-Year Child

Advocacy Program, the National Council of Churches of Christ Child and Family Justice Office, and the Southern Baptist Child Advocacy Network are just some of the denominational efforts that have built on the church's long tradition of ministry to children and advocacy in their behalf. (See Appendix 4.) These efforts illustrate the expertise, leadership, realistic strategies, and broad connections that church agencies can offer.

> ChildServ, a United Methodist child welfare agency in Illinois, formed an advocacy organization a decade ago and named it United Voices for Children. The organization now claims almost 5,000 child advocates in a statewide network. ChildServ provides direction to these advocates in three primary ways. First, the agency involves advocates in education, informing themselves and then others about the needs of children. They may form advocacy groups in their own churches, provide articles for their church newsletters, or involve themselves in community advocacy efforts. Second, ChildServ involves advocates in the public policy arena. These advocates talk to state congressional representatives, city council members, mayors, administrators of departments of child and family services, and others influential in the development and implementation of public policy. Third, advocates also develop service programs for families at risk or in crisis in their communities. For example, the advocacy organization has been instrumental in recruiting and supporting foster parents. [Kirk 1991]

Churches are familiar with the role of advocacy. Many Christians know at least a few facts about the church's historic concern for social justice—the Quakers' stand on slavery and penal reform in early American history, the leadership of the African American church in the civil rights movement of the 1960s, the church as the seedbed for the nineteenth century women's rights movement, and the call of the church throughout its history for social justice. Many churches can embrace without difficulty the appropriateness of an advocacy role for the church, although members may sometimes disagree vehemently about the target of advocacy efforts.

An advocate is defined as one who pleads the cause of or intercedes for another, who is relatively powerless, with one who is relatively powerful. An advocate acts in behalf of others to do for them what they cannot do for themselves. In the context of professional social work practice, advocacy has been defined as the effort to obtain for clients the rights and benefits they are being unjustly denied. Professional social workers distinguish class advocacy from case advocacy. Case advocacy refers to speaking in behalf of one or a small group of clients. Class advocacy refers to speaking not only in behalf of a client, but also in behalf of all persons who share the same predicament. In many respects, it may be helpful to think of the relationship between case advocacy and class advocacy as akin to the relationship between first-order and second-order change [Watzlawick et al. 1974].

First-order change is a corrective response to minor fluctuations in a system, returning it to the status quo without changing the system itself. Either the situation calling for advocacy was an oversight and needs to be corrected, or it was an unusual circumstance and can be handled as a special case. Case advocacy focuses on the manner in which an agency or other social system responds to a particular client or client group in a particular concrete situation, such as presenting the case for a job training agency to accept a particular pregnant teen. Class advocacy involving second-order change is change in the system itself, not just remedial action. It can occur at both the administrative and the policy levels [Sosin and Caulum 1983].

Administrative-level class advocacy tries to convince decision makers to alter the regulations of a particular social system, often a social service agency. Presenting the case for a job training program to accept *any* pregnant teen who meets other acceptance criteria, if up to this point pregnancy had ruled out participation, would be administrative-level advocacy. Policy-level advocacy tries to convince decision makers to alter laws, basic societal policies, and funding structures. Arguing the case for providing funds and support services (such as health care and parent education) in a comprehensive job training program for all pregnant teens who are no longer in school would be policy-level class advocacy.

Volunteers, parents, and others involved directly in the lives of children may engage in case advocacy. Church congregations are more likely to involve themselves in class advocacy, simply because as a large group, they are more often involved when the need extends beyond one unusual circumstance. If they are inflamed by the circumstances of an individual child or group of children, their concern easily spreads to all in like circumstances.

The Agency Role in Child and Family Advocacy

Church agencies have a significant leadership role to play at all levels of the church's advocacy for children and their families. Perhaps one of the most significant functions of the church as an advocate for children and their families is the empowering of children and families to speak for themselves. When empowerment is not enough to achieve the changes, agencies themselves can become the advocates, not only in behalf of those they serve directly as clients or as members of congregations in relationship with the agency, but also in behalf of children and their families in the wider community. Finally, the agency can provide resources and leadership to congregations and denominational groups for their own advocacy efforts.

Empowering Children and Families

Empowering children and their families simply means giving them power to affect their own lives and surroundings. For example, one emphasis of the World Council of Churches has been "family power," providing resources through family life education programs so that families can obtain clean water for their villages (Indonesia), economic support for single mothers (Jamaica), and a credit union for farmers (Indonesia) [Mpolo 1984]. Once empowered, people become active participants in decisions or social processes that affect them, but in which their involvement had previously had been considered unimportant, if considered at all. Empowered parents can advocate for their needs and the needs of their children, and ultimately, can empower their children to shape their own lives.

Rather than churches developing programs, and thus only caring for families whose needs fit the programs, the needs of families should shape programs. Those needs are best defined by families themselves. Empowerment puts the shaping power for social structures in the hands of those for whom the structures were intended. Parents often can say better than anyone else what supports they need for strengthening their families—what kinds of flexibility they need in preschool day care and in programs before and after school for school-age youngsters, what kinds of family education programs would help them most, what respite programs would enable them to cope with their children's special needs.

When the needs are complex and the responses needed are not clear, even to parents, then parents should be involved as partners with professionals and policymakers in determining both needs and responses. Parents indeed may not have ready solutions for problems such as teen pregnancy, drug abuse, and school failure. They are experts on their own children, however, and therefore ought to be partners in the development of prevention services. When empowerment works, parents acquire three characteristics: capacity, awareness and knowledge, and assertiveness.

Capacity

First, parents must gain the skills and resources for solving the problems that impede them, as well as access to the structures that are the target of change. For example, homeless parents are some of the most powerless parents in the nation; they have lost the power even to provide for the most rudimentary needs of their children. In normal circumstances, these parents may have the ability to stand up for their children's needs. Overwhelmed by the crisis that resulted in homelessness and their desperate search for employment and/or housing to provide some rudimentary sense of security, however, they may no longer have the energy and attention to commit to their children's needs.

Their children may desperately need the security and stability of staying in the same school, although they are temporarily living in a shelter in another neighborhood. School board policy, however, may insist that the child transfer to the new district. Few homeless parents have the resources to tackle school board policy. To write a formal letter of request or to speak to such an august body may be far beyond their current capabilities. Even obtaining transportation to an appointment with a school board member or finding appropriate letter-writing materials may be a major task. Finding a forum for telling one's story and being taken seriously, however, can be a medium for empowerment. It can encourage partnership with the professional who is concerned about the child's needs. The woman in the vignette that follows was given a voice as an advocate for her child and other children in the same plight:

> In New York, one girl was placed in special education after the family moved through seven shelters in 10 months. The girl's mother told Dr. Yvonne Rafferty of the Advocates for Children in New York, "I think what she really needs is to stop going to a different school every month. She didn't have this learning disability before we lost our home. I think what she really needs is a permanent home." [Children's Defense Fund 1991: 109]

Awareness and Knowledge

Second, parents gain awareness and knowledge of the issues. Moran [1986] describes advocacy skills for parent organizations. She suggests that group members attain a significant level of shared awareness and consensus about their needs as parents, the needs of their children, and the appropriateness of advocacy in their behalf. Parents do not always understand the complexity of the situations their children face, such as tracking in schools and the development of magnet and special interest educational programs. These issues are not necessarily straightforward and easy to understand. Guidance is necessary to help parents sift through research and understand the arguments on various sides of the issues and the implications of policies for their own and for other people's children.

Assertiveness

Speaking out at a school board meeting about the damaging effects of tracking or the barriers a magnet school system creates for poor children takes considerably more assertiveness than writing a letter or voting in a school board election. All parents require some level of assertiveness, however, recognizing that one has a right to be heard and that being heard ought to make a difference (whether it does or not). Combining an educational approach to the issues with assertiveness training designed to help parents deal with powerful decision makers is an effective package for working with groups of parents toward empowerment. Pizzo [1987] suggests that there are three images of parents in our society that guide the assumptions upon which services to children have been and continue to be built.

The Incompetent Parent is a parent incapable of meeting a child's essential needs. The Victimized Parent is seen as a sympathetic figure, struggling with oppressive economic and social conditions that thwart healthy child development, conditions that can only be countered by professionals and their programs. Both of these images are disempowering. Unfortunately, they can become self-fulfilling prophecies when parents internalize these images of their own capacity to care for their children; they become passive and powerless. In contrast, Resourceful Parents contribute to public policy rather than simply reacting to it; they are partners with professionals in caring for their children; they are protective buffers between vulnerable children and powerful institutions; they have the last word on decisions about their children.

Resourceful parents can tackle the internal/familial and external/ environmental obstacles to nurturing care for their children. They recognize that they cannot stand alone in caring for their children; they need help from competent professionals, extended family and friends, and other parents. Because they cannot do it alone, however, does not mean they are inadequate or that they cannot do it at all. Resourceful parents are empowered parents. Parent networks and self-help groups can enable parents to work together in advocacy efforts. Parents together can accomplish far more than an isolated parent knocking on the doors of unresponsive school, health, and social service systems.[1]

Characteristics of Effective Advocacy

Advocacy seeks to bring about change. Sometimes it is successful and sometimes it is not. An ethnographic study of successful child advocacy efforts found that four ingredients were always present whenever advocacy was successful [Dicker 1990].

First, successful advocates propose concrete solutions to the problems they take on. Simply railing against injustice does not bring about change. Legislators have to learn what programs have worked with a particular problem, and with what resources. Church congregations need concrete suggestions about what they can do to make a difference. It is counterproductive to report statistics of child poverty, drug abuse, teen pregnancy, and school failure without providing hope for change and avenues for action that promise to make a genuine difference. Without the means for an active response, hearers become passive, hopeless, and at some point, insensitive and hardened to the suffering of others.

Second, Dicker's study of successful advocacy efforts found that they empowered parents and/or children to make decisions affecting their lives. Proposed solutions to social problems need to be carefully thought through for both the negative and positive consequences they may have. No one can be more helpful in this process than those directly involved— parents and children. Even when family crises press parents to toss the ball for advocacy to the agency professional, at the very least, parents can serve as consultants—partners with the advocates who speak in their behalf, telling the stories that can be repeated to give flesh to abstract statistics.

Third, successful advocacy rests on finding partners inside governments or other target social systems to achieve successful implementation of changes [Dicker 1990]. Inside these social systems are people who care deeply about the problems and are committed to working for change from within. They are not unlike church professionals who have chosen to stay in church denominational work despite all its frustrations and limitations, because they believe that change has to come from the inside.

Grady Nutt, a Baptist humorist and minister, once said that the church is like Noah's Ark; if it were not for the storm outside, no one could stand the stink inside. Many agencies are filled with people who, despite the "stink" inside, realize that the storms besetting families outside the "arks" of our current social service systems are even worse. They believe that the best way to care for families is to stay inside and work within the system for reform, even if sometimes it means shoveling manure. Relationships with these partners should be cultivated.

Private agencies need friends inside the government agencies with whom they have service contracts. It is important for them to be able to speak into the ears of the state and federal legislators and administrators who shape and implement public policies. Effective advocacy calls for skill in collaboration and coalition building—among agencies, public officials, professional groups and organizations, individuals within organizations, clergy and laypeople in churches, denominational employees in different niches of different denominations, and parent groups. These people may disagree on many points, but they can find points of agreement and speak together on those.

It takes considerable skill to identify and emphasize commonalty, particularly when we are personally or professionally offended by the positions some of these people take on other matters. For example, some denominational networks of child advocates include people who range the spectrum of positions on the issue of abortion. Nevertheless, these networks are speaking in chorus on pro-life issues that affect children after birth—health care, adequate family income, and hope-filled developmental and educational opportunities.

Working in coalition calls for a delicate balance. On the one hand, too close an alliance with any other party may make it difficult to maintain one's own bearings. In some respects, it is the same issue that professionals face in family therapy; one must join the system to the extent of forming alliances with individuals in the family before one can understand the family from the inside out. On the other hand, a professional who becomes too much a member of the family loses the perspective of an outsider, of one who can challenge the rules and alter the structures. It is a difficult role to be in the system but not of the system. Maintaining a network of relationships in a variety of social systems, even some that are in direct conflict with one another, helps to avoid being overly allied with one—and sometimes the target of all.

Finally, successful advocates use a variety of strategies over a prolonged period to achieve their goals [Dicker 1990]. Change must involve educating church members and getting them involved, networking professionally, writing church congregational literature and preaching in churches, and lobbying and writing to legislators. No one strategy by itself is likely to be effective. Advocates must be able to commit themselves to processes that sometimes take a long time, with repeated failures and disappointments, before change comes. Effective advocates keep dreaming, keep believing that what they stand for is right and that right will eventually prevail.

> Sojourner Truth, a woman who could neither read nor write, pointed a way for us. She never gave up talking or fighting against slavery and the mistreatment of women, not even against odds far worse than those we and our children face today. Once a northern Ohio man rudely confronted her, asking, "Old woman, do you think that your talk about slavery does any good? Why I don't care any more for your talk than I do for the bite of a flea." "Perhaps not, but the Lord willing, I'll keep you scratching," Sojourner replied. Every single person can be a flea for justice. Enough fleas can make even the biggest dog—the biggest institutions—mighty uncomfortable. If they flick some of us off, and others of us keep coming back, we will begin to get the basic human needs of the poor heard and attended to and oil the creaks of our institutions that many say no longer work. [Edelman 1987: 112-113]

Strategies for Advocacy

Advocacy strategies should be chosen in response to the current social context in which the problem is being approached. Sosin and Caulum [1983] have suggested a model for designing advocacy strategies based on whether the context is one of alliance, neutrality, or adverseness.

Alliance

In some situations, the advocate has or can form an alliance with the decision maker she or he wants to influence. The advocate and the decision maker have some basic agreement about the importance of caring for children and families, and perhaps even about what the needs are and what the response should be. The advocate serves primarily to point out how the request being made fits the context on which both the advocate and the decision maker agree. This often means providing key information the decision maker may need to describe how the decision to be made fits the overall mission and purposes of his or her agency.

Neutrality

In a neutral situation, there is neither a positive nor a negative relationship between the advocate and the decision maker. The advocate must convince the other of the merit of the request being made. Neutral situations call on the advocate to provide key information and to bargain and negotiate.

Adverseness

Finally, in an adversarial context, disagreement is so great that the advocate has little legitimacy. The advocate must often use coercive strategies in order to be effective, mustering power as leverage for moving the decision maker. For example, threats of or actual media coverage, demonstrations, and disruptions of the social system being challenged are all adversarial strategies. The less adversarial the context, the more probable is a positive outcome of the advocacy effort. Choosing methods of advocacy to fit the context increases that probability, however. Even in a situation of alliance, the outcome of advocacy may be negative if the strategy used is not appropriate.

It is important to use the least amount of power and coercion possible to achieve the stated objective. If the advocate approaches the decision maker with accusations of being insensitive to the needs of children and families and threats of publicity if certain actions are not taken, the previously sympathetic decision maker may decide against the advocate's position out of an unwillingness to give in to coercive tactics. Yet, successful advocacy often requires willingness to use coercive strategies when nothing else will work. These tactics may be the only recourse, and may turn out to be effective, in an adversarial situation where the decision maker has indeed been overtly insensitive to the needs of children and families and where publicity may well generate a public outcry.

The Decision to Become an Advocate

Advocacy costs. It takes staff time and energy to research the issues, to establish and maintain a network of relationships, to involve others in the advocacy effort, to speak out or write letters or lobby legislators. Advocacy may make new friends for an agency, but it may also alienate others. It sometimes creates visibility for the agency in new ways and with mixed effects. It may be a task central to the agency's mission of caring for children and their families, but it may also divert the agency from providing some direct services. Each of these cost/benefit ratios calls for careful consideration.

Clients who become directly involved in advocacy also face costs. Advocacy is not always effective, and results sometimes take too long to be of direct benefit to the clients who invested themselves in the effort. Clients may reap the benefits of empowerment, however, being able to be more assertive in other areas of their lives; recognizing that they are "good" parents may consequently make them even better parents. Children sometimes can share in writing letters, telling their stories, and talking with others who have had similar experiences. But it is also true that families may find the advocacy effort an additional stress for which they simply do not have the resources. The importance of their considering carefully before involving themselves in advocacy for themselves and others should be recognized and respected.

Reid and Billups [1986] have pointed out a danger in advocacy that also must be considered. Advocacy is unjust if it empowers those whose interests are being advocated at the expense of those in a similar position who have no advocates, benefiting some while diminishing the possibility that others will benefit. For example, to advocate for free quality day care for homeless children may be unjust if no additional day care slots are made available for low-income families. Success in such an advocacy attempt would lessen the opportunities of poor families working in minimum wage jobs to obtain the limited number of good child care slots available. Many of these families are already paying a third of their wages for day care, and thus, with rising housing costs, are vulnerable themselves to homelessness.

The decision to advocate, therefore, requires careful attention to the benefits and costs to the agency, the clients, and others who may be inadvertently affected by the advocacy effort.

Involving Congregations and Other Church Organizations

Agency staff members can provide key leadership for church groups and congregations in child and family advocacy. Sometimes, agency staff members are able to inspire church groups to advocacy as they speak of the needs of the families and children they serve. They can also provide access to and develop literature and educational resources for churches to learn about the problems and to respond with social service programs and social action. Appendix 4 lists resources for congregational involvement in child and family advocacy.

Most congregations and agencies should base their advocacy efforts in service to children and their families and stay rooted in that service. The fire of advocacy is fueled by knowing and caring for actual children and families, not families as they are presented in tables of statistics about rising rates of teen pregnancy or school failure. Firsthand experience arouses compassion and commitment; there is no substitute for it.

Congregations would be wise to begin with low-profile issues and advocacy activities and proceed to high-profile, controversial issues and activities [Johnson and Long 1983]. An after-school activity program with tutoring for school-age children and teens is relatively low profile and noncontroversial. Writing to school board members advocating that the school house after-school programs in its facility is not likely to gain the church group a high profile with the general public. Urging the same school board to provide on-site nursery care for the infants and toddlers of teen parents who remain in school is more controversial. Doing so by picketing a school board meeting in collaboration with parents pushing their babies in strollers is even more likely to gain a high and controversial profile with the general public, and perhaps more importantly, with uninvolved others in the congregation, especially if the picketers are using the name of the church.

Clearly, the appropriateness of the strategy to the advocacy group's own identity and preparation for an advocacy role must also be considered seriously. Congregational advocacy begins with simply creating visibility for children in the congregation itself. Compassion for children and their families is nurtured through service programs. Congregational groups can then move from service to advocacy.

Raising the Visibility of Children

One of the first steps toward involving churches in ministry and advocacy with children and their families is helping them simply to see children. Children have been increasingly segregated from the rest of the church community, presumably because their needs are better met in programs designed for them, such as educational programs or a children's worship service. In many congregations, adults seldom see the children of other members. Many adult worship services are no longer disturbed by crying babies and six-year-olds making their way to the rest room or dropping their offering coins to roll noisily under the pews. Reversing this trend toward age segregation would better meet the needs of children—and, indeed, of persons of all ages. Children and adults both grow best in cross-generational communities.

The picture of a believing community where "crawlers, toddlers, walkers, wheelers, and runners all journey together" is a picture of God's covenant people. At the heart of the covenant is an action of being called or brought together—of being included. It is not an action of separation into individual units, but a bringing together into a whole, the forming of community [United Church of Canada 1989: 7].

Organizing a special day for including and recognizing children would begin to reverse the trend toward age segregation. Many churches celebrate a Children's Sabbath and/or Youth Sunday, when children or youths play primary roles in the community's worship. Denominational and ecumenical publications provide sermon outlines, suggested hymns and litanies, and prayers that recognize and celebrate children [e.g., Children's Defense Fund 1992, Guy 1991]. Such special services can underline a particular need of children, such as quality child care for low income families, and may even include the congregation in some advocacy effort, perhaps by providing letter paper and addresses in the worship bulletin so that members can write to legislators about a specific issue as part of an "offering of letters."

Other churches have made concentrated efforts to include children in the ongoing life of the congregation, sometimes in addition to an annual emphasis. Sunday school classes provide cross-generational programs so that persons of all ages can participate in Christian education together. In worship, children light candles, collect the offering with the adults, read scripture, and gather on the steps of the pulpit for the children's sermon. They sit with their parents in the choir, or participate in a family choir of adults and children. Special bulletins for children explain the different worship activities and provide paper-and-pencil puzzles and games related to the worship to help children stay involved. Some churches are including children in the pastoral care of the church, visiting the ill and the homebound. The children participate in committees, particularly those that directly affect them, planning for the present and the future of the church.

Some churches are reconsidering their practice of excluding children from Communion.[2] One six-year-old girl registered her opinion of the restriction: "I'm not going to say, 'We are all one body' again, because we aren't. Me and Ben don't share the bread" [Müller-Fahrenholz 1982: 25]. Groups in a variety of denominations are exploring additional ways that children can be incorporated more effectively into the life of the congregation.[3] It is easy to ignore the needs of a group of people we never see, but it is much harder when they are in our midst. As congregations include their own children in their lives and begin to respond to their needs, they are much more likely to begin to see the needs of children in society. The World Council of Churches has called for inclusion of children throughout the life of the church:

> The *oikos* [the Greek term for house or home] of God is a household within which the whole of humankind has a place. Such a household should have an atmosphere in which all the children, including the youngest, the smallest, the weakest, the most shy— and the boldest and naughtiest—know that they belong. ...There should be no lonely or unwanted child who can either come in or stand outside unregarded. The Church in many parts of the world is set against a dark scenario of oppression—oppression of the weak and, not least, the young. Its activity, and especially the way in which the young are included in its *oikos*, should stand out as a sign against this oppression—a sign which affirms that every child is of infinite value as a child of God. [Müller-Fahrenholz 1982: 13]

Just as children can be included in all arenas of church life, they can also be included in the work of the church in behalf of children and families. Advocacy is not just an adult activity. Children and youths can be powerful advocates for their own interests. Older children have the ability to empathize and a keen sense of fairness and justice. In addition, serving and advocating for others are key experiences for children's own spiritual formation.

Educating about Children

Some urban congregations have all they can do to cope with the needs of the children in their midst. The diverse needs of all our society's children are represented among their own. Other churches, in middle-class suburbs, may have little contact with poor children, although concern runs deep about drugs, alcohol, teen pregnancy, and cultural violence. Whether the needs of children are within their walls or in the community that surrounds them, congregations must learn about those needs if they are to deal with them responsibly and effectively.

Hessel [1982] suggests that education for social justice must heed the voices of four groups in learning about social issues: (1) the vulnerable population and victims of a given policy or facet of society—the children and their families; (2) the change agents who lead voluntary organizations that seek constructive changes for the sake of the vulnerable population and victims—agency staff members, key volunteers; (3) the established powers in public office and managers of corporate entities who are responsible for administering current policy—members of school boards, legislators; and (4) the independent students of major public issues whose analysis is not part of a contracted service to the powers—members of advocacy organizations, such as the Children's Defense Fund, or key faculty members of colleges and seminaries who study child and family issues [Hessel 1982]. Church agency professionals should avoid dominating the learning process with their own perspectives, and should facilitate the congregation's hearing of all four voices.

Education often takes place through the church's programs—a special study undertaken by a mission group, a weeknight fellowship's month-long focus topic, a Sunday School unit, or articles in a denominational journal. These educational programs are most effective when supported by sermons, bulletin inserts, liturgy and music, and the visual symbols of the church. Education involves not only studying the issues but also experiencing them. Congregational groups who are considering advocacy for homeless families can visit family shelters and talk to staff members and residents. Congregations concerned about health can visit neonatal intensive care facilities and public clinics, sit in the waiting rooms, ride the buses or other transportation from public housing projects to the clinics, and talk to the foster parents of children with special physical needs.

A newspaper may quote statistics about infant mortality, but words on a page can be erased from the mind by new impressions. Seeing a three-pound infant connected by tubes to life-support systems leaves a more profound and lasting imprint. Personal experiences can set hearts on fire. [Guy 1991: 53]

Guy suggests that site visits are most effective when the agency director is involved in the planning. The following would help make a visit useful for participants: (1) basic information and brochures about the program provided before the visit; (2) guidance in being as unobtrusive as possible during the visit, especially if clients are present; (3) guidance in not indicating knowledge of any client they may recognize unless the other speaks first, and the importance of confidentiality; and (4) time afterwards to discuss what they learned and how they felt [Guy 1991].

One of the most difficult, but most potentially powerful forms of education is arranging for adults to talk to children. Children can talk about what they do and how they feel when they are home alone during the hours between the end of school and a parent's return from work. Children can describe their schools, their worries, their experiences of poverty. It is not usually appropriate for concerned church groups to interview child clients in an agency's programs. But children can write their stories or tell them on tape, and any identifying data can be changed. Hearing children's stories, together with a visit to the agency and a talk with tutors, child care workers, and other staff members, can galvanize congregational groups into action.

Consider the impact of this story, told by a 10-year-old:

I was asked to tell you what it's like to live in a single-parent home with no money. Sometimes it's sad because I feel different from other kids—for instance, when other kids get to go to fun places and I can't because I don't have enough money and they do. Most of my friends get an allowance but I don't because my mom doesn't have enough money to pay me. They get to get the things they want and need and I don't. The other day in school we had this balloon contest, and it only cost one dollar, and out of three years I haven't been able to get one.

Me and my brother are a little hard on shoes. This summer the only shoes we had were thongs, and when church time came, the only shoes we had to wear were one pair of church shoes. The one that got them first got to wear them. The one that didn't had to wear a pair of my mom's tennis shoes or my sister's.

I have a big brother. He is not my real brother. He is with the Big Brothers and Big Sisters Association. Once I tried to tell my big brother about welfare. It was so embarrassing I was about to cry. I don't like Joe just because he takes me to a fun place every week; I like Joe because he makes me feel special. Sometimes I pray that I won't be poor no more and sometimes I sit up at night and cry. But it didn't change anything. Crying just helps the hurt and the pain. It doesn't change anything. One day, I asked my mom why the kids always tease me and she said because they don't under-stand, but I do understand about being on welfare and being poor, and it can hurt. [Guy 1991: 27-28]

It helps congregations to grasp the issues if they can be localized. National poverty statistics can be brought home by state and community figures. The Children's Defense Fund publishes state statistics annually, as does the Annie E. Casey Foundation's Kids Count project. Local government staff, public and private agencies, and school boards and clinics can provide key information. Day care organizations can give figures for the number of children in day care and the number of children on waiting lists for subsidized care.

Choosing the Issues

The needs of children span the spectrum from education to health care, from the affluent child's need to learn values of social justice to the need of the child in poverty for a decent pair of shoes to wear to church. In many ways, the resources with which we have been entrusted as leaders of the church in ministry to children and their families seem like a widow's mite in the face of the need. We cannot fill all the gaps, feed all the hungry children, stop all the teenage pregnancies, or prevent all child abuse and neglect. The professional's own values, concerns, and contexts, as well as those of the congregation, play a significant role in choosing a target for the church's concern. Some Christians may be familiar with the advice to "grow where we are planted." We cannot be everywhere and do everything, but we can be faithful to service in the place where we find ourselves.

It is wise to choose issues that the congregation can understand, or can come to understand. Specific needs to which specific, effective responses can be made, such as the need of working poor and vulnerable families for affordable, quality child care, will engage a congregation. These needs and responses can then be linked to larger efforts, uniting the congregation with other congregations with similar concerns. Specific issues are usually linked to broader issues, such as child poverty. Clarifying these linkages can highlight how the drop-in-the-bucket efforts of the congregation may have widespread ripple effects.

As Schorr [1988] has pointed out, because the causes of "rotten outcomes" such as teen pregnancy, school failure, and family violence are interrelated, not every factor that contributes to rotten outcomes for children must be changed before the incidence of those outcomes can be reduced. Correcting a vision problem or providing some needed tutoring will improve the chances of school success even for the child of a poor, unmarried teenage parent. This is good news, generating hope and excitement in congregations that otherwise may feel despairing and powerless in the face of overwhelming need.

The advocacy efforts congregations are called on to make should hold out a good chance of making a positive difference. Christians who learn that they can make a difference find strength to commit themselves to some of the longer, harder struggles that have to be taken on. Eventually, congregations can come to terms with the long, hard work, sometimes with imperceptible short-term results, that is part of being leaven in the lump.

> Justice is not cheap. Justice is not quick. It is not ever finally achieved... The Bible is replete with the images and power of small things which achieve great ends when they are grounded in faith: a mustard seed, a jawbone, a stick, a slingshot, a widow's mite. We must not, in trying to think about how we can make a big difference, ignore the small daily differences we can make, which, over time, add up to big differences that we often cannot foresee. [Edelman 1987: 107]

Ultimately, all advocates face dark nights when they feel very small compared to the powers that are arrayed against them. Advocates can feel lonely and vulnerable. Advocacy takes grit and determination, sometimes in the face of what seem impossible odds. In 1934, Grace Abbott, an early head of the U.S. Children's Bureau, described the role of the child advocate this way:

> Sometimes when I get home at night in Washington I feel as though I had been in a great traffic jam. The jam is moving toward the Hill where Congress sits in judgment on all the administrative agencies of the government. In that traffic jam are all kinds of vehicles...There are all kinds of conveyances, for example, that the army can put in the street—tanks, gun carriages, trucks...the handsome limousines in which the Department of Commerce rides...the barouches in which the Department of State rides in such dignity. It seems to me as I stand on the sidewalk watching it becomes more congested and more difficult, and then because the responsibility is mine and I must, I take a very firm hold on

the handles of the baby carriage and I wheel it into the traffic. [Children's Defense Fund 1991: 7]

It helps to know that this is part of advocacy, that Grace Abbott and Marian Wright Edelman and other great advocates for children have also had to come to terms with feeling small in a great battle. It takes more than knowing that others share one's feelings. One needs hope and faith. In the words of Shel Silverstein [1974: 27]:

> Listen to the MUSTN'TS, child, listen to the DON'TS, listen to the SHOULDN'TS, the IMPOSSIBLES, the WON'TS. Listen to the NEVER HAVES, then listen close to me—ANYTHING can happen, child, ANYTHING can be.

Or, in the words of the Apostle Paul:

> Have no anxiety about anything, but in everything by prayer and supplication with thanksgiving let your requests be made known to God. And the peace of God, which passes all understanding, will keep your hearts and your minds in Christ Jesus. Finally, brethren, whatever is true, whatever is honorable, whatever is just, whatever is pure, whatever is lovely, whatever is gracious, if there is any excellence, if there is anything worthy of praise, think about these things. ...I can do all things in him who strengthens me. (Phil. 4:6-8, 13)

Avoid Blaming the Victims

William Ryan's book *Blaming the Victim* became a landmark almost immediately upon its publication in 1971. Most helping professionals are familiar with his premise that making victims responsible for their own plight is terrifyingly simple and absolves others of responsibility. Years after Ryan named the game, it still is played. Those working with congregations must be especially sensitive to how easy it is to reach the conclusion that victims caused their own suffering. Ryan describes four steps in the blame game:

> (1) Identify a social problem (such as the high dropout rate and low job skills of teenagers in underclass families); (2) Study those

affected by the problem and discover in what ways they are different from the rest of us as a consequence of deprivation and injustice (in this case, low reading skills); (3) Define the difference as the cause of the social problem itself (poor teenagers drop out because they do not have reading skills); (4) Develop a humanitarian action program to correct the differences (tutoring and remedial programs). [Ryan 1971]

The game encourages looking sympathetically at those who "have" the problem in question, then separating them out and defining them in some way as a special group, different from the population in general. It is an ideological process, a set of ideas and concepts deriving from systematically motivated, but unintended, distortions of reality. An ideology develops from the collective unconscious of a group or class and is rooted in a class-based interest in maintaining the status quo. Instead, Ryan would suggest that problems are a function of the social arrangements of the community or society, and since society is imperfect and inequitable, that such problems are both predictable and preventable. There is not something inherent in poor children that keeps them from learning to read. There are factors inherent in our community and school structures that make it difficult for them to learn. Children living in poverty do not have the preparation for learning through preschool experiences that middle class families provide. They do not have hope and models for success that encourage them to learn.

Does this mean that churches should not offer tutoring programs for poor children who are having difficulty learning to read? Of course not! But first, church members may need help in discovering the processes that create insurmountable barriers to success in school for many poor children. Tutors can become outstanding advocates for universal programs to prepare young children for school, to help parents help their children, and even to build a more equitable economic system that can lift all children and their families out of poverty. Describing the game is one of the most effective ways of confronting the victim-blaming process in churches and in family support program volunteers, showing how it works in the social problems the congregational group is addressing. The group can then be led to look for the multitude of alternative explanations for the suffering.

For example, they can envision the validity not only of tutoring children vulnerable to school failure, but also of becoming advocates for family support programs and preschool education programs that have been demonstrated to substantially improve the performance of poor children in school.

Nurturing Compassion

Compassion is the opposite of blaming. Blaming looks for how the other is different and assigns pathology to that difference. Compassion puts itself in the place of the other, and experiences with the other. Compassion means "to suffer with"; it is the foundation for advocacy. Jesus was moved to compassion over and over.[4] His compassion was the first step in making visible the abnormality of human suffering that had become accepted as simply the way things are. Compassion is not simply generous good will, but also criticism of the system, forces, and ideologies that produce the hurt. Jesus entered into the hurt of persons and finally came to embody it [Brueggeman 1978]. His life represented God's compassion, God's taking on human form in order to suffer with us, to take on our experiences, even our death, and in taking them on, to challenge them. Christians who live as Christ take on the hurt of victims and challenge the systems that cause the hurt, making it difficult for others to remain blind to human suffering.

The Samaritan (Luke 10:33) and the father of the prodigal son (Luke 15:20) embody this alternative consciousness based on compassion. Those who passed by the wounded traveler were indifferent, numb. The Samaritan noticed the pain and ended the indifference. Feeling the pain led to response. Jesus made it clear that numbness to the suffering of others leads to God's judgment (Luke 16:19-21). To be a Christian is to take on the suffering of brothers and sisters and children, to bear their burdens as one's own, to live compassionately. But this is not the end; compassion brings transformation. The end of numbness brings potential for change.

From Service to Advocacy

The move from service to advocacy, from compassionate ministry to prophetic action, is difficult for many churches. Services—"social ministry"—are feeding the hungry, giving drink to the thirsty, welcoming strangers, caring for hurting neighbors, and other deeds of love and mercy. Social ministry includes case advocacy, advocacy aimed at obtaining goods and services for a particular person or family. Social action attempts to change the sinful social structures that harm a whole class of persons; it is class advocacy.

Delos Miles [1986] uses the story of the good neighbor in Luke 10:25-37 to illustrate the difference between social ministry and social action. The Samaritan who responded to the needs of the wounded traveler, binding up his injuries and paying for lodging until he was well enough to travel, engaged in social ministry. If he had sought to change the conditions that led to the Jericho Road robbery and mugging, however, that would have been social action. The Samaritan's ministry sprang from compassion. Had he chosen to advocate for more police patrolling, programs to provide constructive activities for young people who might otherwise turn to thievery and violence, or a "traveler's watch" program that paired lone travelers so that they did not have to walk alone, those too would have been responses springing from compassion.

Churches and denominations have taken varying stands on whether churches and their organizations should engage in social action. Many Christians think social and political action are inappropriate for the church, although they encourage individual Christians to work toward structural changes. Of particular significance has been the view of the relationship between evangelism—"the attempt to convert persons and structures to the lordship of Jesus Christ" [Miles 1986: 15]—and social action. Are they equally important but independent responsibilities of the church, functions of the church that mutually support one another, or functions in conflict with one another?

Leighton Ford [1982] has suggested that social responsibility can be seen in six ways in relation to evangelism: as a distraction from evangelism ("Why shift furniture when the house is burning?"), as a result of evangelism ("Changed people will change the world"), as preparation for evangelism ("Hungry people can't listen to sermons"), as a partner of evangelism ("Lives change when we treat people like people as well as souls"), as an essential element of evangelism ("A person is woven of one cloth, body and soul"), or as an equivalent of evangelism ("A cup of cold water for the thirsty speaks just as loudly of the love of God as any word that can be said").

A meeting of the World Evangelical Fellowship and the Lausanne Committee for World Evangelization considered the relationship between evangelism and social responsibility in 1982. The delegates concluded that three relationships between the two disciplines are "equally valid": social concern as a consequence of evangelism; social concern as a bridge to evangelism; and social concern as a partner of evangelism [Williamson 1982]. The most balanced approach appears to be seeing the two as partners.

> If you would see evangelism and social involvement in partnership, look at how Jesus combined the two in His life and ministry. His ministry was characterized by both proclamation (*kerygma*) and service (*diaconia*). The two went hand in hand, with His words explaining His works, and His works dramatizing His words. His words and deeds were expressions of compassion for persons. ...The gospel of the kingdom of God is compromised and caricatured by those who reduce it to the changing of social structures or to the changing of individual persons. [Miles 1986: 22]

As churches become more involved in compassionate service to children and their families, as they come to experience what it is like to live in poverty, to see no end to the stresses that plague one's family, to be unable to read as a youngster and see no reason to learn, they become less caught up in arguments about service versus advocacy, evangelism versus social action. These arguments seem ridiculous when bright youngsters are growing up despairing of a life any different from the poverty and powerlessness of their parents, when babies are being born sickly because their mothers received no prenatal care, when infants born addicted to drugs are housed in hospitals because nobody wants them and there are not enough foster homes.

"Sometimes I would like to ask God why He allows poverty, famine and injustice when He could do something about it."

"Well—why don't you ask Him?"

"Because I'm afraid God might ask me the same question." [Anonymous, from Children's Defense Fund 1991: 13]

Notes

1. The Parents—Let's Unite for Kids (PLUK) group has developed an excellent advocacy training program for parents of children with emotional handicaps [Kelker 1987]. Other resources for empowering parents include Boukydis 1986; Children's Defense Fund 1982; Cochran [n.d.]; and Garland 1990b.

2. The communion of infants and children has been practiced in the Orthodox traditions since the days of the early church. The first references to the communion of children are contemporary with references to infant baptism in the apostolic fathers. In 1215, the Fourth Lateran Council stated that the obligation to partake in communion was to be postponed until the "year of discretion," when children could discriminate between the Eucharist and an ordinary meal [Müller-Fahrenholz 1982]. Other Christian faith groups require confirmation before admission to communion. Churches that emphasize believers' baptism often limit participation in communion to those who have been baptized.

3. For resources to help incorporate children into the life of the congregation, see Greater Minneapolis Council of Churches 1990; Garland 1993; Guy 1991; Heusser 1985; Larose 1981; Pople 1986; and United Church of Canada 1989.

4. Matt. 14:14; Mark 6:34; Mark 8:2; Luke 7:12-13; Matt. 9:35-36.

CHAPTER 7

Resources for the Church's Services to Children and Their Families

CHURCH AGENCIES HAVE EXPERIENCED DRAMATIC CHANGES in the population they serve and the kinds of services they provide. Just as dramatic, however, have been the changes in support for agencies' work—funding, staff, and members of governing boards. Obviously, the changes in the work of agencies and the changes in their support bases are interrelated. Changes in the work of church agencies both respond to and shape the changes in their financial support, staff configuration, and governance.

Note: Major contributors to this chapter were David Graves, A.C.S.W., formerly Executive Director of Home of the Innocents, Inc., Louisville, Kentucky, and now Executive Director of Brooklawn Youth Services, Louisville, Kentucky; and Judith A. Lambeth, A.C.S.W., Executive Director of Maryhurst, Inc., Louisville, Kentucky. The contributions of the staffs and boards of directors of Home of the Innocents and Maryhurst are greatly appreciated.

Funding

Virtually all church agencies are by definition not-for-profit, tax-exempt organizations funded by fees for services, by donations and charitable gifts, or, in the majority of cases, by a mix of both. Many agencies are moving to budgets based on fees for services as services become more expensive and, in some cases, as government funds or even private health insurance dollars become available to underwrite particular services to clients.

Church agencies are obtaining funds from government programs by offering client services that government agencies purchase from the private sector rather than providing directly. In many instances, church agencies are operating as franchises of the public child welfare system; the state defines the model (e.g., therapeutic foster care), which is then delivered by the private agency contracting with the state to offer services.

Thus, for many church-related agencies, a large proportion of funding is coming from government sources. Reid and Stimpson [1987] followed the reports of the National Conference of Catholic Charities, one indicator of trends in church agencies. In 1987, government funding constituted approximately half the funding of these Catholic agencies. At the same time, however, Catholic Charities experienced a gradual increase in church support (from 13.3% in 1979 to 17.5% in 1982), while United Way funding gradually decreased (from 11% in 1979 to 8.9% in 1982).[1]

In a regional study of Episcopal, Lutheran, and Salvation Army agencies, Netting [1982] found that no agency was solely supported by its parent religious body; most sponsoring religious bodies contributed only one third or less of the agency's budget. In Netting's study, government funds provided approximately half of these agencies' budgets, as they did for Catholic Charities. United Way support was also decreasing, mainly because agencies felt that the United Way exerted too much control for too little money. Barber's 1990 survey of agencies that were members of the National Association of Homes for Children in one region of the country found no relationship between the size of the agency and the extent of government funding. The agencies surveyed ranged from those with annual budgets of less than $500,000 to those with annual budgets of more than $5,000,000.

In my own 1992 national survey of church-related agencies that belonged to the National Association of Homes for Children, I found that the 79 responding agencies received 28% of their budgets directly from the contributions of churches and religious organizations [Garland 1992]. The majority (61) of the agencies received funding from state and federal grants and contracts as well, averaging 44% of their budgets. Private donations contributed 20% of the budgets for the 61 agencies that received these donations, and 58 agencies received 21% of their budgets from endowment income. Presumably, these private donations and endowments often came from the sponsoring church or religious group's members. Although 44 agencies received client fees, the fees contributed only 10.5% of the agencies' budgets. (It is probable, however, that at least some respondents were including in this figure only fees paid directly by clients or their insurance. Much of the government money they received came from purchase-of-service contracts.) Twenty-seven agencies received an average of 11.8% of their income from other sources (e.g., income from property, United Way, foundations, estates, and fundraisers).

Therapeutic foster care programs, which are relatively expensive compared to other foster care programs, account for some of the increase in government purchase of services from church and other private agencies. Snodgrass and Bryant [1989] surveyed 42 therapeutic foster care programs in predominantly volunteer (private) agencies; they did not indicate how many of these were church-related, however. They found that 93% were funded by state or local public agency contracts or service grants, which, in turn, derived largely from federal programs such as Title XX. Only one program was funded entirely by private foundation support, and one reported 90% funding by direct charitable contributions. Four received supplemental assistance from endowments or foundations. Typically however, therapeutic foster care programs operate on a purchase-of-service basis.

Issues around Government Funding

Some church agencies have been receiving government funds since their beginnings. For others, however, reliance on government funding represents a dramatic, if quiet, metamorphosis from a financial structure that had been dependent almost exclusively on charitable gifts from individuals, congregations, and denominational budgets. Such a working relationship with government is more congenial to some church traditions than to others. For example, some Episcopal traditions see church and state as inseparable aspects of one commonwealth; in general, Episcopalians perceive themselves as part of society, not over against it [Horsburgh 1990]. Baptist tradition, on the other hand, has emphasized separation between church and state and has looked with considerable suspicion on any enterprise jointly undertaken.[2]

In addition to the significance government funding may have for a particular denominational tradition, a reliance on government raises several practical matters that warrant careful consideration by agency administrators, staff members, and governing boards.

Loss of Identity and Independence

The decision to accept government funds and offer expensive per-client services appears to be one that many agencies are making out of expediency rather than careful consideration of the agency's long-term mission and what it may cost to become a quasi-public institution. The funds are available. The need for therapeutic foster care, residential treatment services, or other reimbursable services is pressing, and may even go unmet if the church agency does not respond. The combination of slowed growth and even decline in many mainline denominations during financial recession has stagnated funding for church agencies at a time when the complexities and costs of children's services have greatly increased, and the pull toward government funding is difficult to resist.

Administrators and boards of directors may try to comfort themselves by noting that only a portion of their funding comes from government sources, that the agency retains its role as a church agency because a portion of its funding also comes from church sources, and that its own board of directors still controls its destiny. Some are using a rationale similar to the one Michigan's Hillsdale College has used in its conflict with the federal government: funds given on a student-by-student basis so youths can purchase an education do not make the college a government organization any more than the grocery store is a government agency because it accepts customers' food stamps and Social Security checks [Brendtro 1982]. Nevertheless, the relationship may carry with it some significant risks.

Funding often dictates the parameters of service. An agency may not be free to plan services if the child "belongs" to a state agency with strict limits as to the length or nature of services it will reimburse. In some instances, a state agency determines the length of time a child can receive contracted services, and it retains responsibility for family services while the church agency works with a child in residential care.

> Jimmy, age 12, was placed in a church-related residential child care center 200 miles from his home because he had twice broken into neighbors' homes and stolen from them. Both times, he stole food and camping equipment so that he could run away from home. The juvenile court judge decided not to adjudicate him a delinquent on condition that he be sent outside the county to a residential care facility for six months and that the county child welfare staff work with the family. Accordingly, Jimmy was placed in the residential child care center as a state ward, with fees paid by the state child welfare agency.

> The staff of the residential child care center was discouraged from working with the family, since that responsibility had been assigned by the court to the county child welfare agency and would have been difficult to meet in any case because of the geographical distance. Instead, the residential child care staff was expected to "treat" the boy for six months, at which time he would be returned to the family. No arrangements were made for the impoverished family to visit their son; on two occasions, he was sent alone on the 200-mile trip by bus to visit them for holidays, as arranged by the county child welfare agency. More pressing cases harassed the family's child welfare worker; he was one of a few workers responsible for investigation of child abuse and neglect complaints in the large rural county. Nevertheless, he visited the family home several times while Jimmy was in care, but not during the holidays when Jimmy was at home. Conse-

quently, no work was done with Jimmy and his family concerning the family conflict that twice had driven him to try to run away, much less to prepare for his return home. Jimmy was returned home at the end of six months with the stated agreement that the county worker would provide the family with follow-up services.

Contracts between a church agency and a governmental child welfare program often mean that the church agency loses control over fundamentals, such as the definition of a case and the standards that shape services. Too often, these become defined by cost-saving rather than programmatic criteria [Hart 1988].

Some of the most backward child care programs, however, are those that insist on accepting no government funding, all the while unable to support quality programs on the funds that the church provides [Brendtro 1982]. It is virtually impossible to retain total independence in services or in funding when the problems children and their families face are such a tangle of complexities.

Vulnerability to Changes in Public Policies and Public Agencies
Agencies that receive government money for services find themselves vulnerable to political decisions regarding federal and state expenditures. The shifting demands of the public bureaucracy may require frequent and costly administrative adjustments on the part of the church agency, sometimes entailing large volumes of paperwork [Kramer and Grossman 1987; Snodgrass and Bryant 1989]. Because the agency is not part of the government system, it frequently will not have an inside voice in making decisions. Operating in such a climate requires considerable assertiveness on the part of the agency to build networks with influential individuals in public agencies, to collaborate with other private agencies operating in the same context, and to lobby governmental officials for support of key legislation. All of these activities take time and expertise and consume resources not reimbursable from the public funds that make these activities necessary.

Because of the vulnerability government funds create, many agency administrators [e.g., Baker 1989] recommend that church agencies should limit government contract dollars to under 30% of the total agency budget, so that voluntary dollars are their primary funding source. If an agency does receive a large share of its budget from government contracts (40% or more), contracting with several government agencies with incomes from different sources may reduce the agency's vulnerability. Cahill [1981: 114] states flatly that "an operating budget with less than 50% derived from nongovernmental dollars is an invitation to disaster." The balance between government and private dollars demands consistent review and disciplined attention to the agency's mission and objectives. Agencies become vulnerable to fragmentation and segmentation of services as they adjust to government requirements for the expenditure of funds and for accountability [Kramer and Grossman 1987].

Loss of Freedom to Innovate
The church agency with private funding is often able to develop specialized services that have not yet been recognized as public responsibilities. The hope is that the community in time will recognize the need and respond with public support, sometimes freeing the agency to focus on other needs. The church agency with private support thus has the freedom and responsibility to experiment with new program areas and service methods [Johnson 1981]. For example, the innovative Homebuilders program of intensive home services for families with children at imminent risk for out-of-home placement began as an experimental program in a Catholic agency in Tacoma, Washington [Schorr 1988].

That is not to say that public agencies never develop innovative, experimental programs—they do. Nor is it to ignore the fact that many privately funded church agencies become so absorbed with day-to-day administration and the raising of funds that no energy is left for experimentation or innovation. Even so, privately funded church agencies are usually in a better position to innovate. They can act more quickly than public agencies to meet newly emerging or newly recognized needs, or to implement new methods and approaches. They do not have to wait for legislation to be passed or for large bureaucracies to gear up for change. They are not obligated to serve the whole population, as public agencies are. The obligation to serve everyone sometimes leaves public agencies with little maneuverability in planning specialized, experimental services with specific groups.

Sometimes, this ability to maneuver and innovate is a positive factor in the relationship between agencies and governments. Large government agencies may find it difficult to make dramatic changes in programming or establish new services. The church agency can respond more quickly and be Johnny-on-the-spot when government funds are made available for a new service program. Church agencies may also be able to convince government bodies that services they are already providing are worthy of funding, so these services can be expanded and offered on a larger scale. As the agency begins to accept government funding, however, its role as an innovator, the very role that created the funding in the first place, is diminished.

Loss of Freedom to Advocate

Government funding also has a profound impact on an agency's credibility as an advocate. It is difficult to assume a confrontational role with social systems that are dipping from the same pot or actually funding the church agency. "An agency's freedom and effectiveness in social action or advocacy are in inverse proportions to the amount of public money it receives" [Manser 1974: 426]. Gilbert and Specht [1974] express concern that by developing purchase of care contracts with government agencies, an agency may forfeit some of its ability to express new or unpopular ideas, to be the guardian of pluralistic values, and to critique public policy.

The church agency's role as an advocate of reform in public policy may be at risk, however, whether or not the agency receives public money. In 1934, in an effort to exclude organizations that were mere fronts for private interest lobbying, Congress revised the Internal Revenue Code as applied to "religious" organizations to state that they shall be exempt from taxation so long as no substantial part of their activities attempts to influence legislation. The definition of *substantial* was left to the Internal Revenue Service. On this basis, the IRS can threaten loss of tax-exempt status if churches and their agencies become seriously involved in public affairs. For example, the National Council of Churches, which has been an active voice in public life, was recently threatened with loss of its tax exemption pending a careful examination of its financial records [Wood 1986].

Obviously, the loss of tax exempt status would have dire consequences for most church agencies. There appears to be no resolution of the continuing debate over the extent to which church and state should be separate and its practical applications for the financial relations between government and church agencies and their influence on each other. The debate itself, however, will continue to influence—and be influenced by—church agencies' willingness to speak out as advocates for children and their families.

Establishment of Agency Norms by Government Funding Sources
In addition to the shape that government funding sometimes imposes on services, this funding also brings with it the possibility that the agency will be forced to conform to norms that operate in the public sector, including nondiscrimination in hiring practices. Many church agencies currently hire staff members who identify themselves as Christians or belong to a particular denomination. Norms for the public service sector include proscriptions against promoting religion; many agencies, however, have mission statements and program objectives calling for the promulgation of religious beliefs. To the extent that the agency's mission reflects the church's calling to service and aims at achieving the church's goals, state money received by the agency could be construed as supporting religion [Prince 1991]. This issue has continued to be raised for almost a century without any resolution. Mayer et al. [1977: 205] have concluded that the receipt of government funds causes the "secularization" of child welfare services, and assert that sectarian group child care has practically disappeared, with notable exceptions in some southern states: "Though the sponsorship is sectarian, the institutions are nonsectarian in the use of their services and the sources of most of their income."

On one hand, then, it appears that church agencies will continue to provide services that are reimbursed through government funds. The money is making possible programs that church agencies could not carry out on their own without sacrificing other programs that do not have the possibility for such funding support. In partnership, church agencies and public funds can provide carefully tailored and highly effective services to children and families whom neither church nor state could reach without that partnership. For example, church agencies can recruit, train, and retain highly effective treatment foster parents for children with special needs, paying them with state contract funds. Some of these parents would never have been available for recruitment by a public agency, but they readily identify with and are challenged by the church agency's mission and religious context.

Church agencies should walk down this path carefully, with eyes wide open and looking both behind and ahead for the intended and unintended effects of such funding on the church agency's current programs, historic and future mission, and relationship with churches and church organizations. They should also prepare themselves to respond to accusations that such funding relationships violate the constitutional requirement for separation of church and state.

Funding and Support from Churches and Other Sources

Church agencies face funding considerations not only with regard to government grants and fees for services, but also with regard to churches, denominational and other religious organizations, and other private funding sources that undergird them. Of the $65 billion given to charities in the United States in 1983, religious organizations received 48.8%. Dollar amounts of giving increased from $69 per capita in 1961 to $278.67 in 1983, an increase of 303%. In constant 1967 dollars, however, the increase was only from $77.01 in 1961 to $93.39 in 1983—a gain of 21.3%, in real terms, or slightly less than 1% each year. Therefore, stewardship has been a major focus of church denominations [Jacquet 1985]. Church agencies have often had to carry on with minimal budget increases when the costs of providing professional services to clients were skyrocketing.

Maintaining Diversity of Funding

If agencies subscribe to the fundraising principle that they should never receive more than 30% of their funding from any one source [Pooley and Littell 1986], maintaining diversity may be a demanding and time-consuming task that involves not only administrators, but also service professionals in the community and its churches. It is tempting to view every church consultation and invitation to speak to a congregation as a chance to make an implicit or explicit plea for financial support. Nevertheless, agencies with successful programs and solid finances may find it easier to generate financial support than those that communicate to potential donors their desperate need for money.

Shortly after David Graves assumed directorship of Home of the Innocents, a church-sponsored emergency shelter for children, a local newspaper article described the Home's desperate financial plight. Instead of the hoped-for outpouring of gifts from the community, the agency staff received phone calls from vendors not wanting to sell them food or supplies except on a cash-and-carry basis. Graves commented on this experience [1991]: "If the word gets out that you are going bankrupt or that you can't meet your payroll, you might as well give up on raising any money, because people do not want to give money to an agency that looks like it has mismanaged its resources or that is not going to be around in the future."

People give money to programs that appear to be accomplishing their objectives, programs where they feel their contribution can make a real difference in the lives of children and families, programs that appear to be more focused on service than they are on institutional survival.

Financial Liability

A particularly sensitive issue many agencies wrestle with is that of financial liability: To what extent do churches and denominations that support the agency bear fiscal responsibility for it? The principle of ascending liability suggests that one organization (the denomination) may be held responsible for the liabilities of another (a child welfare agency operating under denominational auspices).

In 1978, Pacific Homes Corporation, a chain of United Methodist retirement communities in California, Arizona, and Hawaii, filed bankruptcy. A class-action suit by residents against the denomination followed. For the first time in history, a major international religious denomination was considered responsible for an unincorporated association. The out-of-court settlement cost the United Methodists 21 million dollars [Netting 1992].

The case has had obvious application to the relationship between church child welfare agencies and supporting denominations; most church agencies have moved toward legally independent status. For some, that has meant a legal change or clarification in status; they now identify themselves not as a "church agency" but as a "church-related agency." It is conceivable that the legal meaning of church affiliation will range in the future from the assumption of total financial responsibility to the use of a church name only as a marketing tool [Netting 1992]. At the same time that the legal distance between many agencies and their supporting denominations is widening, however, concerted efforts are being made to retain and even strengthen the sense of emotional investment and ownership by churches.

Staff Members

Changes toward greater financial and legal independence for church agencies from the churches and religious organizations that created them have been both responsible for, and a response to, greater professionalization in child welfare agencies. The shift to professionalism has often been described as a pull from one side of a continuum to the other. The core staff of agencies has shifted from caring Christian volunteers to professionals hired for their expertise in child and family services; the professional staff member's religious affiliation may not even be considered in the hiring process. In fact, all agencies accredited through the Council on Accreditation of Services for Families and Children must have a clear affirmative action policy and must hire personnel without any discrimination, including discrimination on religious grounds. The Council was formed in 1978 through the joint efforts of the Family Service Association of America and the Child Welfare League of America. Since then it has been joined by some of the larger religious organizations, including the National Conference of Catholic Charities, the Lutheran Social Service System, and the Association of Jewish Family and Children's Agencies [Reid and Stimpson 1987].

This policy of nondiscrimination creates the potential for great tension with the mission, culture, and values of the church agencies affiliated with these bodies.

Many church agencies have avoided choosing between personal faith and professional training as the primary criterion for staff, trying instead to combine them. They apparently do so in spite of the pressure in professional organizations toward religious nondiscrimination. In my survey of agencies that are members of the National Association of Homes for Children (mentioned earlier), 46% of the executive directors responding to the survey stated that their agencies require their social workers to be Christians. Only 16% require that social workers be members of particular denominations or churches, however, while 19% require their staff members to attend church with some degree of regularity. Additionally, 10% of the directors indicated other requirements for social workers, including support of the agency's mission as Christian ministry, attendance at the campus chapel services when on duty, modeling Christian behavior, and commitment to Christian faith.

Almost half of the respondents reported, on the other hand, that none of these religious requirements apply for their social work staff. Apparently, agencies are divided between those that do and those that do not consider personal faith and its expression and professional credentials both critical staff qualifications. One would guess that expectations for religious behavior would be at least as significant for child care workers as for social workers. Many residential agencies still require child care workers and the children for whom they are responsible to attend community church services, thus in effect controlling the church participation of those staff members when they are on duty.

Keith White [1986] offers the Christian community as a model for staffing a residential center. He suggests that in many subtle ways, a monastic model of community has underpinned the ethos and structure of group care facilities. Monastic communities were built on strong vows shared by their members, with a commitment that embraced all of their lives, not just their employment. Communities continue to serve as chosen alternatives to the family for many persons, at least for a portion of their lives. White describes his own experiences at Mill Grove, located in East

London, England. Mill Grove began as a typical children's home, largely cut off from the surrounding community and with a clear demarcation between the staff and the children. Over the decades, however, the boundaries have blurred, instead of becoming more distinct as they have in other children's homes. By now the community at Mill Grove is rather like a rambling foster family, with several retired people, former residents grown to adulthood who have returned for varying periods, and children of various ages. There is no age at which children are required to leave.

Such an alternative community will not be a family in every sense of the word, White notes, nor should it attempt to be so, but the kind of cross-generational, long-term community he describes can meet many of the needs generally provided by family. Mill Grove is supported by a world-wide network held together by informal links. It is independent of any church or denomination. All the adult "carers" are Christians who have committed themselves to being full-time residents, who gather for prayer each morning, and whose shared faith provides the underlying continuity and climate for the family. As a consequence, children in residence experience a security unusual for residential care settings. "If one of the problems of past institutional care was that children languished in it too long, one of the most pressing problems now is that too few children find a secure base in or through the social work system" [White 1986: 91].

Not all residential care programs can offer the kind of community that White describes, nor should they. But the model of Christian community deserves a closer look from church agencies. The decision to hire a staff with religious faith commitments congruent with the religious milieu of the agency is sometimes, in fact, sound professional practice, not narrow-minded discrimination. To the extent that an agency needs to speak the language of church congregations, understand and share their world view, and provide them with leadership in Christian social ministries, the agency needs to hire professionals with the knowledge, skills, and values to do so. At issue may not be only the professional's faith commitment, but also her or his knowledge and experience with church leadership roles.

Undoubtedly, expectations for religious behavior lead to different kinds of agency environments from those where religious faith is not a factor in staff employment. Agencies with restrictive hiring policies are likely to have a more homogeneous staff than agencies that impose no expectations for religious behavior on their staff members. Fewer restrictions mean greater diversity, which may bring a variety of skills and experiences from which to draw, but also differing values and beliefs about the work and aims of the agency. Creativity, innovation, conflict, dissension, and disillusion may all be products of such diversity. One staff supervisor of a church agency described the diversity in her agency:

> A number of my staff are fundamentalist Christians who don't want to try any new program or method unless I can quote chapter and verse out of the Bible as to why we are doing what we are doing. Several of my colleagues are not Christians; for them, this agency is simply a service for family and children who need what we offer; they have no commitment or sense of our relationship to the church. A couple of the program directors are very liberal in their theology and critical of the church; they want us to develop programs that focus more on social justice and social policy and less on direct services, and want to avoid the churches as much as possible. Then there are the church people who claim this as "their" agency and have this picture in their minds of these sweet little children we serve who will be so grateful to receive their hand-me-down clothing and toys, a far cry from the difficult adolescents we actually have in care. Everyone has a different idea of who we serve, what we ought to be doing, and, most importantly, why. I have to relate to all these different groups. No wonder I feel stressed!

Personal Characteristics of Staff Members

Professional staff members and volunteers who work in church agencies in response to a sense of spiritual calling or a living out of their religious beliefs bring personal characteristics to the task that reflect their faith and spiritual development. On the one hand, they may exhibit a narrow moralism, an overly judgmental attitude, a sense of guilt for their own real or perceived shortcomings, and a narrow definition of what families and children ought to be like. On the other hand, they may exhibit an amazing tolerance and flexibility, a willingness to understand and forgive, extraordinary commitment to the task and to the client, and a deep feeling of common humanity and humility. It is not unusual for both sets of characteristics to reside in the same staff person, one set or the other holding sway in different circumstances and at different times. Sometimes, tolerance, flexibility, and empathy will be easily seen in relationships with certain children and families, whereas, to the dismay of administrators, rigidity, moralism, and defensiveness are likely to be expressed in response to policies and programs.

Christian staff members in church agencies are not by definition any more skillful than staff members in agencies with other support bases, although Christian staff members may have more dogged determination and ability to "hang in." Faith-motivated staff members are not always dependent on client outcomes for reinforcement; their reinforcement can also come from the process of serving. Their belief in the fallibility and sinfulness of humanity may make them less susceptible to discouragement at the inevitable disappointments and setbacks that come with child welfare practice. Yet sometimes even this can be a disadvantage: a staff member who places little emphasis on outcomes may not be highly motivated to continue to develop ever more effective professional practices and programs.

The Church Agency as a Mission-Driven Organization

How the agency defines its mission is a primary factor in shaping criteria for hiring staff members. An agency's mission is the special task to which it devotes itself; it is often the task for which the agency was formed. Most church child welfare agencies had a strong, clear mission when they were founded. An agency's history contains statements describing its mission: "its reason for being, its vision of the future, its major goals and philosophy, its commitments and dedications" [Topor 1988: 21].

The term "mission" originally carried religious connotations, but now other organizations and institutions use the word to describe their values and purpose. Druecker [1989] states that business organizations initiate planning by looking at financial returns, whereas not-for-profit organizations initiate planning in light of their mission. The organization's mission helps the organization (1) to focus on action, (2) to define strategies for attaining crucial goals, (3) to create a disciplined organization, (4) to foster innovative ideas, and (5) to clarify why these ideas should be implemented. Thus, the agency's mission provides the foundation and direction for the agency. Effective mission-driven organizations retain their focus by judging the agency's actions in terms of their agreement with the mission of the agency. The mission may undergo amendment and reinterpretation to adapt the agency to changing times and needs, but the basic values reflected in the mission of the agency seldom if ever undergo radical change [Keys and Ginsberg 1988].

Working for the agency requires sharing in a commitment to the mission of the organization, which often leads the agency to develop distinctive cultural characteristics. Its personnel share common customs, idioms, and beliefs that develop through the agency's history and reflect its mission and values. Policies stem from the common values that develop as a consequence of the agency's mission. The mission sets the broad and permanent parameters within which specific and time-limited goals are set and programs are designed [Kettner et al. 1990].

It is possible for an agency to provide effective services but to be ineffective in accomplishing the mission for which it was founded, even though its mission has been redirected through the years in response to changing needs and concerns. This may happen when an agency offers services that are not identified as expressions of its mission, or when staff members are hired who have no commitment to the mission of the agency or appreciation for the values that were foundational for the agency's establishment and development. Consequently, many agencies choose to seek first within the ranks of the denomination or religious group supporting them (or at least within the Christian faith) for professionals who can bring to the agency an insider's understanding of the church, an appreciation for the agency's history and mission, and the professional knowledge, values, and skills to carry out the agency's mission. When persons who bring all these credentials to the agency cannot be found, some balance must be struck between professionalism in the child welfare arena and religious leadership. The agency wants staff members who are "our kind of people"; who have values consistent with the history, clientele, and future of the organization [Keys et al. 1988]; who will fit into the cultural milieu and values of the agency.

In some agencies and for some positions, job candidates do not have to be Christian, much less members of the same denomination, but staff members who will be working in congregational consultation may have to demonstrate expertise in understanding denominational politics and assuming church leadership roles. This kind of experience normally develops only through firsthand involvement with church groups, experience that is difficult to gain unless one is a member. In short, the mission of the agency and the place of a particular staff position within that mission determine the place of personal faith and religious behavior in the qualifications for that position. It may be, for example, that the personal faith and religious behavior of certain support personnel (cooks, janitors, secretaries, maintenance engineers) are not as central to the agency's mission as the faith and religious behavior of others, such as those professional staff members who provide direct services to clients and congregations.

Interestingly, some agencies' practice is the actual reverse of this. Their clerical and other support staff are all members of supporting congregations. The professional staff, however, have been drawn from other faith traditions or have no expressed faith, often because the agency has not been able to recruit qualified staff members from within the ranks of its parent religious body, or because it is adhering to a nondiscrimination policy in the hiring of professional staff.

Whatever the requirements of the particular position being considered, whether as a member of the professional staff or the support staff, employees must believe in the agency's mission and identify with their place in it. This belief and identification must go beyond intellectual assent. They must be able to embrace and be empowered by the mission of the organization.

The Process of Staff Formation

Hiring staff members who have a set of characteristics defined by the tasks of the positions being filled and by the overarching values and mission of the agency begins a process of staff formation. Once staff members are selected, training socializes them to become productive members of the agency. The socialization of new staff members involves transmitting the organization's culture—its beliefs, values, and norms. New staff members learn how the mission is translated into practice. The term *formation*, with its connotations from Christian thought on spiritual discipline and development, can be used to describe the socialization process of church agency staff. It connotes the importance of theology and the agency's role in the church as dimensions of the agency's mission and consequent work.

Formation takes place through training, which is the crucial link between the agency's mission and the empowering of staff members with the necessary knowledge, values, commitment, and skills for carrying out the mission [Austin et al. 1984]. Training informs the staff about the agency's mission so that they will conform to policies and procedures derived from the mission and perform services to children and their families that further the mission.

One way to inform staff members about the agency's mission is to tell them the story of the agency's founding and history. The story should encourage them to see themselves as carrying that history into the future, taking pride in who they are as members of a mission-driven agency with a valuable history, current work, and future calling. The history of the agency is often a saga that lends itself easily to being told as a story, not a dry historical account of dates and names.

Saga is a Norse term for the cumulative history of the struggles and victories of a people or organization. It represents the shared collection of tales of conquests in the face of great difficulties. Saga serves to forge a sense of group identity and purpose, to bind individuals into a cohesive team able to face the challenges of the present by relating to the achievements of the past [Brendtro 1982: 36].

Most church child welfare agencies came into being as Christians responded to some pressing human need, often exhibiting extraordinary resourcefulness and tenacity. Committed founders translated spiritual values into service to persons in crisis, often using revolutionary means. To live out the saga does not mean merely maintaining the programs established in earlier days in relation to the needs of those times. It means continuing to live with the resourcefulness, tenacity, and risk-taking that characterized the agency's founders.

The process of staff formation and the use and importance of the agency's saga are illustrated by the following extended description of one agency's staff orientation and experiences as a mission-driven agency:

> At Maryhurst, a residential treatment facility for adolescent girls, new staff members are introduced to the agency by hearing its story, which has been handed down for nearly 150 years. The current director, a Southern Baptist, emphasizes the importance of retaining the mission and heritage of the founding Good Shepherd Sisters as the soul of the agency's very difficult work. She orients new staff members to the agency on their first day by using the agency's story to communicate the contemporary perception of its place in the continuance of the story:

> "On your first day of orientation, I want you to find out who we are and what we are about. You were selected because you have the fundamental knowledge and abilities to perform the job and because you share a sense of caring needed for this type of work. You seem to be 'our kind of person.'

> "We are a mission-driven agency with very strong values. A strong sense of purpose is reflected in why we do what we do, and very definitely in how we do what we do. Our ministry is to give children hope and to help them heal their broken lives. Our values include how we treat one another; we share a strong sense of camaraderie and love for our coworkers, as well as for the girls we serve here. We also believe in servant-leadership—leading others by serving others—with our children and our staff.

> "I want to share with you a story: our story. This story began in the 18th century in France with an incredibly bright, courageous, sensitive woman who was called to work with those referred to as society's marginal people. This woman had a vision, a sense of purpose and mission that led her to serve outcast women and girls who had "gone astray" and who people of those days

considered forever tainted. Her mission called her to help these women and to provide opportunities for their growth and salvation.

"Rose Virginie Pelletier knew much hardship as a young girl. As a young adult, she experienced a strong call to serve needy women and, for this reason, joined an order of Catholic nuns who did this kind of ministry. Her name as a Catholic Sister became Sr. Mary Euphrasia Pelletier. Her sense of calling to serve women in need was so evident to her Sisters that they made her their leader, their "mother superior," at the young age of 29. This innovative woman enlarged the work of the Sisters, expanding it, taking it to the town of Angers, France. Her dynamism and creativity were not always well received. She was lied about and persecuted by people in church leadership and by women within her own order, especially as she ventured to move beyond the traditional works of her sisterhood. She eventually created a new group of Sisters, the Sisters of the Good Shepherd. The Good Shepherd Sisters believed they were called to go beyond tradition. Their tradition became to break with tradition if change was needed in order to meet the needs of people.

"The first Good Shepherd Sisters sent to America came to Louisville, Kentucky, in 1842. This was in response to Bishop Flaget's request for help for homeless and "wanton" women and orphaned children.

"In 1843, the Sisters established a residence to help prostitutes, abandoned and neglected children, and wayward girls. In 1856, the Sisters founded a second residence, named Maryhurst. The mayor and city council attended the groundbreaking, the local newspaper praised the noble purpose of the venture, and the Commonwealth of Kentucky pledged 33 1/3 cents per day per child for board and care. By 1922, Maryhurst was caring for 125 troubled teenage girls and 98 women from the county jail. The work continued to grow.

"Today, we provide residential treatment and community-based programs for very troubled girls. Our history reaches back to Mother Euphrasia. In her spirit, we have modified and stretched our programs to meet the needs of the very emotionally disturbed child, the hard-to-manage child, the child who at times will be difficult for you to love. The Good Shepherd tradition continues at Maryhurst today; our mission is still to serve 'those in greatest need.'

"A century or so ago, practical rules were handed on, first by word of mouth, and later in writing, to guide the Sisters who worked with the girls. Today, few Sisters work directly with the girls. It is you and I, as staff members, who integrate those practical rules into our work. We have adapted those rules to fit modern approaches to treatment, and as your training as a Maryhurst staff member continues, you will hear more about those 'practical rules' as they are applied in our services today.

"In the tradition of the Good Shepherd Sisters, we are a community of deeply committed professionals dedicated to treating those youths in greatest need, and giving them hope, through love and discipline."

Two years ago, Maryhurst intensified services in one of its dormitories and contracted with the Commonwealth of Kentucky to serve children certified as severely emotionally disturbed. Its mission "to serve those in greatest need" motivated the staff to design and implement a program for this population of children in dire need of effective services. A review of Maryhurst's mission and saga served as the rallying force that empowered the staff and the supporting religious order to develop programs and professional skills to serve these special children. The staff and Sisters saw these new services as the actualization of the agency's ongoing mission.

The initial establishment and/or support of agency services as expressions of the church's mission must be revisited and emphasized periodically, particularly during times of transition. These revisits should include supporting religious groups as well as agency staff. The membership of churches and other religious organizations changes over time;

child welfare agencies develop new programs and hire new staff members. These changes should be accompanied by a reexamination of the agency's mission and its relationship with the faith communities that support it and minister through it.

One caution is necessary, however. As important as the agency's mission is, an agency should not be confused with a church or community of faith. Church child welfare agencies are extensions of the church's mission, but they are not churches. Because the roles of personal faith and professional practice often overlap in church agencies, maintaining appropriately open boundaries between personal lives and professional responsibilities while respecting the personal privacy and rights of staff members is a demanding task that requires considerable discernment and discussion on the part of staff, administration, and governing boards of directors.

Ongoing Staff Formation and Retention

Staff training can motivate employees toward productive compliance with the agency's mission as well as ensuring that they have the necessary knowledge and skills to carry out their duties. Adequate staff salaries are critical in avoiding staff frustration, demoralization, and turnover. Poorly compensated staff members cannot be jollied into a high level of commitment to the agency and its mission or the kind of sacrificial service that is often demanded of child welfare personnel. Motivational speeches, token gifts, and public accolades may be appreciated or may anger poorly paid staff members; either way, however, they will not substitute for adequate salaries in retaining staff and ensuring commitment and enthusiasm for the work of the agency.

Staff members must have adequate salaries if they are to feel valued and justly treated. Money alone, however, is not enough to create commitment and a sense of being appreciated and valued as a contributing member of a professional team. Social reinforcement, both spoken words of appreciation and symbolic gifts, are critical to nurturing the staff's commitment, particularly when they tie the work being done to the foundational mission of the agency:

> During a weekend early in the process of instituting Maryhurst's
> new program for severely emotionally disturbed children, the

living unit was disrupted by the agitated and physically destructive behavior of two residents. In response, several staff members worked overtime, cared for the adolescents in appropriate and therapeutic ways, and supported one another. After that weekend, and upon reflecting on the agency's mission and the changes they were making, staff created the "Order of the Silver Heart." It was symbolized by a small silver heart on a blue ribbon that was awarded to staff demonstrating exemplary service. The silver heart is rooted in Maryhurst's mission; it was worn by Mother Euphrasia and the early Good Shepherd Sisters. In the "Order of the Silver Heart" at Maryhurst, the heart has come to stand for the Good Shepherd value of love for those whose behavior dares others to try to respond in a loving manner. It reinforces conformity to Good Shepherd values: to love and not be put off by the most difficult-to-love child. It also serves as a teaching instrument, reminding staff of the continuity of their work with the early work of the Good Shepherd community.

Breadth of Responsibilities Carried by the Staff

Work with staff members in church agencies has to take into account the breadth of responsibilities the staff carries. Because of the relatively small size of church agencies, as contrasted with many public child welfare agencies, staff members are far less likely to be confined to one or a few professional roles. A social worker, for example, may provide direct services to children and their families, direct a volunteer service program, consult with congregations, conduct parent education programs for churches, and supervise other professional staff members. Some staff members may experience such a spread of responsibilities to be frustrating, particularly if the agency does not recognize the time commitments each requires. If, however, appropriate supports are provided (such as reimbursement of travel costs for working with churches, flexible scheduling, a caseload size that is sensitive to other responsibilities, and secretarial support), this breadth may in fact encourage commitment to the agency's mission as it is reflected in all these services.

Professional staff members who work primarily with troubled children and dysfunctional families may find working in prevention programs and developing community support services a way to retain perspective on the part their work plays in the larger fabric of the church's ministry with children and families and a gratifying and welcome respite from their usual responsibilities. Such experiences may protect against burnout and reduce staff turnover.

Church agency staff members often experience not only a greater breadth of responsibilities at any given time in their career than they would have in a public agency, but also more changes in responsibilities over time. Some clinical staff members find themselves relatively quickly promoted into supervisory and administrative positions, although they may still retain some direct service responsibilities. These promotions almost always require retooling. Staff members often need help in recognizing that behaviors that were so appreciated they led to promotion are not necessarily those required by the new position. It is not intuitively obvious to many that a new job requires new and different behavior [Druecker 1985]. The outstanding family therapist will usually find that the skills needed for consulting with church groups or supervising a group of volunteers or administering an agency are dramatically different from those involved in providing family therapy with severely emotionally disturbed adolescents and their families.

Consequently, to retain the commitment and good work of staff members, church agencies should provide access to professional journals and books, continuing education, outside consultation, and other professional development opportunities for the variety of responsibilities staff members carry.

The Board of Directors

An agency's board of directors profoundly influences how staff members express its mission through programs and services. The board carries legal responsibility for the overall operation of the agency, with specific responsibilities for making policy and overseeing the raising and spending of funds. Effective organizations almost always have committed, energetic, and effective boards of directors. The composition of a board of directors reflects the mission of the agency, including both those who have determined the agency's mission and, sometimes, those who are the target of the agency's work as well—its clients and churches.

Nettings' recent research into the governance of church-related retirement communities discovered that, on the average, 81% of the members of these agencies' boards of directors belong to the parent religious group, contrasted with only 15% of the staff. In fact, it is not unusual for these agencies to have boards composed entirely of church members. Similarly, my survey of church child welfare agencies in 1992 found a strong church representation in the governance of these agencies; 60% of the respondents indicated that 76% to 100% of their boards of directors were official representatives of churches and/or other religious organizations. Only 29% indicated that 25% or less of their board members represented their religious constituency; the other 8% ranged between these two extremes.

Roles and Responsibilities

Churches influence the missions and programs of church agencies through the leadership the board exhibits. The board affects the agency's relationship with the community and its social systems as it carries out its responsibilities for community relations. Finally, the board may even affect the services of the agency, not only indirectly, through the establishment or abolition of policies and programs, but also directly, if the board intervenes as an advocate for clients.

Agency Program and Financial Leadership

The board of directors bears responsibility for oversight of the agency, leading it in pursuit of its mission. It is responsible for setting policies, approving or disapproving new and ongoing programs in light of the agency's mission, and correcting the agency's trajectory when it loses sight of its mission. Sometimes, its responsibility for oversight begins with self-evaluation and change. Again, an extended agency description offers an illustration:

Home of the Innocents was founded in 1880 by a group from the Episcopal Cathedral in Louisville, Kentucky, as a receiving home for small children. It was originally staffed by Episcopal sisters. In 1970, it was a small group home with five employees and an annual budget of $40,000.

During the 1970s, the agency took responsibility for two other agencies, incorporating the county's emergency shelter for children and adolescents and a pediatric nursing home for children. Both the programs it took over were much larger than the Home of the Innocents itself; two new facilities had to be built to accommodate the additions. With too much change coming too quickly, the agency came close to bankruptcy.

Through conversations with others in the community, the Episcopal bishop, a board member, learned that state and county social workers were no longer referring children to the Home of the Innocents and doctors were unwilling to transfer children to the nursing program because the quality of care was considered poor. The bishop commissioned an investigation of the agency. Several major problems were disclosed.

First, it was determined that the board itself had conflicts of interest; several board members were also agency employees or otherwise receiving payment from the agency—the agency's attorney, dietitian, school teacher, and insurance salesman. Second, the board lacked expertise for its tasks. Although board members were well intentioned, few had knowledge or skill in overseeing a child welfare agency. Third, the board had little contact with the daily operations of the agency. For example, the staff kept children outside the building during board meetings, so as not to "disturb" the board. Fourth, to save money, the agency was obtaining its employees through federally subsidized job training and placement programs; only six of the 46 employees had completed high school and only two had college educations. The staff did not have the professional knowledge or skill to operate a pediatric nursing home and an emergency shelter for children.

In response to the report, the bishop arranged to bring in a consultant from the Child Welfare League of America. A women's group in the Episcopal Church paid the expenses. The board adopted the consultant's subsequent recommendations, including a major overhaul of the board itself and the hiring of a new administrator.

The board told the new administrator that since they were heading for bankruptcy in two or three years at the rate of the agency's current spending, the agency should be overhauled to become "the very best agency it possibly can be, and if we go bankrupt, we will just go bankrupt sooner." Management consultants from a local hospital were retained. The entire staff was dismissed, and new job descriptions were prepared. About one-third of the former employees were rehired in new positions, and additional professional staff members were hired.

Over time, the agency's programs earned a reputation for quality care. United Way and government supports grew significantly. Today, the Home of the Innocents serves as the county's emergency shelter for neglected, abused, and abandoned children and adolescents; it also offers the only residential pediatric nursing care program in the state. Service programs have continued to expand to include a community group home for teenage mothers and their children.

Community Relations

The board provides key linkages with the agency's community. Board members themselves represent the community. They also may have relationships with significant persons and groups that provide a variety of resources for the agency—funding, volunteers, and legal and other professional consultation services. As active advocates for the agency, they use these linkages with the community to seek resources for the agency:

It is absolutely essential that every board have aggressive, informed, well connected advocates. ...There has to be recognition that simply going to meetings and planning sessions are not ends in themselves, they are only means. [Cahill 1981: 115]

Often, an auxiliary group expands the linkage of the agency with the community and functions in a supportive role. The auxiliary can be linked to the board through an ex officio seat on the board for the auxiliary president. Auxiliaries are considered membership organizations, and some charge small annual dues; they may require their members to involve themselves in one of the auxiliary activities, such as advocacy, fundraising, and/or public relations:

The auxiliary group of the Home of the Innocents Board of Directors recently invited to the agency all the state social workers, police officers, and judges who make referrals and work with the children who are served in the Home's emergency shelter program. They conducted tours of the facility and handled introductions to staff members, provided a luncheon, and gave a coffee mug embossed with the Home of the Innocents logo to each invited guest. Many of the police officers and social workers had brought children to the agency's admissions office, but they had never seen where children live, play, and go to school. Few judges had ever seen the facility. Since these persons prepare children in a crisis to be placed temporarily in shelter care, they need knowledge of the agency to communicate comfort and reassurance to children. The staff presented a brief program describing how to prepare children who are experiencing the crisis of being removed from their homes for placement in the temporary shelter.

Sometimes, the work of the board and its auxiliaries is directed toward providing ways for laypeople to feel linked to the work of the agency, thus giving the agency visibility in the wider community.

A Georgia United Methodist agency's auxiliary provides a handmade quilt for each child placed in residential care, as a sign of support and care from the churches that sponsor the agency. Handmade quilts are also sold and proceeds used to provide furnishings for the agency. Hundreds of persons all over the state are involved in the work of the agency through the making and "offering" of quilts. Auxiliary members conduct other funding activities, such as yard sales, festivals, and arts and crafts sales. These activities not only raise monies for the agency but also create community visibility and a means for many persons to involve themselves in the work of caring for children and their families [Rumford 1991].

Advocacy for Children and Families

As Gratch [1980: 1] has noted, "Each person who accepts a position on the board of directors of a child welfare agency automatically and without further formality assumes the role of child advocate. There is no choice. The responsibility and duty come with the title and job." Usually, that means advocacy for the client population group served by the agency. Board members concern themselves with public policies and decisions by public agencies and governments that affect the work of the agency or the persons served by the agency. Gratch even suggests that board members are legally bound to be advocates when public policies and practices interfere with the optimal performance of the agency's service, since advocacy is a part of many agencies' corporate charter and purposes. "Novel, but conceivable, is the possibility of consumer lawsuits and mandatory court orders to compel attention to this advocacy purpose" [Gratch: 6].

Less commonly, board members may serve as advocates for specific clients of the agency. Although agency staff members do not normally relish the idea of board members involving themselves directly in work with clients, board members do play a significant role in direct services, particularly when they can obtain resources or serve as advocates beyond what the professional staff is able to do.

> Six years ago, a three-year-old girl and her six-year-old brother were brought from a neighboring county to the Home of the Innocents Emergency Shelter. They were victims of child abuse;

their parents had used them to make pornographic movies of sex acts with dogs, adults, and each other.

Although the children were transferred to another child care facility several weeks later, the Home's program director remained involved in the case. Legal charges were being brought against the parents, and expert testimony by Home of the Innocents staff members would be needed concerning their initial assessment of the children.

The parents were able to retain a prominent, successful attorney. The state was represented by a young attorney who had finished law school one year earlier and had no previous experience in prosecuting child abuse cases. The agency program director learned that the children were going to be returned to the parents because the physical evidence—confiscated pictures and film—had disappeared from the property room of the rural county's police department. The agency program director and executive director explained to the board of directors of Home of the Innocents what had happened. The board voted to retain an attorney to intervene on behalf of the two children.

Over the course of the following six years, in three different legal cases concerning removal of the children from the home, criminal prosecution, and termination of parental rights, board members stayed involved as advocates. When a jurisdictional dispute concerning which judge would hear the case resulted in an appeal to the state court, the board traveled to the state capital in a car caravan to sit in the courtroom as silent witnesses in behalf of the children.

The agency board can also serve as an advocate for children within the agency. At Home of the Innocents, board members talk with children in the shelter periodically to determine their likes and dislikes about the services they are provided. They hear complaints about the food, wishes for more activities, and appreciation and criticism of staff members and programs. When there are problems, the board has access to information from the most important people in the agency—the children. This information can be used to make changes within the agency's staffing or programs, and to deal with other social systems that affect clients and their families. The executive director describes one such change:

> We were faced with a decision concerning school for children in the emergency shelter. The average length of stay for children in the emergency shelter is 10 days, but it is often much shorter. The neighborhood public school would therefore experience considerable disruption if new children came into the classroom from the shelter each day, usually to be there only for a period of a few days. The children themselves would be faced with trying to adjust to a new school at a time of extreme personal crisis. The board members learned in interviews with children that the children did not want to go to the public schools because other children teased them for being from the "Home." We therefore asked the public school system for a separate school facility.

> Two child advocacy organizations in the community publicly opposed the idea, believing the children ought to be mainstreamed into the public school. They obtained local newspaper coverage supporting their position.

> Board members had been so involved in the decision making process and in the research of the issues, however, that they took responsibility for meeting with the opposing organizations to explain their decision and the rationale behind it.

To fulfill its roles and responsibilities, the board has to learn about the work of the agency and continually be informed about changes in the agency's programs and services, its context, and the client population it serves. Board members must know what is going well, what problems develop, and what mistakes are made if they are to provide sensitive leadership and vigorous advocacy for the agency and its clients.

Composition

The composition of the board should reflect the needs and purposes of the programs the board oversees. Pooley and Littell [1986] suggest recruiting board members from the following groups:

- Well-known or important community members: executive directors of other agencies, politicians, superintendents of schools, bank presidents, clergy or other church leaders;

- Persons with skills useful in overseeing the administration of the agency, such as attorneys, accountants, business managers, and fundraisers;

- Persons with expertise in program areas, such as family therapists, social workers, public school educators, and academics;

- Persons who are interested in agency programs because they are active in the community and/or in churches it serves and/or represents;

- Parents, grandparents, or former clients who have been involved in the program;

- Program volunteers; and

- Staff members from other agencies or organizations that serve families.

Small boards tend to be more active and involved as a group in the work of an agency than large boards. A large board may meet only quarterly, but members may reach the same level of active involvement that characterizes a small board by serving on committees that meet frequently. The organization of these committees may reflect the agency's programs and structures—a committee to oversee the work of each agency program and additional administrative and finance committees with general oversight. Committee structures may also be allowed to evolve over time, supplemented by task forces in relation to particular needs. The larger the board, all other things being equal, the greater the amount of time staff members need to expend in providing support to the board's activities. The executive director describes the current composition of the board of the Home of the Innocents and his work with them:

> The 32 current board members all come from this county; the majority are Episcopalian, since this is an Episcopal agency. Almost all the work of the Board takes place in committee meetings, not in the general board meetings. Ten committees meet every month. Over half the members of the committees are not board members; they are other people whom we have included because their expertise is needed for the work of that committee.
>
> Working with 10 committees takes a great deal of my time, but I find it is time very well spent in building a broad network of support for our agency. It involves the community in our programs and the daily work of the agency.
>
> Parents of children in the nursing program and active volunteers in all our programs also serve on the board. They know what is happening in the agency from personal experience and are not dependent upon staff to interpret for them or for the board what is happening. For example, two children ran away from our emergency shelter, found a rowboat, and were out on the river when they were apprehended by the police. The local paper's headline read "Helter Skelter Shelter," building public opinion that the agency had been remiss in not keeping the children in a secure facility. Board members had had enough personal experience with the agency to know, however, that Kentucky state law requires child care agencies to be "open," allowing children to be free to leave at any time they want to do so. In fact, we were required by state law to allow those children to leave.

Denominations and Other Religious Groups: Politics and Change

A church agency relates to religious groups and is profoundly affected by those groups, through funding, staff, and the governance of its board of directors. Even when the religious groups are relatively stable social systems, nurturing and monitoring these vital relationships is a demanding task. Often, however, the religious groups that support church agencies are anything but stable. Denominations and other faith groups are changing, sometimes turbulent, organizations. Subgroups in congregations quarrel with one another; denominations split and proliferate, or, sometimes, join together in new groups united out of different traditions. Developing a supportive, collaborative relationship with one congregation may alienate another.

Many of the mainline denominations in the United States find themselves no longer growing; some are even experiencing shrinkage. These are frequently the denominations that have supported social ministries, including child welfare agencies. At the same time, nondenominational megachurches, often dependent on the leadership of a particularly powerful pastor, are growing rapidly. These churches may not be interested in collaborating with other churches to support shared ministries. Instead, they have the resources and energy to develop family support programs of their own, including counseling centers, community centers, and day care programs.

For child welfare agencies, which have historically been created by, funded by, and consequently related to denominations rather than individual churches, these phenomena create complex questions. Because they have moved toward legal independence to protect their parent denominations from fiscal liability, agencies have the opportunity to expand their relationships to churches of other denominations and of no denomination. To do so, however, carries the risk of compromising the agency's identity, and thus, perhaps, muddying a clear picture of the agency's mission and alienating historically supportive relationships. In such an environment, church agencies will not be able simply to stand still; too much is in movement all about them.

The largest Protestant denomination in the United States, the Southern Baptist Convention, is currently at imminent risk of division, creating serious questions for agencies sponsored by the Convention and identifying themselves as Southern Baptist child welfare agencies. With which side of the controversy will they align themselves? Will alignment with one side preclude continuing relationships with congregations on the other side?

Can an agency that claims to base its practice on theology and to be working toward social justice for children and families remain neutral when broad issues of theology, politics, and worldview distinguish the two sides? One thing is certain; agencies may struggle with these questions, but they cannot simply ignore them if they want to remain viable Baptist agencies. If a formal denominational split comes, agencies will have to either choose sides or choose some form of independent identity that relates to both sides. Whatever choice is made, relationships with churches and denominational bodies that have historically shaped these agencies will change dramatically.

Although the Church as a theological entity, the Bride of Christ, may be eternal, the churches and denominations to which agencies relate are very much of this world, and thus "passing away." Denominations split, die, and arise from ashes. Individual pastors and churches strike out on their own with exciting visions of ministry. Religious groups form within or outside of denominational and church structures, such as the religious order that birthed Maryhurst, the Sisters of the Good Shepherd. And such groups die out—as it seems the Good Shepherd Sisters may someday, as their number continues to diminish—perhaps leaving a legacy to be carried on by other Christians from other faith traditions.

It behooves staff members of church agencies, therefore, to consistently monitor their lifelines to the religious groups that they support in ministry and that support them. The professionals employed in a public child welfare agency are naive to think that all their attention should be focused on work with clients; attention must also be given to the public policies and laws that empower or dismantle their work. Similarly, the professionals employed in a church agency are naive to think that they do not have to tangle with church and denominational politics; this too is part of the context for their professional practice.

Notes

1.   More recent statistics for family service agencies affiliated with Family Service America indicate similar trends in these agencies: United Way support of family service agencies dropped from 68% of total agency budgets in 1962 to 28% in 1988 [Garval 1990: 438].

2.   A survey conducted almost 30 years ago illustrates these different attitudes toward the relationship between the church (and its agencies) and the state. In 1965, Coughlin conducted a survey of church-related agencies (including hospitals, nursing homes, children's institutions, and children's services) in 20 states. He found significant differences in attitudes and policies among Catholic, Protestant, and Jewish agency administrators with regard to government funding, including both government subsidies for agencies and the government purchase of services from agencies. Most Catholic administrators surveyed did not express concern about government subsidies violating the principle of separation of church and state, although Jewish and Protestant administrators were concerned about this potential violation. Nonetheless, all three groups were concerned about the potential threat to their autonomy presented by government subsidies. With regard to the government's purchase of services, Coughlin often found contradictory attitudes among administrators representing the same denomination, and even broader disparity among the different Protestant denominations. Some Southern Baptist administrators regarded even purchase of services unfavorably, whereas Lutherans and Episcopalians were highly favorable toward the government purchasing services from voluntary agencies [Coughlin 1965].

CHAPTER 8

The Future of Services with Children and Families

𝕿HIS BOOK HAS SOUGHT TO ARTICULATE the characteristics of the church as a context for child welfare services and to describe effective practice strategies that are sensitive to this context. It has been a surprisingly difficult task for several reasons. First, as long as the church has been involved in providing child welfare services to children and their families—and it has been involved longer than any other social institution—precious little actual research has been conducted to describe its work, its processes, its staff, and its clients. The focus of church agencies has been caring for children and their families, with little attention to researching or writing about those caring efforts.

Second, the helping professions have not encouraged an examination of the church as a unique context for child welfare services. Why? Perhaps biases about the role of religious groups in professional caring have blinded us to the fact that, whatever our personal beliefs, a significant proportion of the professional care for children and families does take place under church auspices in the United States. Or perhaps the professions have recognized the role of the church but have failed to see it as any different from that of other private providers of social services. Church agency staff members have worked hard to present a professional, competent image to their professional groups. This image is often incongruent with the messier aspects of church practice—narrow theological positions and conservative politics that constrain agency policies and create professional dilemmas in some churches, the involvement of well-meaning but bumbling church volunteers, decisions to hire staff members with the "right" denominational affiliation over those with the needed professional and personal credentials. Consequently, church agency professionals may have de-emphasized the implications of the church as a context for their practice in describing what they do to professional colleagues in other arenas of practice.

Third, the dialogue between the social sciences and theology demanded by a discussion of the church context for professional practice is not easy. Few social scientists, including child welfare theorists, are also theologians. Theological discussion may seem esoteric and idealistic to social scientists, and social scientists may seem reductionist and simplistic in their understanding of church and religion to theologians and Biblical scholars. Practically, the dialogue would necessitate at least a rudimentary knowledge of two different kinds of language as well as two professional cultures that differ sharply from one another.

I am grateful that the Child Welfare League of America recognized the significance of the church as a context for practice and supported this writing project as an initial attempt to describe that context and tease out the significance of its characteristics for effective services to children and their families. It has indeed been simply a beginning; the book is based on my own personal experiences and observations and those of the network of church agency staff members and executives who I know or have met during the research for this project. The future calls us to be more disciplined in describing who we are and what we do—to articulate the processes behind our decisions, such as the reasons church agencies consider but then decide not to offer some services, as well as why they offer those they do offer and their outcomes. Because church agencies are mission-driven agencies, the study of agencies' missions and sagas, and the objectives, programs, and agency processes that develop from them, are just as important as the evaluation of programmatic outcomes.

The church has a unique role in caring for children and their families. That role has constraints, and professional practice in church agencies certainly has its tribulations. Few professionals in church agencies have not been tempted more than once to jump ship. Many stay, however, despite the frustrations of denominational power politics, theological positions that condemn rather than bless, narrow definitions of evangelism that caricature the complexity of the human spirit, inadequate funding, and volunteers who cavalierly ignore client confidentiality and self-determination. They stay because they have a vision of what the church can be and a commitment to the roles church agencies can have in caring for children and their families. They stay because they have experienced a call to serve in this place, in this time, and for these purposes.

The Roles of Church Child Welfare Agencies

The church agency has the potential for providing leadership to church congregations and groups in ministry, for encouraging pluralism in the services available to children and their families, for serving as an advocate for children and their families, and for being an innovator in the development of professional child welfare services.

Church Leader

Most of this book has focused on the leadership that church agencies can offer to individual Christians, groups, and congregations in living out the expectation that Christians care for their neighbors in need. For some agencies, that means serving those whose needs require highly professional care and offering that care in the name of the church. Many agencies, however, have the ability and opportunity to develop congregation- and community-based family support programs, significant child welfare services that have gained increased recognition as indispensable threads in a comprehensive family services network. By offering these services, agencies also turn the flow of resources between church and agency into a mutually reciprocal exchange. Just as the church provides resources for the agency's work, so the agency provides professional consultation and help for the work of the congregation in its own community.

Encourager of Pluralism

Alan Keith-Lucas has argued that there is much danger in seeing the church agency as the filler of gaps in the services offered by public agencies; it is "the danger of actually slowing down the process of government facing up to the real need, and the assimilation of our programs into an auxiliary system of child care in which what we are is obscured." Instead, he has argued, church agencies can offer pluralism and complexity to the array of community services, a complexity that corresponds to the complexity of needs of children and their families.

> [Parents] can entrust their children to the state, to the community, or to the church. Even where the state intervenes and forces this entrustment, it should have available to it a range of different facilities with different values, different methods, different skills. If it controls all the facilities this simply will not happen. For, although there may be local differences, and agencies carefully designed to fulfill different needs, and some administrators with ideas and values of their own, as long as a central government holds the major part of the purse strings, the same philosophies will prevail. Agencies that believe in them will be funded, others not. [Keith-Lucas 1982: 27]

A pluralistic delivery system will continue to be the essence of child and family social services in the United States [Springer 1990]. Church and nonsectarian agencies allow for choice without diminishing the importance of services universally available to all who need them. Community-based human services should often be offered in small agencies that encourage warm, informal, supportive, culturally congruent relationships between staff members and clients if they are to reach and be effective with some high-risk populations. Church agencies can offer such services.

There should be no reason for competition between the voluntary sector and government programs. Certainly, no one would argue that there are not enough human needs to go around! The presence in the community of a rich diversity of voluntary agencies and resources does not decrease the need for a strong public child welfare system. Almost 20 years, ago, Wilda Dailey [1974] noted that the use of public money to fund voluntary agencies might have the positive outcome of promoting the alliance between the public and private human services sectors.

Advocate

One of the roles the church and its agencies may embrace is a prophetic role, speaking out for social justice, criticizing the culture when it oppresses, and putting forward points of view that challenge prevailing cultural norms. Professionals working in church agencies are in the company of a sleeping giant. When awakened, the church can speak with a powerful voice in our culture, and although sometimes slow to speak and slow to move, the church can have an impact, as it has in our country's past on issues such as slavery and child labor.

Some church agencies may be fearful, however, of awakening the sleeping giant. They fear that the church's stand on issues may not be what they would hope, and that, in fact, the church will speak out on the opposite side of issues from their own. The professional may even be caught between two mighty giants, the church as employer and the profession's sanction of practice. Some church groups take stands that differ from those of some professional organizations on abortion, the giving of family planning information and contraception to teens, national health insurance, a guaranteed family income policy, and a great many other matters that vitally affect children and families. It takes considerable courage for the professional to risk raising these questions, encouraging church groups to look at the interface between their values and the needs of children and families. Church agencies have to make choices. Will they try to lie low and avoid controversy, and thus abdicate the leadership role they could embrace in child advocacy? Or will they risk what taking such a role may mean to their lifeline of support with some church groups?

Innovator

The church agency is often able to develop specialized services in response to needs that are not recognized as public responsibilities. The hope is that the community in time will recognize these needs and provide services universally. For example, churches have been at the forefront of offering quality child care for low-income working parents and teenage parents still in school, a service desperately needed but often not available from the public sector. Yet churches cannot provide child care for all who need it.

Sometimes, church agencies develop innovative, experimental, small-scale programs that can serve as models, or at least as sources of ideas, for universal service programs or for other small, community-based family support services. The well-known Homebuilders family preservation program, for example, was begun and nurtured by Catholic Community Services of Tacoma, Washington [Kinney et al. 1991]. Innovation sometimes means that an agency will outgrow its connections to one church or religious organization, as Homebuilders did, becoming an institution that belongs to the larger community and receives public and/or diversified private funds.

> The aim here is not to keep the agency in the control of the church, nor to seek to maintain its identity as Christian, but to see the role of the church as initiator and catalyst of a necessary process that seeks to overcome evident injustice." [Grierson 1991: 16]

Churches and faith groups may also serve as catalysts for the development of programs in which they participate but do not attempt to control.

> The Parish of St. John's became increasingly concerned about the high rates of single teen pregnancy and parenting in its inner-city community. Because the parish has a limited budget and church members saw the need as much larger than their own resources, they called a public meeting with a view to developing a commu-

nity response. Forty people attended the meeting, many in response to special invitations, representing other churches, social service agencies, public schools, concerned citizens, and a sprinkling of teen parents (actively encouraged to attend by providing child care and transportation).

A committee was formed to examine the feasibility of a community-based teen health resource center that could provide comprehensive health services, including pregnancy prevention counseling, located in or adjacent to the public schools. The committee also examined possible models of teen parenting resource centers. Funding for the subsequent services was provided by county government, several local businesses, a state agency providing seed money to develop "community-based family resource centers," and several neighborhood churches. St. John's was among these supporting churches, and was represented by one seat on the feasibility committee and the subsequent boards of directors of the two newly established community service centers.

Unfortunately, state officials often believe that "nonprofit agencies concentrate almost exclusively on generating program dollars and rarely behave as problem solvers who have solutions to offer the public sector" [Langley 1991:434]. Patricia Langley has challenged church agencies to see and portray themselves as "crafters of solutions" [433] rather than simply as critics of public policies and services. Church agencies can advocate and encourage the development of service coalitions to incorporate all the agencies that serve children and their families in a geographical area, public and private, sectarian and nonsectarian.

Challenges to Church Agencies

Church agencies face many challenges. First, the roles of church leader, advocate, and innovator can all be allowed to go unclaimed. Agencies may passively react to changes in the church: rather than asserting a leadership role, they may avoid speaking out on political issues and community attitudes that have an impact on children and families, and continue to provide services in which they have established expertise rather than risk innovation. For the most part, these are challenges internal to the church agency. They are played out in relationships among mission and programs and services, and among board and staff members and clients. They are part of the intrasystemic environment of the agency.

Other challenges also confront the church agency in its external environment, in its relationship with church groups, denominations, voluntary grass-roots religious organizations, the social work profession and other professional child welfare groups, the legal child welfare system, and the changing community.

Energetic, Value-Driven, Damaging Actions by Individual Volunteers and Volunteer Groups

Work with congregations and voluntary, grass-roots church organizations is fraught with problems, often making the agency vulnerable to attack from both professionals and church groups. Janet Spressart, Director of Volunteer Programs for the New Jersey Mental Health Association, described such a situation [1988]:

> Louella spent the last three months of her pregnancy in a host home offered through a pro-life action group sponsored by several churches in her community. Her parents knew of her pregnancy, but her father's serious illness precluded her spending the last trimester at home as a constant visual reminder to him of something that upset him even more than his own terminal illness. Her mother was supportive of Louella staying in a Christian home, but could not provide many tangible supports due to the pressures of her husband's illness. Louella wanted to keep her baby, but two days after delivery, while she was still in the hospital, her father died.

> The host home in which Louella had been housed was that of a childless couple. The adoption scene had turned bleak and barren in the years since the host family had made contacts with agencies. The family had entered the pro-life movement with the expressed intent of enabling a life to come into the world that

might otherwise be lost to abortion. Their covert, and perhaps yet unconscious, wish was to be able to adopt a baby born to an unmarried mother who found refuge in their home.

Louella left her baby in the hospital and returned home to her grieving mother. Both women faced weeks of depression and grief. Louella understood that the infant would be released to a representative of the pro-life group, who, she believed, would see that the child had a good temporary home while she and her mother dealt with their crisis. Louella was somewhat relieved to learn that the child had been placed in her host's home. She was told that she could visit the child there once a week, which she did for two consecutive weeks. However, her depression deepened and she reported later that she felt very uncomfortable visiting the child in that home. She felt that she was an intruder.

After one month of no contact from Louella to arrange for visitation, the pro-life organization advised the host family that they could keep the infant and adopt him. Knowing that adoption required some kind of court action, a representative from the group contacted a Christian social service agency requesting whatever services were necessary to formalize the adoption.

The problems faced in a matter such as this are many. The independent grass-roots organization went beyond its own purpose in deciding what action should be taken on behalf of the child. Serious misjudgments were made regarding what was best for the child and what were the intentions of the biological mother. The pro-life group interpreted her depression and intimidation by the host family as a lack of interest in her child. The entrance of a professional Christian social worker on the scene was expected to provide a conclusion to the matter. It might have, if the social worker, versed in child placement policy, procedure, law, and regulations, had not confronted the volunteer-run program with the illegalities inherent in their actions. The vulnerability of the social worker and the agency represented surfaced in the threat by the Christian pro-life group to withdraw referrals from the agency and to expose the agency as desirous of stealing babies from appropriate Christian homes for its own gain [Spressart 1988: 48-49].

Unfortunately, an agency's first reaction to such an experience is to protect itself by withdrawing from visibility with such groups and churches. Instead, an offer of professional consultation that could help the pro-life group use its energies to serve babies and their families more effectively, though challenging and even risky, might also be extremely rewarding for both sides.

Decreasing Denominational Loyalty

Many church members have considerably less "brand loyalty" than church members had in the past; they have no strong commitment to a particular denomination. The growth of nondenominational churches is one indication of this. Some churches—both independent and denomination-affiliated— revolve around the personality of the pastor. Consequently, people may not be willing to support an agency simply because it has a denominational seal of approval. Church agencies can no longer assume that they will receive support as long as they retain their close denominational ties. They have to nurture relationships directly and consistently with the congregations and individual Christians with whom they work and who support them.

Adapting to Minority Status

Newton Daddow has noted that "the Church's self-perception is changing as it comes to terms with the contemporary reality of the Christian Diaspora, its marginal role and its minority status" [Pollard 1991: 8]. As a culturally and religiously diverse society broadens, churches will no longer be able to presume that they speak for the majority culture. This trend has been less obvious in the United States, where Christianity is still normative, than in other Western countries. Even so, it appears that connection with the church as an institution is less and less a cultural expectation and is ever more dependent on individual and active choices. This trend will continue, no doubt, despite the posturing of political figures and the presumption of some religious leaders that they can speak for all that is American. Current pendulum swings toward political and religious conservatism do not appear to be permanent shifts in the process of societal secularization. Even the current swing to greater religiosity appears to emphasize personal spirituality rather than commitment to religious organizations [Naisbitt and Aburdene 1990].

Consequently, church agencies that embrace and seek to shore up their ties with supporting churches and denominations will be confronted increasingly with their role as leaders of the social action of a minority group in society. They will not be able to assume automatic acceptance and credibility on the basis of their identity with a communitywide shared faith. Their credibility and legitimacy as caregivers will have to be earned. "Whilst in the past parishes claimed a centrality in community life, they must now earn a place as one centre among many in most communities— they must therefore be prepared to be part of a network and to be accountable to it" [Burke 1989: 3].

An Aging Population

Our population is aging. In 1970, the 57 million children and youths from 10 to 24 years of age represented 28% of the total population of the United States. In less than 40 years, adolescents and youths in this age group will make up only 18% of the population, and their actual numbers will have declined by more than three million. In 1970, there were almost three teens and young adults for every person age 65 and older. By 2030, the ratio of youths to elderly will drop to 1:1 [Children's Defense Fund 1991]. Not only are there fewer children, but there are fewer parents, the adults who often care the most about children. With more adults choosing not to become parents at all, it may be much more difficult to generate support for services for children and their families. Characteristically, people have difficulty empathizing with, and thus caring for, those whose experience differs from their own. It may be difficult for young career-focused adults who have chosen not to have children to muster any empathy for poor, unemployed parents who, they may feel, should have realized they did not have the resources to parent children.

Consequently, advocates for children and families must appeal to people's self-interest and to fiscal reasoning, not simply to disinterested compassion. With a shrinking pool of children and youths, each one becomes increasingly precious as a potential worker and taxpayer who will (or will not) support the social services to which we will be entitled as older persons. If we do not attend to their needs, we will be squandering not only their futures, but our own.

The Children's Defense Fund garners statistics concerning children and develops responsible and hard-hitting interpretations for use in state and federal government policy-making. They speak the language of government, demonstrating the short-term and long-term fiscal wisdom of caring for the needs of children and their families. Similarly, church agencies ought to provide interpretation of statistics about children for the churches. As the population ages, agencies will have to be increasingly creative in nurturing the compassion, caring, and servant theology that undergird and motivate the church's ministry to children and their families. This is particularly difficult in a society that views children as a "personal indulgence" of parents, and that believes "public policy should not relieve the burden of families in having them" [Schorr 1974: 197].

The Church's Emphasis on Family Ministry

Concern about supporting and strengthening all families will continue to draw increasing attention from churches. As important as sporadic marriage enrichment weekends and parent education seminars may be, they are in no way a substitute for the societal and community supports that sustain healthy, functional families throughout lifetimes of changes and crises. These supports include child care, networks of caring adults to back up parents, educational and developmental programs for family members of all ages, and professional services for families in trouble. They require social policies that ensure families affordable housing, reliable income, health care, quality education for their children, and professional services for special needs. All families need these supports, and churches will more and more be seeking ways to facilitate comprehensive supportive services for their families, as well as for families outside their congregations. Innovative church child welfare agencies will be seeking ways to help congregations find resources to provide community-based services and voices in public policy development.

A Shrinking Pool of Volunteers

In an age when the pool of volunteers is shrinking, it may seem ludicrous to call for renewed attention to, and roles for, volunteers in the work of the agency and congregation. Only a minority of married women, the major group of volunteers in the past century, do not carry the multiple responsibilities of employment and caregiving for children and/or aging parents. Fewer able-bodied senior citizens will be choosing to retire early, with the repeal of mandatory retirement, and others will find some paid work necessary to survival. The character of the volunteer has changed substantially, from one who has hours of time to devote to service outside of family responsibilities to one who wants to find ways to serve within his or her current roles and relationships, and who wants to fit service into the very limited time between these other responsibilities.

Undoubtedly, the number of volunteers who devote hours to making quilts and other time-consuming fundraising activities will decline. In their place, agencies must find opportunities for service for very busy persons already carrying multiple demands. Some of these opportunities will be within the agency, but they will not be the extensive roles that in the past could supplement or serve in place of employees.

Growing Emphasis on Results and Evaluation

One cannot write a book about child welfare services without at least some call for more research on program outcomes and more attention to evaluation. Certain aspects are unique to church agencies.

First, with the exception of counting new converts and members, budget size, and the percentage of church income that is sent on to mission causes, churches do not focus much on outcomes. They tend to put resources into causes rather than results. As Prince noted [1991], with tongue in cheek:

> You think how many years folks have been preaching against fornication. You look at the results, and one has to wonder if that preaching has had any effect at all. Yet we are still preaching.

It is easy to point out the problems in attending to causes rather than outcomes; agencies can continue to offer the same tired, ineffective services they have offered for the past 20 years or more, because they are responding to causes that concern the church. This focus on causes, however, indicates one of the important and valuable characteristics of the church's response to children's needs—its foundation in compassionate response to the needs of others, even when that response does not bring about the anticipated change. Church programs are not tied directly to the effectiveness of social change efforts. This does not mean that church programs do not have to be accountable or evaluate the outcomes of their services. They do. But evaluation cannot stop there.

Church agencies also have to consider how they can evaluate the effectiveness of their leadership in the mission of the church: for example, how to include as part of an evaluation the extent to which laypersons have been involved in the financial support and actual services provided by the agency, and the consequence of that involvement for the laypersons, their churches, and their awareness and concern for children and families. The extent to which the church has been empowered to serve is just as significant as the effects of the service itself.

Finally, the church-related agency has to evaluate the consequences of its inevitable choices concerning the use of its limited resources in the face of almost limitless possibilities for service. What did the choice to offer expensive residential treatment and treatment foster homes cost in terms of other services that could not be implemented? What inadvertent consequences did the agency's leadership in a congregation-based child advocacy program have for the financial support from that congregation for services to seriously emotionally disturbed children? What are the advantages and costs incurred when a formerly centralized staff is dispersed to community-based centers?

Only after considering these wider issues, and keeping them continually in focus, should a church agency design its program evaluation. Certainly, the effectiveness of specific services in relation to client needs must be evaluated, but this is only one portion of the agency's responsibility for accountability. Even the evaluation of specific services must heed the warning that many of the kinds of programs the church agency is beginning to offer under the rubric of family support services take time to implement. Community-based services by their nature must be sensitive to their community, and thus are not simply replications of services elsewhere. Campbell [1987: 347] has warned against premature evaluations that do not give programs time to work out the bugs: "We should have no external evaluations until a program sends up a flag that says, 'We've got something special that we know works and think others ought to borrow.'"

Making Changes in the Church Agency

Challenges both within and without make it certain that no church agency can remain unchanged. To try to continue "as is" in the changing professional and church context of today is like trying to tread water a few hundred yards from the top of Niagara Falls. One may be doing everything one can to stay in place, but the current is too strong.

At the same time, the agency's roots in its current services and programs may be deep. For example, the church's physical resources often do not lend themselves to a change from residential to community services. The church agency is often located in a facility built decades ago as a "children's home" in the quiet countryside outside the city. Now it finds itself in suburbia, because the city has grown out and around it—often affluent suburbia, not the place one would locate a community-based service center for families at risk. The residential facilities often have alumni who are key supporters and are emotionally attached to the facility itself; it may have been their actual childhood home. Other members of the church constituency may also have identified with the children's home, a location that figures significantly in their involvement with the agency.

Most church agencies therefore cannot risk a complete overhaul and redefinition of their objectives and program services. Instead, agencies approach change incrementally, adding congregational and community services, revising and enhancing current program services. The agency asks itself:

- What are the needs of children and families in the community and churches we serve?

- What are the needs of the churches we serve who want to involve themselves in ministry with children and families?

- How do these two sets of needs interface? Are we the right system to respond to these needs? Is this a part of our mission?

- Which of the multitude of possible services will be most effective in responding to needs?

- How will those services fit with other programs and services we offer?

- Do we have the values, knowledge, and skills to develop those services?

- Can we generate the resources of staff members and time, facilities and finances, and excitement and energy?

This decision-making process links needs assessment with the tasks, values, and politics of already established programs and relationships; it links community needs assessment with church resource assessment; it links services with the mission of agency and church.

Change inevitably comes with considerable difficulty and stress to an agency, particularly when it affects established practices and daily patterns of living and working. Wolins and Wozner [1982] state that the ease of change is inversely related to the level of the change. That is, global modifications require less effort than limited modifications; policy is easier to change than strategy, and strategies are in turn easier to change than actual practice. The tactics and techniques of the work done, because it is carried out by numerous individuals with their own established patterns of working, are the most difficult element of the agency to change. It may be far easier to establish agency goals for working with the various congregations and religious groups that relate to the agency than to change the behavior of receptionists and social workers and child care workers who actually implement—or fail to implement—those goals in the ways that they think about their tasks, structure their work, and talk with these religious groups.

Conclusions

In centuries past, early Christians in Rome, a young nun in France, Baptist women in Louisville, a pastor in the slums of New York, and United Methodist women in Chicago had clear visions of what needed to happen: orphaned children needed shelter and care, troubled and troubling children needed help, and the people of God needed to respond. The situation facing church-related child welfare agencies today seems much more complex. Our resources of money and staff seem so limited in the face of a whole array of complex needs. What congregations often want to give— a party for "orphans" on a holiday, or used clothing and toys—does not fit the needs of the children and families whom we serve.

Effective professionals in a church-related agency need far more than skills in family therapy with troubled children and their families; they need to be students of theology and the Bible who can firmly root what they do in the values and mission of the church community, fervent speakers who can help churches understand the needs and their role in responding to those needs, visionaries who can look at the church's resources and the needs of children and families and bring them together in creative new services, program planners and implementers who understand the strengths and limitations of the church as a voluntary religious organization, and consultants who can train and support laypersons for key roles in their own social networks, as well as with the children and families who are directly served by the agency. Thank God that the power and Spirit Christians had within them in the past is the same power and Spirit on which we can draw in the work before us.

Biblical Texts Related to Children and Child Welfare Services

$\mathcal{F}$ AMILIAR STORIES FROM THEIR OWN HERITAGE can help churches recognize and embrace their responsibility to care for, and to respond to, children and their families in crisis. The Bible and the history of the church are rich sources of information about the response of saints and martyrs, and churches and other groups of Christians, to children and their families.

In speaking with, or writing for, church groups, appropriate illustrations from scripture and from the church's history can communicate understanding and respect for the audience. It is a part of the process of "joining," which Minuchin [1974] has described so eloquently in talking about the family therapist becoming a part of the family system in the therapeutic relationship. The pages that follow suggest ways for professionals to communicate a connection with the belief system and culture of the church community.

This appendix is by no means complete; it is simply meant as an illustration. The history of the church, the stories of its martyrs and saints, and its scriptures can be explored for other content that relates to children and their families. One must make sure, however, that stories used to illustrate current issues or to draw connections between those issues and the church's scriptural or historical heritage are not distorted. The original historical context and/or the broader messages the biblical authors meant to communicate are necessary to inform meanings and values drawn from such material.

Exodus 2. The Infant Moses

This story touches on the difficult decisions that often have to be made in protecting children. We have to weigh the risks of remaining in a precarious home situation against the risks of out-of-home placement. It is also a story of foster care and adoption and the role biological family members may continue to have, even when a child cannot live at home.

1 Samuel 1:9-20. The Conception and Birth of Samuel

Samuel's birth gives us a picture of the wanted child that should be the experience of all children. Hannah pleaded with God for a child, promising to dedicate him to God. Her story can illustrate that wanted babies are often better cared for—both before and after birth—than babies who are not. Working to nurture and support expectant parents, particularly those who, unlike Hannah, experienced pregnancy as an "accident," can help ensure that all babies have the best chance at life, and of a life dedicated to God, that a community can give.

II Samuel 12:7-23. The Death of King David's Son

David took the blame for the illness and eventual death of his child because of his own sin. The story helps one see the awesome consequences parents' decisions often have for their children. Many of today's infant deaths and lifelong disabilities are preventable, the tragic consequences of substance abuse or poor nutrition. When a child dies, guilt and anguish wrack those who feel they could have or should have done something to prevent the tragedy. The experience of David's servants also echoes our own uncertainty and helplessness about how to comfort others who experience such a family devastation.

Luke 2. The Birth of Jesus

Services for homeless children and families can draw on the story of Jesus, born in the shelter of a lowly manger.

Matthew 2:1-12, Luke 2:16-38. The Shepherds and Magi, the Prophet Simeon and the Prophetess Anna

Family support services can draw on the experiences of Jesus' father and his mother, who was most probably a teenager. The shepherds, the magi, the prophet Simeon, and the prophetess Anna were "significant others" who, in reaching out to Jesus' parents and blessing their baby, provided critical social support to this young family at a time when they faced forced emigration and an uncertain future. Later, other caring persons supported Mary as she had to stand by and watch her son suffer (e.g. John 19:25-26). All parents need to be surrounded by a community of persons who can bless, encourage, and support them in the difficult tasks of parenting, a community that can also stand with parents during life crises when they feel helpless to intervene for their children.

Matthew 2:13-23. The Flight into Egypt and the Move to Nazareth

Programs that work with migrants and refugees can identify with Jesus' parents, who became political refugees and fled to Egypt. They gave up home and security for the welfare of their son, moving from place to place.

$\mathcal{A}$PPENDIX 2

Tools for Congregational Assessment

Annotated References

> Carroll, Jackson W.; Dudley, Carl S.; and McKinney, William, eds. *Handbook for Congregational Studies*. Nashville: Abingdon, 1986.

An excellent handbook for consulting with congregations and helping congregations study themselves, before and as part of developing new programs and approaches to ministry. A number of very useful assessment instruments are provided in the handbook, as well as guidance for interpreting them with the congregation. This handbook is highly recommended for any major assessment process with a congregation.

> Dudley, Carl S., ed. *Building Effective Ministry: Theory and Practice in the Local Church*. San Francisco: Harper & Row, 1983.

Authors describe the study of the church as an organization from the various perspectives of psychology, ethnography, literary symbolism, sociology, theological ethics, and philosophical theology. This volume describes multidisciplinary approaches for consulting with congregations in assessing and planning change.

> Hessel, Dieter T. *Social Ministry*. Philadelphia: Westminster Press, 1982.

This volume gives pastors and other church leaders a theological challenge and excellent resources for involving churches in social ministry. Believing that all church members share social ministry, Hessel shows its central function in liturgy, Bible study, pastoral care, social service, community organization, and public policy action.

> Hopewell, James, F., ed. *The Whole Church Catalog: Where to Get Tools for Congregational Study and Intervention.* Washington, DC: The Alban Institute, Inc. (Mount St. Alban, Washington, DC 20016), 1984.

The Project Team for Congregational Studies compiled in this notebook descriptions of survey instruments and other instruments for learning about the identity that characterizes a particular church and about the church's community context, organizational structures and programs, interpersonal relations, and corporate processes. Each entry affords suggested applications and where to obtain further information or copies of the resource. No actual research instruments are included in the catalog, however.

> Roozen, David A.; McKinney, William; and Carroll, Jackson, W. *Varieties of Religious Presence: Mission in Public Life.* New York: Pilgrim Press, 1984.

These researchers took a sociological approach to the study of congregations as open systems. They classified congregations in terms of the dominant way each defines its relationship to its community, which they called a church's "mission orientation." Their research methods included interviews with community leaders, a telephone survey of area residents, a survey of pastoral leaders of congregations, and case studies of individual congregations based on directed participant observation. Their methods are described in detail, and invite use in other communities and with other congregations.

Learning Techniques

What follows are some suggestions for learning about a congregation that will help shape a consultation concerning the church's ministry with children and their families. These have been selected because they are relevant to a broad understanding of the church, and, more specifically, its historic and current concerns for children and their families, as expressed in social justice positions the church has taken, actions related to those positions, and ministries the church has offered. These methods are merely illustrations, however, and are in no way meant to be construed as an exhaustive compilation of congregational study methods.

The information gathered by the use of such methods can be a critical resource in consulting with the church about its ministries with children and their families. The church, however, may benefit from placing this assessment within a much larger and more comprehensive self-assessment that can help shape its future in a wide variety of areas, not only its social ministries with children and families. The references above can be very helpful in undertaking such a congregational study.

Gathering Oral History
(from Carroll, Dudley, and McKinney 1986)

Guided interviews with members of different age groups and lengths of membership in the church can help you and the congregation understand its history. Be sure to interview children and young people as well as adults. The following questions can guide the interview:

- Tell me about your association with the church.

- What changes have you noticed about the church during the time you have been associated with it?

- What has happened that you wish had not occurred?

- What has happened that you would have liked to see followed up in a different way?

- In what ways has the church demonstrated concern for children, youths, and their families in the congregation? in the larger community?

- How has that changed during the time you have been associated with the church?

Time Line
(from Carroll, Dudley, and McKinney 1986)

One can also learn about a congregation's history by gathering a group of members for an evening of disciplined recollection. Tape a long sheet of wide paper (such as butcher paper) down one wall at a comfortable height for writing. Draw a line from one end to the other. Put the congregation's founding date at the left end of the line and the present date at the right end. Mark off the intervening period in suitable time intervals: single years, five- or ten-year periods, and so on. Above the line, for each time period, describe the significant events in the neighborhood, region, nation, and world.

Encourage members to recall important events in the church's past and note them below the line on the paper near each date. Discuss connections between community events and the life of the church. Leave the paper up so that participants may add to it later. The church may want to save the information for other uses.

During this process you will probably want to focus particularly on the ministries of the church to children and families. You can later consult church documents or talk to church members to gather more information about critical events. For example, if you learn that the church at one time had a day care center that is no longer a part of its ministry, ask what happened to it.

Exploring a Congregation's Heritage of Care for Children

Explore church documents for indications of ministries the church has undertaken with children, youths, and families and for social justice concerns as they have been expressed in the church's actions. Depending on the amount of time you can invest, the following documents can be helpful:

- A written congregational history, if one exists

- Annual reports and minutes of meetings

- Annual budgets

- The church covenant, statements of faith, and other written statements of the congregation's purpose and ministries

Looking for Children and Youths in the Life of the Church

Look at church programs (worship, Bible study, mission groups and activities, recreation) and administrative structures to find where children and youths are included in activities with the congregation and where they are not included or are segregated in age groupings. Where children are incorporated into the life of the congregation, examine the following:

- What roles do they play?

- Do they share leadership?

- In what other ways are they participants?

- Which community rituals include children? Which exclude them?

- Where are the children of different ages located in the church building(s)? For example, are they scattered throughout the congregation in a worship service, or do they choose to sit together in the back or balcony? Do they sit with families, in groups of peers, or in some other grouping (for example, with a friend and the family of a friend)? Or are they segregated in a children's worship service for part or all of the time of the congregational gathering?

- What effect does this have on their inclusion?

Conduct the same kind of analysis for other cross-generational events, such as church suppers, recreational events, and informal social gatherings.

- In what ways have programs and functions been accommodated to the needs of children and youths? For example, do committee meetings include activities that invite intergenerational participation?

- Is the business explained in such a way that a child or youth committee member can understand and become a participant?

- What physical changes or facilities have been provided to encourage children's participation? (For example, carpeting a portion or all of the sanctuary floor to quiet the sounds of scuffling feet or to invite children to play quietly on the floor)

Look at the facility from the perspective of a child or youth.

- Is it possible to see what is going on in worship?

- Are bulletins written in a way that children can understand, or are special bulletins prepared for them?

- Can water fountains be reached?

- When asked, how many children can adults in the church name with whom they have a close relationship, other than those in their own family? How do they know those children? In what ways do they continue to relate to them?

- When asked, how many adults in the church can children name, other than their own parents, whom they consider friends they can talk to personally? How do they know those adults? In what ways do they continue to relate to them?

In programs designed especially for children and youths, examine the following:

- What portion of the church's budget is spent on activities for children and youths, in comparison with other age groups in the church?

- Are the physical facilities and equipment appropriate, safe, adequate, and appealing?

- What kinds of adult staffing are used?

- Are training and ongoing support available for volunteers?

- Is there an adequate number of adults for the number and needs of the children and youths being served?

- Where do the children and youths in the church's programs come from? Are they all children of adult members? Do they come from the surrounding community? Are poor and at-risk children actively sought and included in the church's programs?

- To what extent are volunteers who serve in these programs considered to be carrying out the central mission of the church, versus simply providing care for the children of adult members?

- How does the church address the particular needs of children and youths in the community that are not being met by other community organizations?

- What are the indicators of sensitivity and lack of sensitivity to the needs of poor and vulnerable children and their families?

As you put together this information, it may be helpful to write a summary report describing the role of children and youths in the worship, fellowship, ministry, and administration of the church community. You may draw some conclusions about the significance of ministry to children and youths in the church's budget, in its programs and activities, and in the informal relationships among members. You can begin to form hypotheses about the importance of the needs of children and youths relative to other aims of the church's mission. This may then lay a foundation for ministry efforts being considered, or, alternatively, suggest that attention should be given to enhancing the role and importance of children and youths in all aspects of the church's life before undertaking ministry programs with children and youths outside the church's life. Involving the church staff and the members of the church in preparing the report can yield particulars you have overlooked, bring in additional data, and continue their active involvement in the assessment of their community.

A Demographic Portrait of the Congregation

Gather information about the demographic characteristics of children, youths, and their families within the congregation. Pertinent information includes age, gender, marital status, race, ethnicity, and socioeconomic status. Some congregations routinely collect this information when people join the congregation, but it may not have been updated. Other churches regularly conduct churchwide surveys. If the congregation does not have demographic information, you may have to conduct a survey.

The Parish Profile Inventory in Carroll, Dudley, and McKinney's *Handbook for Congregational Studies* is an excellent resource for such a survey. It includes not only demographic information, but also members' comprehensive assessments of the church's functioning, members' beliefs and attitudes, and their preferences in ministry styles. This information can then be compared with the demographic characteristics of the church's community (available in U.S. census data) and conclusions drawn about particular groups the church is serving and special needs that are being met, as well as groups in the community that are not represented in the church. Hypotheses about the reasons for this lack of participation by some demographic groups in the community can then be the basis for further assessment.

The conclusion that the church is serving a particular target group can be discussed in making decisions about the shape of future ministries. For example, a church that finds itself composed primarily of young middle-class families with dual-career spouses in a community with a large population of single mothers may examine its programs and ministries from the perspective of the needs of single mothers and their children.

Carroll, Dudley, and McKinney [1986: 43] suggest the following uses for a demographic survey:

- To provide a profile of the congregation's typical member

- To indicate the degree of diversity that exists in a given congregation

- To compare the congregation's presumed demographic picture with its actual one

- To compare the congregation's demographic picture with that of the community the congregation serves

- To provide important clues for program development for both present and potential members

- To help a congregation reflect on its given demographic identity in comparison with what it would like to become

- To assist denominational leaders (and church agencies) in understanding the congregations with which they work

Mapping the Church Community
(adapted from Carroll, Dudley, and McKinney 1986)

Place a map of the church's community on a bulletin board. Have church members place pins on the map to mark the location of their households. A completed membership map will illustrate the extent to which a church is a neighborhood church or draws members from a larger geographical area, and whether it skips over some residential neighborhoods. One might also invite youngsters to place pins (perhaps with a different color head) on the location of their schools, and parents to place pins where they have children enrolled in day care and/or preschool programs. The location of public recreational facilities, children's treatment facilities, hospitals, and other resources and locations for possible ministries can also be noted.

Mission Opportunity Questionnaire
(from Carroll, Dudley, and McKinney 1986)

Jackson Carroll and his colleagues developed a brief 32-item anonymous questionnaire to elicit information from a congregation about reports made to it concerning its community's needs and demography (as drawn from census data and interviews with key informants). It lists a number of projects and activities for the church to consider. Room is available on the questionnaire for additional suggestions. Items pertaining to the needs of children, youths, and families could be developed—for example, recruiting and supporting foster parents, developing a ministry with teen parents, and so on. Respondents are asked to check one of the following categories for each question: (a) not needed in our community, (b) not appropriate for our church, (c) low priority at this time, (d) only moderate priority at this time, (e) high priority/needs immediate attention. The following are sample items from the original survey:

- Develop more effective outreach to members of minority groups.

- Review our church's ministry to families and family members.

- Look for ways we can minister to people in nontraditional families.

- Review our congregation's stewardship potential in light of community income data.

$\mathcal{A}$PPENDIX 3

Agencies and Other Resources

Sources of Information

The Child Advocacy Network of the Health and Welfare Ministries Program Department, General Board of Global Ministries, The United Methodist Church, 475 Riverside Drive, Room 350, New York, NY 10115-0050.

The Child Advocacy Network helps annual church conferences establish conferencewide child advocacy networks and resources. It publishes a newsletter, *The Child Advocate.*

Child and Family Justice Office, The National Council of Churches of Christ, 475 Riverside Drive, Room 572, New York, NY 10115-0050.

The Office supports child advocates and educators by offering leadership training, resources, and technical assistance and by coordinating the ecumenical community's efforts to inform and empower churches to respond to the needs of children and families.

The Child Welfare League of America, 440 First Street, NW, Suite 310, Washington, DC 20001-2085.

The Child Welfare League establishes standards and accredits child welfare agencies. It researches current policy and legislative agendas that affect children, reviews innovative policies and programs, advocates for legislation to benefit vulnerable families and children, and publishes child welfare-related literature, including a wide range of books and the journal *CHILD WELFARE.*

Children's Defense Fund, 25 E Street NW, Washington, DC 20001.

The Children's Defense Fund is an advocate for children, particularly poor, minority, and disabled children. CDF gathers and disseminates information on key issues affecting children at federal, state, and local levels. It pursues an annual legislative agenda in the U.S. Congress and litigates selected cases of major importance to children. The Children's Defense Fund is supported by foundations, corporate grants, and individual donations. *The State of America's Children*, produced annually by CDF, contains a wealth of statistics and interpretation concerning children and youths in the states, the nation, and the world. It covers research and developments in family income and employment, child care, health, education, youth development, housing and homelessness, and vulnerable children and families.

The Ecumenical Child Care Network, 1119 Dauphine Street, #5, New Orleans, LA 70116.

The Network provides technical assistance and leadership for churches that provide community child care programs, and also offers conferences, publications, and training resources.

The Family Resource Coalition, 230 North Michigan Avenue, Suite 1625, Chicago, IL 60601.

The Family Resource Coalition is a cooperative network of professionals, including social workers, clergy, health professionals, academics, early childhood educators, family therapists, and others who are working in parent support programs. It reviews prevention program models, strategies, and research, and provides publications, including a journal, and information about parent support programs.

Presbyterian Church (USA) Child Advocacy Project, 100 Witherspoon Street, Room 3066, Louisville, KY 40202-1396.

The Project focuses on service, education, and networking, forming partnerships with other child advocacy groups.

The Southern Baptist Child Advocacy Network, The Gheens Center for Christian Family Ministry, Southern Baptist Theological Seminary, 2825 Lexington Road, Louisville, KY 40280.

The Network is a gathering of denominational leaders, congregational staff members, and lay persons who seek to coordinate efforts and collaborate in providing resources and models for ministry and advocacy for children and families.

United Methodist Women's Campaign for Children. The Women's Division, General Board of Global Ministries, the United Methodist Church, 475 Riverside Drive, New York, NY 10115-0050.

The campaign has been designed to help local units of United Methodist women make a concrete difference in children's lives through education and training resources for ministry and advocacy.

Addresses

Adopt a Child Abuse Caseworker Ministry
Corpus Christi Metro Ministries
1906 Leopard
Corpus Christi, TX 78408

Adopt a Social Worker Program
Covenant to Care, Inc.
26 Wintonbury Avenue
Bloomfield, CT 06002-2416
203/243-1806

Center for Family Life in Sunset Park
345 43rd Street
Brooklyn, NY 11232
718/788-3500

Child Welfare League of America
440 First Street, NW, Suite 310
Washington, DC 20001-2085
202/638-2952

Children's Defense Fund
25 E Street, NW
Washington, DC 20001
202/628-8787

ChildServ
Church/Community Consultation Services
1580 N. Northwest Highway
Park Ridge, IL 60068

Covenant Children's Home and Family Services
502 Elm Place
Princeton, IL 61356
815/875-1129

Family Care
First United Methodist Church
Wilmington, IL 60481

The Methodist Children's Home of Louisiana
P. O. Box 929
Ruston, LA 71273-0929
318/255-5020

Operation Getting It Together (OGIT)
500 North Main Street
Sebastopol, CA 95472
707/823-6967

Parent Mentor Program
National Crime Prevention Council
1700 K Street, NW, Second Floor
Washington, DC 20007
202/466-6272

The Philpott Parent Aide Program
Baptist Children's Homes of North Carolina, Inc.
Box 338
Thomasville, NC 27361-0338
919/472-4605

Rainbow After-School Program
Presbyterian Church of the Covenant
For information, write to:
Texas Department of Human Services
701 West 51st Street
PO Box 2960, M.C. 537-W
Austin, TX 78769
512/450-3289

Soulard Family Center
2200 South 12th Street
St. Louis, MO 63104
314/773-2328

Voice of Calvary Ministries
1655 St. Charles Street
Jackson, MS 39209
601/353-1635

APPENDIX 4

Child and Family Advocacy for Congregations and Church Agencies: Written Resources

Bruland, Esther Byle, and Mott, Stephen Charles. *A Passion for Jesus, A Passion for Justice.* Valley Forge, PA: Judson Press, 1983.

This book was written as a guide for Bible study groups and church social concerns committees. It offers a biblical theology of Christian social responsibility and provides practical guidance in responding to matters of social justice. It supports churches taking corporate stands on social justice issues, even when not all members agree.

Edelman, Marian Wright. *Families in Peril: An Agenda for Social Change.* Cambridge, MA: Harvard University Press, 1987.

The president of the Children's Defense Fund describes the overall status of African American and Caucasian children and families in America, the human and financial costs of our widespread child and family poverty, and how we are failing our children. Although the book carefully documents its conclusions with statistics and research, it is written in a style that compels the reader to keep reading. It is a substantive, moving commentary on what our nation is doing—or not doing—for all our children.

Garland, Diana. *Precious in His Sight.* Birmingham, AL: New Hope, 1993.

A study guide written for church members to encourage their involvement in services to children and their families and advocacy in their behalf. The book offers ways of incorporating children and youths into the worship,

Christian care, administration, and ministry of the congregation, as well as particular considerations that directly affect children and youths, with concrete suggestions for how church groups and individuals can respond. Target conditions include child care; poverty, hunger, and homelessness; school failure, teen pregnancy, and substance abuse; and family violence, sexual abuse, and chronic mental illness of a parent. Practical guidance is offered for becoming a child advocate.

Guy, Kathleen. *Welcome the Child: A Child Advocacy Guide for Churches.* Washington, DC: The Children's Defense Fund, 1991.

Excellent resource for planning a Children's Sunday, with worship resources and suggestions for sermons. Guides the study of children's lives and the development of action programs concerning child care and Head Start, education, vulnerable children and families, homelessness and housing, maternal and child health, self-sufficiency of young people, and prevention of teen pregnancy.

Johnson, Ronald, and Long, Russell. *Social Ministry: A Congregational Manual.* Philadelphia: Parish Life Press, 1983.

A manual for members of a congregational social ministry committee or task force, congregational directors of social ministry projects, pastors, and others interested in exploring the responsibility of the congregation for social ministry. It describes a model of study, service, and social action and how to involve congregations in each of these dimensions of social ministry.

Schorr, Lisbeth B. *Within Our Reach: Breaking the Cycle of Disadvantage.* New York: Doubleday, 1988.

Schorr reviews the risk factors for children that lead to too early pregnancy, leaving school illiterate and unemployable, and delinquency, and describes programs that actually work in reducing these risks, with a clear agenda for action. This volume creates excitement and hope that we can make a difference for children.

REFERENCES

Adams, L. Cecile. "Caring for the Children: Advocacy, Children, and You." *Information: Children's Ministries* 36 (Summer 1990): 1.

Addams, Jane. *Twenty Years at Hull House*. New York: The Macmillan Company, 1910.

American Association of Retired Persons (AARP). "Results of a Nationwide Survey of Parent Aide Programs: Older Volunteers in Partnership with Parents Project." Washington DC: AARP, Social Outreach and Support Program Department,1987.

Anderson, Ray S., and Guernsey, Dennis B. *On Being Family: A Social Theology of the Family*. Grand Rapids, MI: Eerdmans Publishing Company, 1985.

Aries, Philippe. *Centuries of Childhood: A Social History of Family Life*. New York: Vintage Books, 1962.

Astrachan, M., and Harris, D. "Weekend Only: An Alternate Model in Residential Treatment Centers." *CHILD WELFARE* LXII (May/June 1983): 253-261.

Attneave, C. L. "Social Networks as the Unit of Intervention." In *Family Therapy: Theory and Practice*, edited by P. Guerin. New York: Gardner Press, 1976.

Austin, M. J.; Brannon, D.; and Pecora, P. J. *Managing Staff Development Programs in Human Service Agencies*. Chicago: Nelson-Hall Publishers, 1984.

Bailey, Patricia L. "Community Ministries." In *Church Social Work*, edited by Diana R. Garland. St. Davids, PA: The North American Association of Christians in Social Work, 1991.

Baker, Charles. Presentation at the Church-Related Child Welfare Agency Conference, the Gheens Center for Christian Family Ministry, Southern Baptist Theological Seminary, Louisville, KY, March 1991.

Baker, C. Truett. "Should Church-Related Agencies Accept Purchase of Care?" Paper presented at the Annual Meeting of the Southern Baptist Child Care Executives, Phoenix, AZ, February 21-23, 1989.

Bampfylde, G. "John ix. 28: A Case for a Different Translation." *Novum Testamentum* 11 (1969): 247-260.

Banks, Robert. *Paul's Idea of Community.* Grand Rapids, MI: Eerdmans, 1980.

Barber, Cyril A. "Residential Care Quiz Produces Surprising Results." *Caring* 6, 1 (1990): 25-26.

Barth, Richard P. "On Their Own: The Experiences of Youth after Foster Care. *Child and Adolescent Social Work* 7, 5 (1990): 419-440.

Beavers, Jeanette; Hampson, Hulgus; and Beavers, Robert. "Coping with Families with a Retarded Child." *Family Process* 25 (1986): 365-378.

Billingsley, A., and Giovannoni, J. *Children of the Storm.* New York: Harcourt, Brace Jovanovich, 1972.

Blankenhorn, David; Bayme, Steven; and Elshtain, Jean Bethke, eds. *Rebuilding the Nest: A New Commitment to the American Family.* Milwaukee, WI: Family Service America, 1990.

Bossard, James H. S., and Boll, Eleanor S. *The Sociology of Childhood,* 4th ed. New York: Harper and Row, 1966.

Boukydis, C. F. Z., ed. *Support for Parents and Infants.* New York: Routledge & Kegan Paul, 1986.

Bowman, Ted. "Living with Contradictions: Training Natural Helpers for Lay Ministry." In *The Church's Ministry with Families: A Practical Guide,* edited by D. R. Garland and D. L. Pancoast. Irving, TX: Word, 1990: 224-234.

Bremner, Robert H. *Children and Youth in America: A Documentary History* (3 vols.). Cambridge, MA: Harvard University Press, 1970-1974.

Brendtro, Larry K. "The Church, Caesar, and Child Care." In *Sacred Shelters: Church-Related Children's Homes,* edited by Robert R. Gillogly. Topeka, KS: The Villages, Inc., 1982: 36-52.

Brieland, Donald. "The Hull House Tradition and the Contemporary Social Worker: Was Jane Addams Really a Social Worker?" *Social Work* 35, 2 (1990): 134-138.

Brueggemann, Walter. *The Prophetic Imagination.* Philadelphia: Fortress, 1978.

Burke, Peter. "Honouring Each Other's Caring: Parish-Agency Partnership in Community Service." A paper delivered at the Fourth National Anglican

Welfare Conference, Christ College, University of Tasmania, Hobart, Tasmania, Australia, February 7, 1989.

Byrne, Eva. "Planning and Policy and Community-Based Services for Children and Families." In *Community-Based Services for Children and Families,* edited by Frank Maas and Susan Sach. Melbourne, Australia: Institute of Family Studies, 1984: 54-60.

Cahill, Brian F. "The Future of Voluntary Children's and Family Services." *CHILD WELFARE* LX, 2 (February 1981): 113-117.

Campbell, Donald T. "Problems for the Experimenting Society in the Interface between Evaluation and Service Providers." In *America's Family Support Programs: Perspectives and Prospects,* edited by Sharon L. Kagan, Douglass R. Powell, Bernice Weissbourd, and Edward F. Zigler. New Haven, CT: Yale University Press, 1987: 345-351.

Carnegie, Andrew. *The Gospel of Wealth and Other Timely Essays,* edited by Edward C. Kirkland. Cambridge, MA: Harvard University Press, 1962.

Carroll, Jackson W.; Dudley, Carl S.; and McKinney, William, eds. *Handbook for Congregational Studies.* Nashville, TN: Abingdon, 1986.

Carter, Forrest. *The Education of Little Tree.* Albuquerque: University of New Mexico Press, 1976.

Caulfield, Ernest. *The Infant Welfare Movement of the Eighteenth Century.* New York: Paul Hocker, 1931.

Chapman, Kathryn. Presentation at the Church-Related Child Welfare Conference, the Gheens Center for Christian Family Ministry, Southern Baptist Theological Seminary, Louisville, KY, March 1991.

The Chicago Home for the Friendless. Minutes of January 21, 1935, Child and Family Services, Chicago. As quoted in McCarthy 1982.

Children's Defense Fund. *A Little Child Shall Lead Us: A Christian Guide for the National Observance of Children's Sabbaths.* Washington, DC: Children's Defense Fund, 1992.

Children's Defense Fund. *It's Time to Stand Up for Your Children: A Parent's Guide to Child Advocacy.* Washington, DC: Children's Defense Fund, 1982.

Children's Defense Fund. *The State of America's Children: 1988.* Washington, DC: Children's Defense Fund, 1988.

Children's Defense Fund. *The State of America's Children: 1991.* Washington, DC: Children's Defense Fund, 1991.

Clark, Linda. "Hymn-Singing: The Congregation Making Faith." In *Carriers of Faith: Lessons from Congregational Studies,* edited by Carl S. Dudley, Jackson W. Carroll, and James P. Wind. Louisville, KY: Westminster/John Knox Press, 1991: 49-64.

Clark, Merrell; Fields, Carl; and Coleman, Ora. "Congregations, Parenting, and the Prevention of Delinquency." As quoted in *Mission Possible: Churches Supporting Fragile Families,* Washington, DC: National Crime Prevention Council, 1990.

Cobb, Sidney. "Social Support as a Moderator of Life Stress." *Psychosomatic Medicine* 38 (1976): 300-314.

Cochran, Mon. "Child Care and the Empowerment Process." *Networking Bulletin: Empowerment & Family Support* 2, 1 (1991): 1-3.

Cochran, Mon. *Empowering Families: Home Visiting and Building Clusters.* Distribution Center, 7 Research Park, Cornell University, Ithaca, NY 14850 (no date).

Cochran, Mon M., and Hogskolesenteret, Inge Bo. "Connections between the Social Networks, Family Involvement, and Behavior of Adolescent Males in Norway." Paper presented at the 1987 Meeting of the Society for Research in Child Development, Baltimore, MD, April 20-24, 1987.

Coleman, Loren. "Many Agencies Were Guilty of 'Placing Out' Children." *Social Work* 36 (January 1991): 94-95.

Coles, Robert. *The Spiritual Life of Children.* Boston: Houghton Mifflin, 1990.

Colletta, N. D., and Gregg, C. H. "Adolescent Mothers' Vulnerability to Stress." *Journal of Nervous and Mental Disease* 169 (1981): 50-54.

Collins, A. H., and Pancoast, D. L. *Natural Helping Networks.* Washington, DC: National Association of Social Workers, 1976.

Combrinck-Graham, Lee. "Introduction." In *Children in Family Contexts: Perspectives on Treatment,* edited by Lee Combrinck-Graham. New York: The Guilford Press, 1989: ix-xiv.

Cooklin, A.; Miller, A. C.; and McHugh, B. "An Institution for Change: Developing a Family Day Unit." *Family Process* 22 (1983): 453-468.

Costin, Lela B. "The Historical Context of Child Welfare." In _A Handbook of Child Welfare_, edited by Joan Laird and Ann Hartman. New York: The Free Press, 1985: 34-60.

Coughlin, Bernard J. _Church and State in Social Welfare_. New York: Columbia University Press, 1965.

Coyne, James C.; Wortman, Camille B.; and Lehman, Darrin R. "The Other Side of Support: Emotional Overinvolvement and Miscarried Helping." In _Marshaling Social Support: Formats, Processes, and Effects_, edited by Benjamin H. Gottlieb. Newbury Park, CA: Sage Publications, 1988: 305-330.

Crase, Dixie, et al. _Parenting by Grace: Discipline and Spiritual Growth_. Nashville: Sunday School Board of the Southern Baptist Convention, 1986.

Cuninggim, Merrimon. "Myths of Church-Relatedness." In _Church-Related Higher Education_, edited by Robert R. Parsonage. Valley Forge, PA: Judson Press, 1978.

Curran, Dolores. _Family: A Church Challenge for the '80s_. Minneapolis, MN: Winston Press, 1980.

Dailey, Wilda J. "Professionalism and the Public Dollar." _Social Casework_ 55 (July 1974): 428-434.

Daniels, W. H. _Moody, His Words_. New York, 1877. As quoted in Martin E. Marty, "Social Service: Godly and Godless." _Social Service Review_ 54, 4 (December 1980): 463-481.

Davis, Allen F. _American Heroine: The Life and Legend of Jane Addams_. London: Oxford University Press, 1973.

Davis, Allen F. _Spearheads for Reform: The Social Settlements and the Progressive Movement, 1890-1914_. New York: Oxford University Press, 1967.

Davis, C. Anne. "History of the Carver School of Church Social Work." _Review and Expositor_ 85 (1988): 209-220.

Dicker, Sheryl. _Stepping Stones: Successful Advocacy for Children_. New York: The Foundation for Child Development, 1990.

Druecker, Peter F. "How to Make People Decisions." _Harvard Business Review_ 63, 4 (July-August 1985): 22-25.

Druecker, Peter F. "What Business Can Learn from Non-Profits." *Harvard Business Review* 67, 4 (July-August 1989): 89-90.

Dudley, Carl S., and Johnson, Sally A. "Congregational Self-Images for Social Ministry." In *Carriers of Faith: Lessons from Congregational Studies*, edited by Carl S. Dudley, Jackson W. Carroll, and James P. Wind. Louisville, KY: Westminster/John Knox Press, 1991: 104-121.

Dumas, J. E., and Wahler, R. G. "Prediction of Treatment Outcome in Parent Skills Training: Mother Insularity and Socioeconomic Disadvantages." *Behavior Assessment* 5 (1983): 301-313.

Duncan, Dick; Myers, Ellen C.; Davies, Donna R.; and Casey, Diane E. *Adopting Child Protection Workers: A New Response by the Religious Community to the Crisis of Child Abuse and Neglect.* Austin TX: Texas Department of Human Services, 1988.

Dunst, Carl; Trivett, Carol; and Deal, Angela. *Enabling and Empowering Families.* Cambridge, MA: Brookline, 1988.

Eckman, George Peck. "Christianity and the Social Situation." In *The Social Application of Religion: The Merrick Lectures, 1907-1908,* by Charles Stelzle, Jane Addams, Charles P. Neill, Graham Taylor, and George P. Eckman. Cincinnati, OH: Jennings and Graham, 1908: 107-139.

Edelman, Marian Wright. *Families in Peril: An Agenda for Social Change.* Cambridge, MA: Harvard University Press, 1987.

Evans, Alice Frazer; Evans, Robert A.; and Kennedy, William Bean. *Pedagogies for the Non-Poor.* Maryknoll, NY: Orbis Books, 1987.

The Family Touch. "Parenting by Grace/Covenant Marriage Goes to the Bahamas." *The Family Touch: Family Enrichment News and Views* (Fall 1990): 1.

Fanshel, David, and Shinn, Eugene B. *Children in Foster Care: A Longitudinal Investigation.* New York: Columbia University Press, 1978.

Ferguson, G. Jane. "Social Work Practice in the Congregation." In *Church Social Work,* edited by Diana R. Garland. St. Davids, PA: The North American Association of Christians in Social Work, 1992.

Ferguson, G. Jane. "Sociomoral Dilemma Group Model: A Sociomoral Reasoning Model for Small Group Discussions in an Adolescent Residential Treatment Setting." In *Models for Ministry III*, edited by Patricia L. Bailey. Louisville, KY: Paul Adkins Institute for Research and Training in Church Social Work, Southern Baptist Theological Seminary, 1988.

Folks, Homer. *Care of Destitute, Neglected and Delinquent Children.* New York: J. B. Lyon, 1900.

Ford, Leighton. "Evangelism and Social Responsibility." *World Evangelization Information Bulletin* 26 (March 1982): 6.

Forman, Wendy, and Slap, Laura. "Preventing Burnout." In *Working for Peace: A Handbook of Practical Psychology and Other Tools,* edited by Neil Wollman. San Luis Obispo, CA: Impact Publishers, 1985: 63-79.

Freeman, Margery. *Called to Act: Stories of Child Care Advocacy in Our Churches.* New York: Child Advocacy Office, Division of Church and Society, National Council of the Churches of Christ in the U.S.A., 1986.

Freeman, Margery. *Helping Churches Mind the Children: A Guide for Church-Housed Child Day Care Programs.* New York: National Council of the Churches of Christ in the U.S.A, 1987.

Friedman, E. *Generation to Generation: Family Process in Church and Synagogue.* New York: Guilford Press, 1985.

Friedrich, Laura Dean Ford. "Serving Children and Families through Agency Consultation." In *The Church's Ministry with Families: A Practical Guide,* edited by Diana R. Garland and Diane L. Pancoast. Irving, TX: Word, 1990: 155-170.

Garbarino, James; Burston, Nancy; Raber, Suzanne; Russell, Robert; and Crouter, Ann. "The Social Maps of Children Approaching Adolescence: Studying the Ecology of Youth Development." *Journal of Youth and Adolescence* 7 (1978): 417-428.

Garbarino, James. "Using Natural Helping Networks to Meet the Problem of Child Maltreatment." In *Schools and the Problem of Child Abuse,* edited by R. Volpe, M. Breton, and J. Mitton. Toronto: University of Toronto, 1979: 129-136.

Garbarino, James, and Sherman, D. "High-Risk Neighborhoods and High-Risk Families: The Human Ecology of Child Maltreatment." *Child Development* 51 (1980): 188-198.

Garland, David E., and Garland, Diana R. "The Family: Biblical and Theological Perspectives." In *Incarnational Ministry: The Presence of Christ in Church, Society, and Family,* edited by Christian D. Kettler and Todd H. Speidell. Colorado Springs, CO: Helmers & Howard, 1990.

Garland, Diana R. "Christians in Social Work, Christian Social Ministry, and Church Social Work: Necessary Distinctions." *Social Work and Christianity* 13 (1986): 18-25.

Garland, Diana R. "The Church's Ministry with Families: An Introduction." In *The Church's Ministry with Families: A Practical Guide*, edited by Diana R. Garland and Diane L. Pancoast. Irving, TX: Word, 1990a: 3-19.

Garland, Diana R. "Developing and Empowering Parent Networks." In *The Church's Ministry with Families: A Practical Guide*, edited by Diana R. Garland and Diane L. Pancoast. Irving, TX: Word, 1990b: 91-109.

Garland, Diana R. *Precious in His Sight*. Birmingham, AL: New Hope, 1993.

Garland, Diana R. "Residential Child Care Workers as Primary Agents of Family Intervention." *Child Care Quarterly* 16 (1987): 21-34.

Garland, Diana R. "Social Work Practice in Church-Supported Child Welfare Services." In *Church Social Work*, edited by Diana R. Garland. St. Davids, PA: The North American Association of Christians in Social Work, 1992.

Garland, Diana R. "Volunteer Ministry to Families of Prisoners and the Christian Social Worker's Role." *Social Work and Christianity* 12 (1985): 13-25.

Garland, Diana R. *Working with Couples for Marriage Enrichment*. San Francisco: Jossey-Bass, 1983.

Garland, Diana R., and Bailey, Pat. "Effective Work with Religious Organizations by Social Workers in Other Settings." *Social Work and Christianity* 17 (1990): 79-95.

Garland, Diana R.; Chapman, Katherine C.; and Pounds, J. *Christian Self-Esteem: Parenting by Grace*. Nashville, TN: The Southern Baptist Convention Sunday School Board, 1991.

Garland, Diana R., and Conrad, Ann P. "The Church as a Context for Professional Practice." In *The Church's Ministry with Families: A Practical Guide*, edited by Diana R. Garland and Diane L. Pancoast. Irving, TX: Word, 1990: 71-87.

Garland, Diana R., and Garland, David E. *Beyond Companionship: Christians in Marriage*. Philadelphia: Westminster Press, 1986.

Garland, Diana R., and Garland, David E. *Marriage for Better or For Worse*. Nashville, TN: Broadman, 1989.

Garland, Diana R., and Pancoast, Diane L., eds. *The Church's Ministry with Families: A Practical Guide*. Irving, TX: Word, 1990.

Garval, Howard S. "Counterpoint: The Changes Are Challenging and Exciting." *Families in Society* 71 (September 1990): 438-441.

Gilbert, Dan. Presentation at the Church-Related Child Welfare Agency Conference, the Gheens Center for Christian Family Ministry, Southern Baptist Theological Seminary, Louisville, KY, March 1991.

Gilbert, Neil, and Specht, Harry. *Dimensions of Social Welfare Policy.* Englewood Cliffs, NJ: Prentice-Hall, 1974.

Gillogly, Robert R. "Primary Prevention: The Church's Role in Residential Care." In *Sacred Shelters: Church-Related Children's Homes,* edited by Robert R. Gillogly. Topeka, KS: The Villages, Inc., 1982a: 1-10.

Gillogly, Robert R., ed. *Sacred Shelters: Church-Related Children's Homes.* Topeka, KS: The Villages, Inc., 1982b.

Gillogly, Robert, R. "Wisdom Is Justified by All Her Children." Paper presented at the Church-Related Child Welfare Conference, the Gheens Center for Christian Family Ministry, Southern Baptist Theological Seminary, Louisville, KY, March 1991.

Gottlieb, B. H. "Social Networks and Social Support in Community Mental Health." In *Social Networks and Social Support,* edited by B. H. Gottlieb. Beverly Hills, CA: Sage Publications, 1981.

Gratch, Alan S. *Board Members Are Child Advocates.* New York: Child Welfare League of America, 1980.

Graves, David A. Presentation at the Church-Related Child Welfare Conference, the Gheens Center for Christian Family Ministry, Southern Baptist Theological Seminary, Louisville, KY, March 1991.

Greater Minneapolis Council of Churches. *Congregations Concerned for Children: Recognizing and Celebrating Children.* Minneapolis, MN: Greater Minneapolis Council of Churches, 1990.

Greeley, A. *The Young Catholic Family: Religious Images and Marital Fulfillment.* Chicago: The Thomas More Press, 1980.

Grey, J.; Cutler, C.; Dean, J.; and Kempe, C. H. "Prediction and Prevention of Child Abuse and Neglect." *Journal of Social Issues* 35 (1979): 127-138.

Grierson, Denham. "Catalyst or In Control?" In *Church Agency or Christian Response? Exploring Issues that Confront Church-Related Welfare Organisations,* edited by Newton Daddow. Melbourne, Victoria, Australia: The Victorian Council of Christian Education, 1991: 15-18.

Groze, Victor, and Gruenewald, Anne. "PARTNERS: A Model Program for Special-Needs Adoptive Families in Stress." *CHILD WELFARE LXX* (September/October 1991): 581-589.

Grusec, J. E., and Redler, E. "Attribution, Reinforcement and Altruism." *Developmental Psychology* 16 (1980): 525-534.

Grusec, J. E.; Kyczynski, L.; Rushton, J. P.; and Simutis, Z. "Modeling, Direct Instruction, and Attributions: Effects on Altruism." *Developmental Psychology* 14 (1978): 51-57.

Guernsey, Dennis B. *A New Design for Family Ministry*. Elgin, IL: David C. Cook, 1982.

Guy, Kathleen. Presentation at the Church-Related Child Welfare Agency Conference, the Gheens Center for Christian Family Ministry, Southern Baptist Theological Seminary, Louisville, KY, March 1991.

Guy, Kathleen. *Welcome the Child: A Child Advocacy Guide for Churches*. Washington, DC: The Children's Defense Fund, 1991.

Guy, Kathleen, and Smith, Chiquita G. *Campaign for Children*. Cincinnati, OH: Women's Division, General Board of Global Ministries, The United Methodist Church, 1988.

Hart, Aileen F. "Contracting for Child Welfare Services in Massachusetts: Emerging Issues for Policy and Practice." *Social Work* 33 (1988): 511-515.

Hartman, Ann, and Laird, Joan. *Family-Centered Social Work Practice*. New York: The Free Press, 1983.

Hauerwas, Stanley. "The Nonresistant Church: The Theological Ethics of John Howard Yoder." In *Vision and Virtue*, Notre Dame, IN: Fides Publishers, 1974.

Hawkins, Robert P., and Breiling, James, eds. *Therapeutic Foster Care: Critical Issues*. Washington, DC: Child Welfare League of America, 1989.

Heller, David. *The Children's God*. Chicago: University of Chicago Press, 1986.

Herrick, Allan. *You Don't Have to Be Rich*. New York: Davies Appleton-Century Co., 1940. As quoted in McCarthy 1982.

Hessel, Dieter T. *Social Ministry*. Philadelphia: Westminster Press, 1982.

Hetherington, E. M.; Cox, M.; and Cox, R. "Divorced Fathers." *Family Coordinator* 25 (1976): 417-428.

Heusser, D-Band, and Heusser, Phyllis. *Children as Partners in the Church.* Valley Forge, PA: Judson, 1985.

Himes, Kenneth R. "The Local Church as a Mediating Structure." *Social Thought* 12, 1 (Winter 1985): 22-30.

Hinson, E. Glenn. "The Historical Involvement of the Church in Social Ministries and Social Action." *Review and Expositor* 85, 2 (1988): 233-241.

Hoch, Charles, and Hemmens, George C. "Linking Informal and Formal Help: Conflict along the Continuum of Care." *Social Service Review* 61 (1987): 432-446.

Horsburgh, Michael. "Parish or Agency Based Welfare? The Client Perspective: A Response to Peter Burke and Peter Allen." A paper delivered at the Fourth National Anglican Welfare Conference, Christ College, University of Tasmania, Hobart, Tasmania, Australia, February 7, 1989.

Horsburgh, Michael. "Towards a Theology for Anglican Welfare." A paper delivered at the Anglican Caring Organisations Network Conference, Morpeth, Australia, June 1990.

Horsburgh, Michael. "Words and Deeds: Christianity and Social Welfare." *Australian Social Work* 41, 2 (1988): 17-23.

Houghton, E. W., and Grant, N. J. *The Parent Peer Group Solution.* Deerfield, IL: Deerfield Citizens for Drug Awareness, 1982.

Hunt, Gerard J., and Paschall, Nancy C. *Volunteers: Forming Effective Citizen Groups.* New York: University Press, 1984.

Itzkowitz, Ann. "Children in Placement: A Place for Family Therapy." In *Children in Family Contexts*, edited by Lee Combrinck-Graham. New York: Guilford Press, 1989: 391-412.

Jacobs, Francine H. "The Five-Tiered Approach to Evaluation: Context and Implementation." In *Evaluating Family Programs*, edited by Heather B. Weiss and Francine H. Jacobs. New York: Aldine de Gruyter, 1988: 37-68.

Jacquet, Constant H., Jr., ed. *Yearbook of American and Canadian Churches, 1985.* Nashville: Abingdon Press, 1985.

James, Beverly. *Treating Traumatized Children.* Lexington, MA: Lexington Books, 1989.

Johns, Mary Lee. *Developing Church Programs to Prevent Child Abuse.* Austin, TX: Texas Conference of Churches, 1988.

Johnson, F. Ernest. "Protestant Social Work." In *Social Work Year Book,* edited by R. H. Kurtz. New York: Russell Sage Foundation, 1941: 403-412.

Johnson, Norman. *Voluntary Social Services.* Oxford, England: Basil Blackwell & Martin Robertson, 1981.

Johnson, Ronald, and Long, Russell. *Social Ministry: A Congregational Manual.* Philadelphia: Parish Life Press, 1983.

Johnston, E., and Gabor, P. "Parent Counselors: A Foster Care Program with New Roles for Major Participants." In *The Challenge of Partnership: Working with Parents of Children in Foster Care,* edited by A. N. Maluccio and P. A. Sinanoglu. New York: Child Welfare League of America, 1981.

Jones, Marshall B. "Crisis of the American Orphanage, 1931-1940." *Social Service Review* 63 (December 1989): 613-629.

Joseph, Sister Mary Vincentia. "The Parish as a Social Service and Social Action Center: An Ecological Systems Approach." *Social Thought* I (Fall 1975): 43-59.

Kadushin, Alfred. *Child Welfare Services,* 2nd ed. New York: Macmillan, 1974.

Kagan, Richard, and Schlosberg, Shirley. *Families in Perpetual Crisis.* New York: W. W. Norton & Company, Inc., 1989.

Kagan, Sharon L.; Powell, Douglas R.; Weissbourd, Bernice; and Zigler, Edward F., eds. *America's Family Support Programs: Perspectives and Prospects.* New Haven, CT: Yale University Press, 1987.

Kahn, Alfred J., and Kamerman, Sheila B. "Do the Public Social Services Have a Future?" *Families in Society* 71 (March 1990): 165-171.

Kamerman, Sheila B., and Kahn, Alfred J. *Social Services for Children, Youth and Families in the United States.* Report for the Annie E. Casey Foundation, June 1989.

Kaplan, Kalman J.; Schwartz, M. W.; and Markus-Kaplan, Moriah. "The Family: Biblical and Psychological Foundations." Special issue of *Journal of Psychology and Judaism* 8, 2 (1984).

Kazak, Anne E. "Families with Physically Handicapped Children: Social Ecology and Family Systems." *Family Process* 25 (1986): 265-281.

Keegan, Robert F. "Catholic Social Work." In *Social Work Year Book*, edited by R. H. Kurtz. New York: Russell Sage Foundation, 1941: 91-97.

Keith-Lucas, Alan. *The Church Children's Home in a Changing World*. Chapel Hill, NC: The University of North Carolina Press, 1962.

Keith-Lucas, Alan. "The Church-Sponsored Children's Home in a Plural Society." In *Sacred Shelters: Church-Related Children's Homes*, edited by Robert R. Gillogly. Topeka, KS: The Villages, Inc., 1982: 24-34.

Keith-Lucas, Alan. Presentation at the Church-Related Child Welfare Agency Conference, the Gheens Center for Christian Family Ministry, Southern Baptist Theological Seminary, Louisville, KY, March 1991.

Keith-Lucas, Alan. Presentation at the First Annual Child Care Institute, Baptist General Convention of Texas, Highland Lakes Baptist Encampment, June 1958. (Later published in Keith-Lucas, Alan, *The Church Children's Home in a Changing World*, Chapel Hill, NC: University of North Carolina Press, 1962.)

Keith-Lucas, Alan. "What Else Can Residential Care Do? And Do Well?" *Residential Treatment for Children and Youth* 4 (Summer 1987): 25-38.

Keith-Lucas, Alan, and Sanford, Clifford W. *Group Child Care as a Family Service*. Chapel Hill, NC: University of North Carolina Press, 1977.

Kelker, Katharin A. *Making the System Work: An Advocacy Workshop for Parents*. Portland, OR: Families as Allies Project, Regional Research Institute for Human Services, Portland State University, 1987.

Kettner, P. M.; Morohey, R. M.; and Martin, L. L. *Designing and Managing Programs: An Effectiveness-Based Approach*. Newbury Park, CA: Sage Publications, 1990.

Keys, P., and Ginsberg, L. H., eds. *New Management in Human Services*. Silver Spring, MD: National Association of Social Workers, 1988.

Kingdon, David. *Children of Abraham*. Sussex, England: Carey Publications Ltd., 1973.

Kinney, Jill; Haapala, David; and Booth, Charlotte. *Keeping Families Together: The Homebuilders Model*. New York: Aldine de Gruyter, 1991.

Kirk, David. Presentation at the Church-Related Child Welfare Conference, the Gheens Center for Christian Family Ministry, Southern Baptist Theological Seminary, Louisville, KY, March 1991.

Klefbeck, J.; Bergerhed, E.; Forsberg G.; Hultkrantz-Jeppson, A.; and Marklund, K. *Natverksarbete i multiproblemfamiljer—Forskningsprojekt i Botkyrka.* Tumba: Botkyrka Kommun Kommungemansam Socialtjanst. As translated by Gunnar Forsberg in *Netletter* 5, 2 (1991): 9-15.

Kramer, Ralph M., and Grossman, Bart. "Contracting for Social Services: Process Management and Resource Dependencies." *Social Service Review* 61, 1 (1987): 32-55.

Laird, Joan. "Using Church and Family Ritual." In *The Church's Ministry with Families: A Practical Guide*, edited by Diana R. Garland and Diane L. Pancoast. Irving, TX: Word, 1990: 110-130.

Lambeth, Judith A. Presentation at the Church-Related Child Welfare Conference, the Gheens Center for Christian Family Ministry, Southern Baptist Theological Seminary, Louisville, KY, March 1991.

Lane, Dermot A. *Foundations for a Social Theology.* New York: Paulist Press, 1984.

Langley, Patricia A. "The Public Sector and Voluntary Agencies—A Time for Partnership." *Families in Society* 72, 7 (1991): 433-434.

Larose, Paul F. *Working with Children and the Liturgy.* New York: Alba House, 1981.

Leonard, Bill J. "Extending the Kingdom." In *Community in Diversity: A History of the Walnut Street Baptist Church, 1815-1990*, edited by Bill J. Leonard. Louisville, KY: Simons-Neely Publishing Co., 1990.

Leonard, Bill J. "The Modern Church and Social Action." *Review and Expositor* 85 (1988): 243-253.

Levine, C. *Programs to Strengthen Families: A Resource Guide.* Chicago: Family Resource Coalition, 1988.

Lewis, C. S. *The Screwtape Letters.* London: Geoffrey Bles, 1942.

Lieber, L. L. "The Self-Help Approach: Parents Anonymous." *Journal of Clinical Child Psychology* 12 (1983): 288-291.

Lincoln, C. Eric, and Mamiya, Lawrence H. "The Black Church and Social Ministry in Politics and Economics: Historical and Contemporary Perspectives." In *Carriers of Faith: Lessons from Congregational Studies*, edited by Carl S. Dudley, Jackson W. Carroll, and James P. Wind. Louisville, KY: Westminster/John Knox Press, 1991: 65-85.

Lourie, Ira S., and Katz-Leavy, Judith. "New Directions for Mental Health Services for Families and Children." *Families in Society* 72, 5 (1991): 277-285.

Louv, Richard. "Weaving a New Web." *Family Affairs* 4, 1-2 (1991): 6.

Lowe, Marion I. "The Challenge of Partnership: A National Foster Care Charter in the United Kingdom." *CHILD WELFARE* LXX, 2 (1991): 151-156.

Lundberg, Emma Octavia. *Unto the Least of These: Social Services for Children*. New York: Appleton-Century-Crofts, 1947.

Magnuson, Norris. *Salvation in the Slums: Evangelical Social Work, 1865-1920*. Metuchen, NJ: The Scarecrow Press and the American Theological Library Association, 1977.

Maluccio, Anthony N., and Fein, E. "Permanency Planning: A Redefinition." *CHILD WELFARE* LXII, 3 (May-June 1983): 195-201.

Maluccio, Anthony N.; Krieger, Robin; and Pine, Barbara A. *Reconnecting Families: Family Reunification Competencies for Social Workers*. West Hartford, CT: Center for the Study of Child Welfare, University of Connecticut School of Social Work, 1990.

Manser, Gordon. "Further Thoughts on Purchase of Service." *Social Casework* 55 (July 1974): 421-474.

Martone, William P.; Kemp, Gerald F.; and Pearson, Susan J. "The Continuum of Parental Involvement in Residential Treatment: Engagement—Participation—Empowerment—Discharge." *Residential Treatment for Children & Youth* 6, 3 (1989): 11-37.

Marty, Martin E. "The Difference in Being a Christian and the Difference It Makes." In *Sacred Shelters: Church-Related Children's Homes*, edited by Robert R. Gillogly. Topeka, KS: The Villages, Inc., 1982: 12-21.

Marty, Martin E. "Social Service: Godly and Godless." *Social Service Review* 54, 4 (December 1980): 463-481.

Marx, Jerry D. "An Outdoor Adventure Counseling Program for Adolescents." *Social Work* 33 (1988): 517-520.

Mayer, Morris F.; Richman, Leon H.; and Balcerzak, Edwin A. *Group Care of Children: Crossroads and Transitions*. New York: The Child Welfare League of America, 1977.

McCarthy, Kathleen D. *Noblesse Oblige: Charity and Cultural Philanthrophy in Chicago, 1849-1929*. Chicago: University of Chicago Press, 1982.

McCaughey, Jean. "Families' Access to and Use of Support Networks—Some Case Studies." In *Community Based Services for Children and Families*, edited by Frank

Maas and Susan Sach. Melbourne, Australia: Institute of Family Studies, 1984: 33-42.

McDonald, M. M. "Involving the Community in Prevention Efforts." *Prevention Forum* 9, 3 (1989): 1-4.

McGinnis, Kathleen, and McGinnis, James. *Parenting for Peace and Justice.* Maryknoll, NY: Orbis, 1981.

McMahon, Robert J.; Geraldine, Mary; and Paul, Mary. Unpublished Progress Report of the Center for Family Life in Sunset Park, 345 43rd Street, Brooklyn, New York, July 1991.

Michielse, H. C. M., and van Krieken, Robert. "Policing the Poor: J. L. Vives and the Sixteenth-Century Origins of Modern Social Administration." *Social Service Review* 64 (March 1990): 1-21.

Miles, Delos. *Evangelism and Social Involvement.* Nashville, TN: Broadman, 1986.

Minuchin, Salvador. *Families and Family Therapy.* Boston: Harvard University Press, 1974.

Minuchin, Salvador. *Family Kaleidoscope.* Boston: Harvard University Press, 1984.

Minuchin, Salvador, and Elizur, Joel. "The Foster Care Crisis." *The Family Therapy Networker* 14, 1 (1990): 44-50, 62.

Moberg, David O. *The Church as a Social Institution,* revised edition. Grand Rapids: Baker Book House, 1984.

Mock, Alan K.; Davidson, James D.; and Johnson, C. Lincoln. "Threading the Needle: Faith and Works in Affluent Churches." In *Carriers of Faith: Lessons from Congregational Studies,* edited by Carl S. Dudley, Jackson W. Carroll, and James P. Wind. Louisville, KY: Westminster/John Knox Press, 1991: 86-103.

Moran, Mary A. "Advocacy Skills for Parenting Organizations." In *Support for Parents and Infants,* edited by C. F. Zachariah Boukydis. New York: Routledge & Kegan Paul, 1986: 117-130.

Morton, Marian J. "Fallen Women, Federated Charities, and Maternity Homes, 1913-1973." *Social Service Review* 62, 1 (1988): 61-82.

Mott, S. C. "The Power of Giving and Receiving: Reciprocity in Hellenistic Benevolence." In *Current Issues in Biblical and Patristic Interpretation,* edited by G. F. Hawthorne. Grand Rapids, MI: Eerdmans Publishing Company, 1974: 60-72.

Mpolo, Masamba. *Family Profiles*. Geneva: World Council of Churches, 1984.

Müller-Fahrenholz, Geiko. *...and do not hinder them: An Ecumenical Plea for the Admission of Children to the Eucharist*. Geneva, Switzerland: World Council of Churches, 1982.

Mulry, Thomas M. "The Home vs. the Institution." *Proceedings of the 25th NCCC*, 1898. As quoted in Tiffin 1982.

Mykytiuk, Gerald. "Enhancing Residential Care through Effective Volunteer Programming." *The Child and Youth Care Administrator* 2, 1 (1989): 41-46.

Naisbitt, John, and Aburdene, Patricia. *Megatrends 2000: Ten New Directions for the 1990s*. New York: William Morrow and Company, Inc., 1990.

National Conference of Catholic Bishops. *A Family Perspective in Church and Society: A Manual for All Pastoral Leaders*. Washington, DC: United States Catholic Conference, 1988.

National Crime Prevention Council. *Mission Possible: Churches Supporting Fragile Families*. Washington, DC: National Crime Prevention Council, 1990.

Netting, F. Ellen. "The Meaning of Church Affiliation for Continuum of Care Retirement Communities." *Journal of Religious Gerontology* 8, 2 (1992): 79-99.

Netting, F. Ellen. "Secular and Religious Funding of Church-Related Agencies." *Social Service Review* 56, 4 (December 1982): 586-604.

Newbigin, Lesslie. *The Open Secret*. Grand Rapids, MI: Eerdmans Publishing Company, 1978.

Niebuhr, Reinhold. *The Contribution of Religion to Social Work*. New York: Columbia University Press, 1932.

Nightingale, Benedict. *Charities*. London, England: Allen Lane, 1973.

Nouwen, Henri J. M.; McNeill, Donald P.; and Morrison, Douglas A. *Compassion*. New York: Doubleday, 1983.

Olson, Richard P., and Leonard, Joe H. *Ministry with Families in Flux: The Church and Changing Patterns of Life*. Louisville, KY: Westminster/John Knox Press, 1990.

Pancoast, Diane L. "A Network Focus for Family Ministry." In *The Church's Ministry with Families: A Practical Guide*, edited by Diana R. Garland and Diane L. Pancoast. Irving, TX: Word, 1990a: 56-70.

Pancoast, Diane L. "Helping Natural Helpers." In *The Church's Ministry with Families: A Practical Guide,* edited by Diana R. Garland and Diane L. Pancoast. Irving, TX: Word, 1990b: 210-223.

Pancoast, Diane L.; Parker, P.; and Froland, C. *Rediscovering Self-Help: Its Role in Social Care.* Newbury Park, CA: Sage Publications, 1983.

Pattison, E. M. *Pastor and Parish: A Systems Approach.* Philadelphia, PA: Fortress, 1977.

Peabody, Francis Greenwood. *Jesus Christ and the Social Question.* London, England: Macmillan & Co., Ltd., 1923.

Perkins, John. *Let Justice Roll Down.* Glendale, CA: Regal Books, 1976.

Perkins, John. *With Justice for All.* Ventura, CA: Regal Books, 1982.

Peterson, R. W., and Brown, R. "The Child Care Worker as Treatment Coordinator and Parent Trainer. " *Child Care Quarterly* 11 (1982): 188-203.

Pilisuk, Marc. "Delivery of Social Support: The Social Innoculation." *American Journal of Orthopsychiatry* 52 (1982): 20-31.

Pilisuk, Marc, and Parks, Susan H. "Social Support and Family Stress." *Marriage and Family Review* 6 (1983): 137-156.

Pizzo, Peggy. "Parent-to-Parent Support Groups: Advocates for Social Change." In *America's Family Support Programs,* edited by Sharon L. Kagan, Douglas R. Powell, Bernice Weissbourd, and Edward F. Zigler. New Haven, CT: Yale University Press, 1987: 228-242.

Pollard, David. "The Contemporary Role of the Christian Welfare Agencies." In *Church Agency or Christian Response? Exploring Issues that Confront Church-Related Welfare Organisations,* edited by Newton Daddow. Melbourne, Victoria, Australia: The Victorian Council of Christian Education, 1991: 6-14.

Pollock, Linda A. *Forgotten Children: Parent-Child Relations from 1500 to 1900.* London, England: Cambridge University Press, 1983.

Pooley, Lynn, and Littell, Julia H. *Family Resource Program Builder: Blueprints for Designing and Operating Programs for Parents.* Chicago: Family Resource Coalition, 1986.

Pople, Leigh. *Helping Children Participate in Holy Communion.* Melbourne, Australia: Uniting Church Press, 1986.

Powell, D.; Halpern, R.; Roberts, R.; and Raimey, C. "Home-Based Family Supports." Presentation at the Second National Conference of the Family Resource Coalition, Chicago, October 1988.

Powell, Thomas J. *Self-Help Organizations and Professional Practice*. Silver Spring, MD: NASW, 1987.

"Preventing Abuse before It Starts." *Ecumenical Child Care Newsletter* 8, 6 (November/December 1990): 2.

Prince, Heyward. Presentation at the Church-Related Child Welfare Conference, the Gheens Center for Christian Family Ministry, Southern Baptist Theological Seminary, Louisville, KY, March 1991.

Radbill, Samuel X. "A History of Child Abuse and Infanticide." In *The Battered Child*, edited by Ray E. Helfer and C. Henry Kempe. Chicago: University of Chicago Press, 1968.

Rappaport, Julian; Hess, R.; and Swift, C. *Studies in Empowerment*. New York: Haworth, 1984.

Rauschenbusch, Walter. *A Theology for the Social Gospel*. New York: Macmillan, 1917.

Ravnsborg, I. S. "The Inpatient Care of Families at Vikersund." In *The International Book of Family Therapy*, edited by F. W. Kaslow. New York: Brunner/Mazel, 1982.

Reid, P. Nelson, and Billups, James O. "Distributional Ethics and Social Work Education." *Journal of Social Work Education* 67 (1986): 6-17.

Reid, William, and Stimpson, Peter K. "Sectarian Agencies." *Encyclopedia of Social Work*, 18th ed. Silver Spring, MD: National Association of Social Workers, 1987: 545-556.

Reis, Janet; Barbara-Stein, Linda; and Bennett, Susan. "Ecological Determinants of Parenting." *Family Relations* 35 (1986): 547-554.

Religious News Service. "Fastest Growing USA Churches are African-American." *Baptists Today* 10, 6 (March 12, 1992): 12.

Rice, Kerry. Presentation at the Church-Related Child Welfare Agency Conference, the Gheens Center for Christian Family Ministry, Southern Baptist Theological Seminary, Louisville, KY, March 1991.

Richards, Lawrence O. *A Theology of Children's Ministry*. Grand Rapids, MI: Zondervan, 1983.

Robinson, Nancy Day. "Supplemental Services for Families and Children." In *A Handbook of Child Welfare*, edited by Joan Laird and Ann Hartman. New York: The Free Press, 1985: 397-416.

Roozen, David A.; McKinney, William; and Carroll, Jackson W. *Varieties of Religious Presence: Mission in Public Life*. New York: Pilgrim Press, 1984.

Rumford, Steve L. Presentation at the Church-Related Child Welfare Conference, the Gheens Center for Christian Family Ministry, Southern Baptist Theological Seminary, Louisville, KY, March 1991.

Ryan, William. *Blaming the Victim*. New York: Vintage Books, 1971.

Schaller, Lyle E. "A Practitioner's Perspective: Policy Planning." In *Building Effective Ministry: Theory and Practice in the Local Church*, edited by Carl S. Dudley. San Francisco: Harper & Row, 1983: 160-174.

Scheinfeld, D.; Bowles, D.; Tuck, S.; and Gold, R. "Parent's Values, Family Networks and Family Development: Working with Disadvantaged Families." *American Journal of Orthopsychiatry* 40 (1970): 413-425.

Schillebeeckx, E. *Marriage: Human Reality and Saving Mystery*. New York: Sheed and Ward, 1965.

Schilling, Don. "Operation Getting It Together." Unpublished document: 1991 Annual Summary Report and Evaluation. OGIT, 500 North Main St., Sebastopol CA 95472, February 1992.

Schorr, Alvin L. "Poor Care for Poor Children—What Way Out?" In *Children and Decent People*, edited by Alvin L. Schorr. New York: Basic Books, 1974: 186-212.

Schorr, Lisbeth B. *Within Our Reach: Breaking the Cycle of Disadvantage*. New York: Doubleday, 1988.

Sell, Charles M. *Family Ministry: The Enrichment of Family Life through the Church*. Grand Rapids, MI: Zondervan, 1981.

Sheek, G. William. *The Word on Families*. Nashville, TN: Abingdon, 1985.

Shyne, Anne W., and Schroeder, Anita G. *Public Social Services for Children and Their Families*. Rockville, MD: Westat, 1978.

Silverstein, Shel. *Where the Sidewalk Ends*. New York: Harper & Row, 1974.

Simms, Mark D., and Bolden, Barbara J. "The Family Reunification Project: Facilitating Regular Contact among Foster Children, Biological Families, and Foster Families." _CHILD WELFARE_ LXX (1991): 679-690.

Smith, Timothy L. _Revivalism and Social Reform in Mid-Nineteenth-Century America._ Nashville, TN: Abingdon Press, 1957.

Snodgrass, Robert D., and Bryant, Brad. "Therapeutic Foster Care: A National Program Survey." In _Therapeutic Foster Care: Critical Issues,_ edited by Robert P. Hawkins and James Breiling. Washington, DC: Child Welfare League of America, 1989: 37-76.

Sosin, Michael, and Caulum, Sharon. "Advocacy: A Conceptualization for Social Work Practice." _Social Work_ 28 (1983): 12-17.

Spressart, Janet Furness. "The Vulnerable Christian Social Worker: 'Wise as Serpents and Harmless as Doves.' " _Social Work and Christianity_ 15 (Fall 1988): 44-54.

Springer, Merle E. "Privatization: Options and Opportunities in Public/Private Relations." _The Child and Youth Care Administrator_ 3, 2 (1990): 25-27.

Stephens, Cinde. "Volunteers Helping At-Risk Families Define, Attain Goals." _High Point [NC] Enterprise_ (March 5, 1990), 8a.

Talbert, Charles H. _Reading Luke: A Literary and Theological Commentary on the Third Gospel._ New York: Crossroad, 1982.

Tiffin, Susan. _In Whose Best Interest? Child Welfare Reform in the Progressive Era._ Westport, CT: Greenwood Press, 1982.

Tillapaugh, Frank R. _Unleashing the Church._ Ventura CA: Regal Books, 1982.

Topor, R. S. _Your Personal Guide to Marketing a Non-Profit Organization._ Washington, DC: Council for Advancement and Support of Education, 1988.

Tracy, Elizabeth, and Whittaker, James K. "The Evidence Base for Social Support Interventions in Child and Family Practice: Emerging Issues for Research and Practice." _Children and Youth Services Review_ 9 (1987): 249-270.

Trute, Barry, and Hauch, Christopher. "Building on Family Strength: A Study of Families with Positive Adjustment to the Birth of a Developmentally Disabled Child." _Journal of Marital and Family Therapy_ 14 (1988): 185-193.

Turner, R. Jay, and Avison, William R. "Assessing Risk Factors for Problem Parenting: The Significance of Social Support." *Journal of Marriage and the Family* 47 (1985): 881-892.

Turpin, Claud Alden. "A History of the Kentucky Baptist Board of Child Care." M.S.S.W. thesis, Kent School of Social Work, Louisville, KY, 1962.

United Church of Canada. *A Place for You: Toward the Integration of Children into the Life of the Church.* Toronto, ON: Division of Mission in Canada, United Church of Canada, 1989.

United Church of Christ, Office of Church Life and Leadership. *The Ministry of Volunteers: A Guidebook for Churches.* St. Louis, MO: United Church of Christ, 1979.

United Methodist Association of Health and Welfare Ministries. *A Theology for United Methodist-Related Residential Agencies Serving Children, Youth and Families.* Dayton, OH: United Methodist Association of Health and Welfare Ministries, undated.

Unsworth, Tim. "Love 'em and Leave 'em: Why Society Keeps Abandoning its Kids." *Salt* 11 (September 1991): 14-17.

Vogel, E. E., and Bell, N. W. "The Emotionally Disturbed Child as the Family Scapegoat." In *A Modern Introduction to the Family*, edited by N. W. Bell and E. F. Vogel. New York: The Free Press, 1960.

Wandersman, Lois Pall. "New Directions for Parent Education." In *America's Family Support Programs: Perspectives and Prospects,* edited by Sharon L. Kagan, Douglas R. Powell, Bernice Weissbourd, and Edward F. Zigler. New Haven, CT: Yale University Press, 1987: 207-227.

Wasik, Barbara Hanna; Bryant, Donna M.; and Lyons, Claudia M. *Home Visiting: Procedures for Helping Families.* Newbury Park, CA: Sage Publications, 1990.

Watkins, Sallie A. "The Mary Ellen Myth: Correcting Child Welfare History." *Social Work* 35 (November 1990): 500-503.

Watzlawick, Paul; Weakland, J. H.; and Fisch, R. *Change: Principles of Problem Formation and Problem Resolution.* New York: Norton, 1974.

Way, Peggy. "The Care of Strangers." Transcript of the Harvey S. Murdoch Memorial Lecture, Buckhorn Lake State Park, Buckhorn, KY, August 1989.

Weber, Hans-Ruedi. *Jesus and the Children: Biblical Resources for Study and Preaching.* Atlanta, GA: John Knox Press, 1979.

Webster, C. D., et al. "The Child Care Worker in the Family: Some Case Examples and Implications for the Design of Family-Centered Programs." _Child Care Quarterly_ 8 (1979): 5-18.

Weissbourd, Bernice, and Kagan, Sharon L. "Family Support Programs: Catalysts for Change." _American Journal of Orthopsychiatry_ 59 (January 1989): 20-31.

Westman, Jack C. _Child Advocacy: New Professional Roles for Helping Families._ New York: The Free Press, 1979.

White, Keith. "Residential Social Work." In _Social Work: A Christian Perspective,_ edited by Terry Philpot. Tring, England: Lion, 1986: 75-93.

White, Ronald C., and Hopkins, C. Howard. _The Social Gospel: Religion and Reform in Changing America._ Philadelphia: Temple University Press, 1976.

Whitehead, Barbara Dafoe. "Why Are Parents Afraid?" _Family Affairs_ 4, 1-2 (1991): 15.

Whittaker, James K. "Colonial Child Care Institutions: Our Heritage of Care." _CHILD WELFARE_ L, 7 (January/February 1971): 396-400.

Whittaker, James K. "Family Support and Group Child Care: Rethinking Resources." In _Permanence and Family Support: Changing Practice in Group Child Care,_ edited by Gary O. Carman and Richard W. Small. Washington, DC: Child Welfare League of America, 1988: 29-55.

Whittaker, James K.; Kinney, Jill; Tracy, Elizabeth M.; and Booth, Charlotte, eds. _Improving Practice Technology for Work with High Risk Families: Lessons from the "Homebuilders" Social Work Education Project._ Seattle: Center for Social Welfare Research, University of Washington School of Social Work, 1988.

Williamson, Arthur. "Evangelicals Study the Link between Social Action and Gospel." _Christianity Today_ 26, 13 (August 6, 1982): 54, 56.

Willimon, William H. "Receiving Little Jesus." _The Christian Century_ (December 4, 1985): 1109-1110.

Wilson, M. _How to Mobilize Church Volunteers._ Minneapolis, MN: Augsburg, 1983.

Withey, Virginia; Anderson, Rosalie; and Lauderdale, Michael. "Volunteers as Mentors for Abusing Parents: A Natural Helping Relationship." _CHILD WELFARE_ LIX, 10 (December 1980): 637-644.

Wolins, Martin, and Wozner, Yochanan. _Revitalizing Residential Settings._ San Francisco: Jossey-Bass, 1982.

Wollman, Neil. "Motivating Others to Work with You." In *Working for Peace: A Handbook of Practical Psychology and Other Tools*, edited by Neil Wollman. San Luis Obispo, CA: Impact Publishers, 1985: 71-79.

Wood, James E. "Tax Exemption of Religion and the Separation of Church and State." *Review and Expositor* 83, 2 (1986): 235-258.

Wynn, Joan, and Costello, Joan. "Children's Services: Directions for the Future." *Family Resource Coalition Report* 9, 3 (1990): 8-9.

Young, L. *Wednesday's Children*. New York: McGraw-Hill, 1964.

Young, Thomas M.; Dore, Martha M.; and Pappenfort, Donnell M. "Residential Group Care for Children Considered Emotionally Disturbed, 1966-1981." *Social Service Review* 62, 1 (1988): 158-170.

Zelkowitz, Phyllis. "Social Support and Aggressive Behavior in Young Children." *Family Relations* 36 (1987): 129-134.

Ziefert, Nancy Day. "Supplemental Services for Families and Children." In *A Handbook of Child Welfare*, edited by Joan Laird and Ann Hartman. New York: The Free Press, 1985: 397-416.

Zigler, Edward F., and Gilman, Elizabeth P. "An Agenda for the 1990s: Supporting Families." In *Rebuilding the Nest: A New Commitment to the American Family*, edited by David Blankenhorn, Steven Bayme, and Jean Bethke Elshtain. Milwaukee, WI: Family Service America, 1990: 237-250.

Zuckerman, Erva. *Child Welfare*. New York: The Free Press, 1983.

ABOUT THE AUTHOR

Diana R. Garland, Ph.D., is Dean of the Carver School of Church Social Work of the Southern Baptist Theological Seminary, Louisville, KY. The only accredited M.S.W. program in a seminary, Carver School focuses on preparing professional social workers for practice in churches and church agencies. Garland also directs the Gheens Center for Christian Family Ministry, a center for continuing education and research in congregational family ministries. She has authored, co-authored, or edited 11 other books, including *Precious in His Sight: A Guide to Child Advoacacy, Church Social Work, The Church's Ministry with Families, Christian Self-Esteem: Parenting by Grace, Covenant Marriage,* and *Beyond Companionship: Christians in Marriage.* She and her husband, David, have two children, Sarah and John.